FIVE NEW YORK PLAYS

by
JIM GEOGHAN

Five New York Plays
All Rights Reserved.
Copyright © 2017 Jim Geoghan
v1.0

This is a work of fiction. The events and characters described herein are imaginary and are not intended to refer to specific places or living persons. The opinions expressed in this manuscript are solely the opinions of the author and do not represent the opinions or thoughts of the publisher. The author has represented and warranted full ownership and/or legal right to publish all the materials in this book.

This book may not be reproduced, transmitted, or stored in whole or in part by any means, including graphic, electronic, or mechanical without the express written consent of the publisher except in the case of brief quotations embodied in critical articles and reviews.

© 2017 Literary Arts/Play.
Cover Photo Credit: Sinitar All rights reserved - used with permission.
Book Design by Lizzy Ross

PRINTED IN THE UNITED STATES OF AMERICA

For my wife Annie Gagen, aka Ruth Ann Poons Geoghan.

All you need is someone who believes in you.

TABLE OF CONTENTS

LIGHT SENSITIVE • 1

ONLY KIDDING! • 81

TWO GENTLEMEN OF CORONA • 180

THE KING OF CITY ISLAND • 274

OF MEN AND CARS • 356

LIGHT SENSITIVE

CAST

TOM, late twenties to fifties, blue collar cab driver and freelance photographer. Has lived his entire life in Manhattan's Hell's Kitchen. A former neighborhood hero turned sour by a disability.

LOU, the same age, Tom's best friend and bartender. Also a product of Hell's Kitchen. Sweet natured, uneducated, unsophisticated, a colorful and faithful friend.

EDNA, the same age, quiet, slightly timid, also slightly lame, could be attractive but has never tried. Kept at home all these years by selfish parents fearful of being lonely.

LIGHT SENSITIVE premiered at the Old Globe Theatre, San Diego, California, Artistic Director, Jack O'Brien; Managing Director, Thomas Hall. The play premiered December, 1992, with the following cast:

    TOM..........................Joel Anderson

    LOU ....Matt Landers

    EDNA................... Victoria-Ann Lewis

Director: Andrew Traister
Set Designer: Nick Reid
Costume Designer: Clair Henkel
Lighting Designer: Barth Ballard
Sound Designer: Jeff Ladman
Production Stage Manager: Douglas Pagliotti

LIGHT SENSITIVE also premiered at the same time under the title TRIPLE EXPOSURE at the Wisdom Bridge Theatre in Chicago where it was nominated for the Joseph Jefferson Award.

CAUTION: Professionals and amateurs are hereby warned that "ONLY KIDDING," "LIGHT SENSITIVE," and "TWO GENTLEMEN OF CORONA", being fully protected under the copyright laws of the United States of America, the British Commonwealth countries, including Canada, and the other countries of the Copyright Union, are subject to a royalty. All rights, including professional, amateur, motion picture, recitation, public reading, radio, television and cable broadcasting, and the rights of translation into foreign languages, are strictly reserved. Any inquiry regarding the availability of performance rights, or the purchase of individual copies of the authorized acting edition, must be directed to Samuel French Inc., 235 Park Avenue South, Fifth Floor, New York, NY 10003, with other locations in Hollywood and London.

ACT ONE

TOM HANRATTY sits at his kitchen table in his dimly lit, tenement apartment in Hell's Kitchen. The unique feature of many of these apartments is that the bathtub is often located in the kitchen, and Tom's apartment is no exception. Both Tom and his home are in a shabby state. Tom hasn't shaved or bathed in days and he probably hasn't changed his clothes either. Dishes lie unwashed, the garbage overflows, pieces of clothing lie about and a lone plant near a greasy window died long ago.

There are a number of things in Tom's apartment that seem to contrast his current state of affairs however, a fair number of black and white photos decorate the walls. These photos (Tom's) depict life on the streets of New York City, unsweetened and real. They range from gritty to joyous and show more than just a little insight. A 35mm camera hangs from a hook on the wall. There is also a collection of books on one shelf and, while everything else in the apartment is in disarray, these books are arranged neatly and with great care.

It is early morning, the day before Christmas Eve. Tom is drinking whiskey from a glass that once was a jelly jar. One of the reasons the kitchen is so dim is that Tom has unscrewed a light bulb from one of his few lighting fixtures and has plugged in a record player. As we begin Tom is listening to a much-played, scratchy recording of Elvis Presley's "Here Comes Santa Claus." He listens for several beats when the record suddenly begins to skip. Tom taps the floor good with his foot and the record resumes playing. He listens for several more moments. There is a knock at the door.

          TOM

Yeah?

          LOU *(O.S.)*

It's Lou.

          TOM

It's open.

          LOU *(O.S.)*

What?

          TOM

It's open!

The door opens but the safety chain has been set. We can only see a little bit of LOU.

          LOU

It's not open.

          TOM

Huh?

          LOU

You got the chain thing here.

TOM

Hold on.

Tom silences the record player then crosses to the door. If we didn't know it yet, we know it now – Tom is blind.

TOM *(cont'd)*

Hold on. Chee. Thought I left this open. Lemme close this.

LOU

Go ahead.

TOM

Don't push.

LOU

I'm not.

TOM

Don't push. I've got to close it.

LOU

I'm not pushin'!

TOM

Watch it. Hold on. Damn it. Hold on, hold on...

LOU

Not the latch. The chain thing.

TOM

Shut up.

LOU

The chain. The chain!

TOM

Got it. Got it. All these frikkin' locks and bolts, chains and latches... I got it.

The door opens and LOU D'MARCO ENTERS. He is near Tom's age and is bundled well against the cold. He warms himself over a radiator.

LOU

Man, it's cold this morning! Must be ten degrees outside.

TOM

Seven.

LOU

Is that what it is?

TOM

Just heard it on the radio. Seven degrees.

LOU

Man, that's ridiculous. It's Christmas time. It never gets this cold around Christmas.

TOM

You believe it?

LOU

January, February, sure. But not Christmas. I think I seen a dead guy.

TOM

Where?

LOU

In front of Smiler's. Some old geezer. I think he tried comin' in the bar a few times but I tossed him right out. He was in bad shape. You know, a bum.

TOM

Please. You mean "homeless."

LOU

Homeless, whatever. Now he's <u>life</u>less.

TOM

He really dead?

LOU

I think so. Cops was there. He wasn't movin'. They covered his head with somethin'.

TOM

Sounds like he's dead.

LOU

Mind if I turn on a few more lights?

TOM

Go ahead.

Lou tries a wall switch, then a wall fixture. Neither seems to be working. As he does so:

LOU

It's so dark in here I can hardly see nothin'. I could trip and break a leg or somethin'. What is this? None of your lights work?

TOM

You tell me.

LOU

You got any more bulbs?

                                TOM
    Under the sink.

Lou looks under the sink.

                                LOU
    Who keeps light bulbs under the sink?
                                TOM
    I keep light bulbs under the sink! It's my house, it's where I keep them!
                                LOU
    Well, it's a stupid place. You sure you got some?
                                TOM
    Yeah. I saw some this morning!
                                LOU
    You got a thing they come in but there ain't no bulbs in it.
                                TOM
    Then I'm out. I don't believe this! You can see – I'm blind as a bat and
    I'm telling you everything!
                                LOU
    Hold on. Wait a minute. Yeah...

Lou opens the door and unscrews a light bulb in a hallway lighting fixture nearby.

                                TOM
    What're you doing?

                                LOU
    Got an idea.
                                TOM
    What's going on?

                                LOU
    Hold on. I'm doing somethin'. Ow! It's hot!
                                TOM
    What are you doing?

                                LOU
    I'm takin' a bulb from the hallway.
                                TOM
    Great. Hey, if you get me in trouble with the landlord --
                                LOU
        (interrupts)
    Shhh... I don't want no one to...
        (to someone down the hall)
    It's an emergency.

TOM

Who's that?

LOU

(to other person)
I'll replace it. I promise.

TOM

Who is it?

LOU

Some guy. Giving me dirty looks.
(to other person)
Just for an hour or two. I swear. It's for my friend.

TOM

Is it a fat guy?

LOU

Yeah.
(to other person)
It's just for a little bit.

TOM

A fat Puerto Rican guy?

LOU

Shhh!

Tom speaks loudly so the person down the hallway can hear him.

TOM

You're talking to "El Jerko?!"

LOU

Tommy...

TOM

(yelling out the door)
The deadbeat who lets his dog go right in the hallways? The guy with eight kids on welfare? You're worried about him? What he thinks of you?

LOU

Shut up.

TOM

Don't worry about him! He ain't sayin' nothin' to the landlord! He owes too much rent! That's right, pal! The whole building knows about you!

Tom reaches into his pocket and flings coins down the hallway.

TOM *(cont'd)*

Here you go! Buy yourself some more crack, you frikkin' drug addict!

LOU
He's gone.

TOM
(still yelling)
Hey! If I see that dog around here again I'm gonna --

LOU
(interrupts)
He's gone! C'mon, Tommy. The guy's gone.

TOM
Some day I'll...

LOU
Man, you got some mouth on you.

TOM
I hate that guy.

LOU
I heard. So did the whole building.

Lou closes the door and screws the borrowed light bulb into a lighting fixture. Lights come up to full.

TOM
Doesn't take his dog out. Just comes home, opens his apartment door, lets his dog go out in the hallway. The dog goes right in the hallway!

LOU
All right.

TOM
Know how many times I've gone down the hall to the toilet and stepped in a pile?

LOU
Okay, so that happens sometimes.

TOM
That's one thing they never really come out and tell you when you go blind. They tell you this, they tell you that, but they never really come out and say it in so many words: "You're blind. You're gonna step in a lotta dog shit."

LOU
Okay, so you're mad at the guy but you don't have to yell like that at 'im.

TOM
Yes, I do.

LOU
Why?

TOM
'Cause he's trash.

LOU
You make him angry enough, you'll be in trouble.

TOM
Aw...

LOU
You don't know. You could go down the hall to the can one night and he could come at you with a knife or somethin'.

TOM
I'll kill 'im with it.

LOU
He could sneak up on you easy. Wait a minute. He wouldn't have to sneak up on you at all. He could stand right in front of you! You would <u>walk</u> right into his knife. He wouldn't have to move a muscle.

TOM
I would <u>smell</u> 'im first.

LOU
Well, it's Christmas. Peace on earth, stuff like that.

TOM
Pshew...

LOU
I got your mail. Want to go through it?

TOM
Naw.

LOU
Might be somethin' special in here, huh? Maybe a letter from Santa.

TOM
Right.

LOU
Uh-oh! An envelope with no stamp. How'd that get delivered?

TOM
Huh?

LOU
Probably 'cause the postman didn't bring it, huh?

TOM
What're you talking?

LOU
Let's take a look. See what gives.

Lou opens the envelope.

LOU *(cont'd)*
Uh-oh! It's a Christmas card from <u>me</u>!

TOM

Pshew!

LOU

And all the guys at the Terminal Bar. Look at this. They all signed it. Kenny, Fat Freddy, George, the two Bobbys, Carmine, Roy and Howard...

TOM

Lemme have.

Lou hands the card to Tom. Tom holds the card close to his face feeling every bit of it with his hands. He sniffs the card as well.

TOM *(cont'd)*

They all signed it, huh?

LOU

Yup.

TOM

All those guys?

LOU

You bet.

TOM

The card smells like cigarettes and beer.

LOU

Well, it ain't gonna smell like flowers.

TOM

Hey, what's the card say? What's it look like?

LOU

Well, there's this chick on the cover and she has got some body on her!

TOM

Yeah?

LOU

She's wearin' a top, like the top of a bikini, you know?

TOM

Yeah.

LOU

But skimpy.

TOM

Right.

LOU

Real skimpy. She looks like five pounds of potato salad in a two-pound bag. She must be from California.

TOM

Right, right.

LOU

And inside the card it says "Merry Christmas."

TOM

All right!

LOU

You like that, eh?

TOM

Woo!

LOU

You wanna go through the rest of your mail? Maybe pay your gas bill?

TOM

Naw. Put it in the tub.

LOU

Yeah, well uh... The thing is, Tom... the tub's gettin' kinda full.

TOM

So?

LOU

So maybe you oughta take a crack at payin' some of these bills. And you get to take a bath. Your lifestyle improves by leaps and bounds.

TOM

Eh!

LOU

How you fixed for cash? You got cash for the holidays?

TOM

I got a little.

LOU

How much is a little?

TOM

A few bucks.

LOU

You want me to cash one of these checks?

TOM

Naw. I'll cash a check with the Chinaman.

LOU

I've got cash on me.

TOM
You got cash?

LOU
Yeah.

TOM
On you?

LOU
Five hundred bucks. Here. Here's a check for a hundred twenty-two dollars. You endorse this check and I'll deposit it in my account.

Lou goes about the task of finding Tom's checkbook, deposit slips, opening disability checks and does all the necessary work during the following:

TOM
How come you got so much cash on you?

LOU
I'm takin' a trip.

TOM
Yeah?

LOU
I'm goin' out of town. Almost a whole week. Right after work.

TOM
Where you goin'?

LOU
Vermont.

TOM
Vermont?

LOU
Yeah. Vermont. Where they make the syrup.

TOM
I know where they make the syrup! What're you going there for? There ain't nothing in Vermont.

LOU
There's trees.

TOM
Excuse me, yes, of course. How stupid of me. Yes, Lou, there are trees... sitting in forests... where it's a hundred degrees below zero!

LOU
Yeah, but in Vermont it's a <u>dry</u> cold.

TOM
Get away!

LOU

Naw, naw, you don't feel it that much. We'll have a good time no matter what.

TOM

"We?" What "we?" Who's "we?"

LOU

Me an' Mona.

TOM

Who's Mona?

LOU

What do you mean, "Who's Mona?!" Mona. The Mona I been tellin' you about.

TOM

You haven't told me about any Mona.

LOU

Sure I did. I've been tellin' you about Mona for weeks. You just don't listen is all.

TOM

Where'd you meet her? At the bar?

LOU

Are you kiddin'? I wouldn't go out with the scuz that crawls in there.

TOM

So where'd you meet her?

LOU

At school.

TOM

What school? You don't go to school.

LOU

Sure I do. See, I told you but you don't listen.

TOM

Where? Where you going to school?

LOU

It's just one course. It finished last week.

TOM

Where was this?

LOU

The New School.

TOM

That college downtown?

LOU

Yeah.

TOM

You're going to college?

LOU

It ain't like a real college. No one ever graduates from the New School. I just took one class. At night.

TOM

What class you take?

LOU

"Early American Cinema and Its Effect on Shaping the Racist, Sexist and Anti-Semitic Values of Modern Industrial America. Part One."

TOM

Wow!

LOU

I sat in that class for twelve weeks and all I learned was the title.

TOM

Why in hell would you take a class like that?

LOU

To meet women! There was maybe a hundred people in my class. And it was loaded with women. Single women who don't look too bad yet.

TOM

You were hanging out with college women?

LOU

Yeah. Me, Lou D'Marco, talkin' cinema with college women.

TOM

Didn't they find out?

LOU

Find out what?

TOM

That you don't know nothin'.

LOU

Naw. Easiest thing to do is shut up an' listen. These college type gals love that. They live in worlds full of men who never listen to them. They meet someone like me willing to listen about their careers and how their biological clocks are tickin' and they go nuts. I just button up and nod a lot. When you don't talk, women think you're sensitive.

TOM

Aw, they love that.

LOU

So you talk with some gal after class, she tells you she thinks the film had a lotta "symbolism," then you go to her place an' have sex. But first you have coffee. That's how you get to have sex with college women, Tommy. You gotta have coffee with 'em.

TOM

Really?

LOU

I'm finding out the more education a woman has, the less it costs to take her out.

TOM

Something's wrong with the world.

LOU

You ain't kiddin'. They ask me out, they want to pay the check, then they want to go to bed with me where they can't <u>wait</u> to do stuff a lot of hookers charge extra for.

TOM

Wow... and this is how you met Mona?

LOU

Yeah. She's divorced. All these women are divorced. Get this. She's an attorney.

TOM

Phew!

LOU

Not bad, huh?

TOM

A bartender who works in the worst bar on Ninth Avenue and a lawyer.

LOU

America's an unbelievable place, huh? See, me an' Mona, we're gonna visit her family, take walks in the snow, go antiquin'... fresh air, sunshine. A nice change of pace. It'll do us good. You need to get out more, Tom.

TOM

I get out plenty.

LOU

Out to Smiler's, the liquor store... You should, I dunno, just get "out" more. Go places, do things.

TOM

It's like a million below outside. Who the hell wants to go out?

LOU

It's not the point. There's such a thing as stayin' in too much. You get stale. Maybe get in a little rut or somethin'.

TOM

I'm not in a rut!

LOU

But you should be with other people. They can help you with stuff.

TOM

I don't need other people. I've got you.

Lou sneaks a pamphlet out of his pocket and tries to quote from it undetected.

LOU

But still, when an adult is stricken with blindness, well, when that happens...
   (reading)
"A vast reliable network of support must be drawn upon so that the disabled individual may cope satisfactorily."

TOM

What're you reading?

LOU

Nothin'.

TOM

What're you reading?

LOU

I wasn't readin' nothin'. I swear on my mother's grave!

TOM

What've you got there?

LOU

Just this pamphlet thing here is all. I was on the east side a while back and I passed the blind place is all.

TOM

Aho!

LOU

Hey, some guy shoved this in my hand. I couldn't help it. I figured I'd read up on this blind stuff is all.

TOM

Well, keep it to yourself.

Lou finds a stapler, counts money, then folds and staples various bills.

LOU

Wouldn't be such a bad idea. Get somebody else in here. I mean in addition to me. Someone who could pick up some of the slack.

TOM
We don't have any slack.

LOU
Well, I dunno. Maybe in a way you do. This place don't look as clean like it used to.

TOM
Hey, I like my place the way it is.

LOU
Tom, it's a mess.

TOM
I like my place the way it is!

LOU
This place looks like a giant ashtray.

TOM
I can't see it!

LOU
But you... now you got me confused!

(becomes confused with the stapling of the money)

What is it? Twenties in half?

TOM
No, twenties fold into fours, then staple.

LOU
Right.

TOM
Tens in half. Fives in half the long way. Staple at both ends. Ones are regular.

LOU
You know, blind people got their own special way of foldin' money.

TOM
So?

LOU
So they don't go around puttin' staples in their money. They teach 'em that at the blind place.

TOM
Hey, I'm doing fine, thank you. "The blind place!" You're some piece of work! You know that?

LOU
These volunteers. All they wanna do is help.

TOM

Bull.

LOU

You don't know what you're talkin'.

TOM

I know exactly what I'm talkin'! I know these volunteer types. I picked up plenty of them in my cab. Plenty of them. "The Lighthouse for the Blind, driver, and please don't drive too fast. Don't smoke, driver. Slow down. Are you trying to kill us both? What's the matter with you, driver? Are you stupid? Do you speak English?" You want to know someone? Really know someone? Watch them deal with someone low. Like a cab driver. Watch how they deal with someone like that. Tells you everything. Two faced hypocrites. I picked up plenty of them in my cab. Plenty of them. And all of them, each and every last one of them, women. Never young. Never pretty. East side women. Nothing but time and money on their hands. You getting tired of reading to me? Is it getting to be too much helping me out a little, huh? Is that it? Well, don't let me get in the way! Don't let me slow down your lifestyle!

Tom makes his way to the door.

TOM *(cont'd)*

Go on! Do all the things there are in life that please you! Go on! Get out! Hear me? Get...

Tom throws open the door. EDNA MILES is standing there.

TOM *(cont'd)*

(screams)
Out!!!
(then)
I don't need some plain, east side frump too scared and stupid to know what to do with her life come here and mess up mine! Understand?

There is a pregnant silence. Finally:

EDNA

Hello, I...

Tom jumps out of his skin.

TOM

(gasps)
Who's that!

EDNA

I didn't know if I should knock. I heard voices.

LOU

It's a woman from the blind place, Tom.

TOM

Aha! Yes! Yes! It all makes sense now. Yup. Fits together perfectly. Makes <u>perfect</u> sense.

LOU

(to Edna)
Would you just give us a minute?

EDNA

Well, I... uh...

LOU

Just one minute. I swear. A minute is all.

Lou closes the door leaving Edna out in the hallway.

LOU *(cont'd)*

Listen, Tom, I didn't tell you the whole truth before because I didn't want you to get upset.

TOM

And it worked like a charm, Lou.

LOU

I ain't just goin' on a vacation to Vermont, Tom. I'm gonna be movin' there. For real.

TOM

You're moving? To Vermont?

LOU

Yeah.

TOM

You've never even been there.

LOU

So?

TOM

So you don't even know what it's like in Vermont.

LOU

I seen calendars.

TOM

I don't believe this. Vermont's not a place you move <u>to</u>. It's a place you move <u>from</u>!

LOU
Me an' Mona. We're gonna look around. See what's up there. Jobs an' stuff.

TOM
Just like that.

LOU
Mona might be a lawyer for one of them environmental groups. The pay would be a lot less for her but then again it's cheaper to live in Vermont. There's nothing you wanna buy. And me, well, there's lots of bars up there. There's always work for lawyers and bartenders, huh?

TOM
The two kind of go hand-in-hand.

LOU
The thing is -- if I move out of the city, you'll be left with no one to --

TOM
(interrupts)
I've got people! I've got lots of people!

LOU
No, Tom -- you got no one and we both know it. You know how long it took to get this woman? Six months! That's how long ago I went down there!

TOM
Been plotting against me all along.

LOU
They got a waiting list like you wouldn't believe. This woman's a trained volunteer. She wants to help.

TOM
She can go to hell.

There is a knock at the door.

TOM *(cont'd)*
(calling to door)
Go to hell!

LOU
Shh! C'mon, she'll hear ya.

TOM
You go to hell. No wait. Go to Vermont!

There is a knock at the door again. Lou crosses and opens the door.

EDNA

I'm sorry but it's dark out here. The light bulb is missing and it's pitch black. There's also a dog roaming the hallway...

LOU

Yeah, come in. We were just... You're a little early is all. We weren't expecting you.

Edna enters. She walks with a slight, almost undetectable limp. She also seems to have some weakness in her hand -- the same side she limps on.

EDNA

They said Saturday morning.

LOU

It's not even nine o'clock yet.

EDNA

I didn't want to be late.

LOU

What's your name?

EDNA

Edna Miles.

Lou readies to leave.

LOU

Yeah, well, hi. I'm Lou. I called the blind place for my friend Tom here. He's the one who's blind.
   (sotto to Edna)
He's a proud man. Having somebody help him is not easy for him.

EDNA

I understand. Are you going?

LOU

I'd only be in the way. Tom, this is uh...

EDNA

Edna.

LOU

Edna. She's from the blind place, Tommy. She's here to read to you, help you answer your mail, go shoppin', whatever.
   (to Edna)
Right?

EDNA

Certainly.

LOU

Yeah, good. Edna, this is Thomas Hanratty. Raconteur, former kick-ass stickball player and, at one time, the most dangerous white cab driver in

21

New York City. Right, Tommy? Huh? Huh!

(no reply)

Good luck. Hey, Tom. Merry Christmas.

(no reply)

Merry Christmas, huh?

(no reply)

Hey, c'mon. Merry Christmas.

TOM

Drop dead.

Lou shrugs to Edna, then exits. Edna stands there not knowing quite what to say or do. Neither Edna nor Tom speak for the longest time. Finally:

EDNA

So, you were a cab driver?

(no reply)

That must have been interesting work.

(no reply)

Driving here and there, to and fro. Picking up all kinds of interesting people. Traveling to interesting destinations.

(no reply)

How long did you drive a taxicab, Thomas?

(no reply)

Perhaps I rode in your taxicab once. Wouldn't that be something? That we've already met only we don't know it. That would be interesting. Yes, very. I can remember when taxis were not just yellow. Remember?

(no reply)

I think they had to be two-tone. That was the only rule. Remember? They were blue and white, red and white, red and yellow, black and yellow... The black and yellow taxis looked like bumble bees. I rather liked that. Didn't you?

(no reply)

I remember being fond of black and yellow taxis. I would always hope we'd get one when father or the doorman hailed a cab. It gave you something to look forward to...

(no reply)

Did you take these photos? They're quite good. Look at this one. It's beautiful. A little girl running through an open fire hydrant. It must've been such a hot summer day. You can almost feel the water and hear her scream... The Brooklyn Bridge... This one's interesting. A bumpy cobblestone street. Looks like you had to lie down in the street to take it. Did you?

(no reply)

A bag lady sleeping... she looks so serene. These are beautiful photos. Is that Madison Avenue under all that snow?

(no reply)

I guess driving a taxi gave you plenty of chances to take pictures.

No reply. Edna spies an empty beer bottle on the counter and she drops it into the trash. The discarded beer bottle clinks loudly.

TOM

What's that?!

EDNA

A beer bottle. It was empty. I threw it away.

TOM

Don't go doing that. Leave everything just the way it is.

EDNA

I'm sorry.

TOM

Make sounds like that. Startle me with noises every which way.

EDNA

Sorry.

TOM

Don't you know how to be around a blind person?

EDNA

I just --

TOM

(interrupting)
Wadda ya got next? A tuba?

EDNA

Sorry.

TOM

You're here like ten seconds you're already banging around the place like a maniac. I'll have a heart attack or something. Listen, Ida.

EDNA

Edna.

TOM

My friend Lou was whadda ya callit... he acted what you might call prematurely.

EDNA

Prematurely?

TOM

You see, he thought I was in need of someone to help out because he's feeling kind of guilty he's taking off with some chick but uh, the fact is, Edna, I really don't need any help. I'm doing fine. I've got lots of people

23

who drop by. Too many, in fact. I've got a whole network of people.

EDNA

What are you saying?

TOM

I'm saying I really don't need any help.

EDNA

From the looks of things, I'd say you need a great deal of help.

TOM

So thank you and adios.

EDNA

You want me to leave?

TOM

No! "Adios" is Spanish for "Have some milk and cookies!" Yes, I want you to leave.

EDNA

But I moved things aside for this today. I made other arrangements.

TOM

So read to one of your other people.

EDNA

I don't have any other people. You're my only client.

TOM

Ho boy...

EDNA

You're also my first.

TOM

Ugh!

EDNA

On the way over here my father said reading for the blind was the stupidest idea I've ever had.

TOM

Smart man.

EDNA

He's never been right about anything. I'll be damned if he's right about this! You don't have a network.

TOM

She's serious!

EDNA

If you had a network, I don't think this place would look like this.

TOM

Look, lady. I don't care what you think. There's been a mistake. You should never've come in the first place, understand? It's nothing personal. I just don't need any help. Okay? Thank you. Goodbye.

EDNA

No.

TOM

What?

EDNA

I said no. I'm not leaving.

TOM

You're not what?!

EDNA

I put aside these four hours and I'm going to spend them here. I don't care if we just sit here. I'll do it. I will.

TOM

I don't believe this...

EDNA

I don't care if you feel so bad for yourself that you just want to rot away. I'll stand here and watch you rot. At least you won't rot alone. I'm not going. For all I care we can both stay here in stone silence listening to the sound of your insides getting hard and crusty.

TOM

You're not going to go?

EDNA

That's right.

TOM

I've asked you to leave but you're not going to.

EDNA

Correct.

TOM

(flabbergasted)

This is... it's... I can't believe you would... Hey! All right, all right. Enough, sister. Scram. Get your ass out of here!

EDNA

I'm not leaving.

TOM

Hey, enough! Get out!

EDNA

No.

TOM

Get out!

EDNA

I said no.

TOM

(*screaming*)
Get out!!! How could you... I said get out!!! Get... out!!!
   (*no reply*)
I could toss you out of here. I hope you know that, lady. I could eject you <u>physically</u>.

EDNA

Perhaps.

TOM

No "perhaps" about it! I've lived thirty years in this apartment. I know every square inch. I'd have you in a corner in no time and out the door five seconds after that.

EDNA

Like I said... perhaps.

TOM

Please just go and the whole thing'll be forgotten.

EDNA

Uh-uh.

TOM

Look, it's not your fault. It's nothing personal against you, Edna. There was just a mix-up... a misunderstanding. Lou thought I might need some help -- it turns out I don't. Thank you very much, but I won't be needing you. Goodbye.

EDNA

No.

TOM

Hey, c'mon. I want you out of here.

EDNA

No.

TOM

Get out.

EDNA

No.

TOM

Get out, damn it!!! I said get out!!!

(no reply)
Do a thing like this to me? My own home?!

Tom begins to slowly circle the table as Edna keeps her distance.

TOM *(cont'd)*
This is my home, understand? I want someone out -- they're out.

EDNA
Go ahead. Just try and catch me.

TOM
You're out of here...

EDNA
Not so. I'm like a jungle cat. I can move like you wouldn't believe. I'll just skip and twirl my way around this room. Zip! Twirl!

Tom makes a sudden grab for Edna and stumbles. His hand comes to rest upon a broom. He breaks off the bristle end of the broom with astonishing ease, then brandishes the stick.

TOM
Okay, fine... Let's see you zip your way around this.

EDNA
What are you doing?

TOM
Real smartass, aren't you?
(mocking her)
"I'm not going." We'll see about that.

EDNA
You're not going to hit me with that, are you?

TOM
It's up to you, babe.

EDNA
You wouldn't.

TOM
A man has the right to choose who stays in his own home.

EDNA
Put that down.

TOM
No.

EDNA
Put that down!!!

TOM
(mocking her)
No!!!

EDNA
You swing that at me...

TOM
Uh-huh.

EDNA
You just swing that at me...

TOM
Oh, I'm going to swing it at you all right...

EDNA
You do and I'll... I'll...

TOM
You'll what?

EDNA
I'll...
(thinks -- then)
I'll shoot you.

TOM
What?!

EDNA
I'll shoot you. I've got a gun. And, believe me, I know how to use it.

Edna opens her purse, then snaps it shut.

EDNA *(cont'd)*
There, it's out. If you do anything that looks like an act of violence against me -- so help me God -- I'll drop you like a rock.

TOM
A gun...

EDNA
That's right. I don't want to use it but if I have to I will.

TOM
And what kind of gun is this, if I might ask?

EDNA
A silver one.

TOM
A silver one. Sounds dangerous.

EDNA
It does the job.

TOM
You carry a gun?

EDNA
This is New York. Doesn't everyone?

TOM
You don't have no gun.

EDNA
Think so?

TOM
Yeah.

EDNA
Pretty sure of yourself, aren't you?

TOM
East side lady from the Lighthouse don't carry no gun.

EDNA
Not even one who was mugged? ... and told herself "Never again. No one does that to me again... <u>ever</u>!"

TOM
You're lyin'.

EDNA
You're positive?

TOM
Total bull.

EDNA
Then go ahead. Take a swing.

Edna crosses nearer to Tom and stands before him.

EDNA *(cont'd)*
If you're so sure about your ability to know a complete stranger you can't even see... then knock my block off. Go on.

Edna silently picks up an empty beer bottle and holds the top end against Tom's head.

EDNA *(cont'd)*
I'll put a bullet right in your thick head. Maybe it'll knock some sense into you.

Tom and Edna stay like this for the longest time as he tries to figure out if she is bluffing or not. He finally lowers his broom handle.

TOM
I need a drink.

Tom pours from his scotch bottle but it's empty.

                    EDNA

It's empty...

                    TOM

I can tell that!!!

Tom crosses to a cupboard and takes out a gift-wrapped bottle of scotch. He unwraps it quickly and pours himself some.

                    EDNA

Giftwrapped. Someone give you scotch for Christmas?

                    TOM

No, I was going to give it to Lou, but...
        (catches himself)
What am I doing talking to you?! I don't want you here -- you're not here!

                    EDNA

Lord, you're thick...

                    TOM

I'm thick. You're waving a loaded gun around and I'm thick. Look. Lady. Here it is plain and simple. As of this very moment, you are not even here.

                    EDNA

I see.

                    TOM

I tried to deal with you rationally, but it didn't work. So you want to stay -- stay. But you're not here. I'm going to go about my business like I always do. As if you're not even in this room.

                    EDNA

Do as you wish.

                    TOM

I will. You've got the dullest four hours of your life coming up.

                    EDNA

You've obviously never been to the opera.

                    TOM

Huh?

                    EDNA

Nothing.

                    TOM

I don't even know what I'm talking to you for. You're not here! I'm going about my day like I'm alone. You're blocked out completely. I'm just going to have my normal routine like I always do.

>   *(struck by a thought)*
> In fact, about this time every day, I take my bath. Yeah. That's what I do.
> I take my bath about this time every day.

                                EDNA

It looks like you skipped a few months.

Tom begins to clean the mail out of his bathtub.

                                TOM

Climb in there, take a nice, long, hot bath. That's what I'm going to do.
Fill up the tub, strip down and hop in.

                                EDNA

That's my favorite part.

                                TOM

Somebody say something?

                                EDNA

Definitely. The strip-down part. It's my favorite. I'm a big fan of the
male anatomy. You bet I am.

                                TOM

Uh-huh.

                                EDNA

Those male strip clubs like Chippendale's and such, I go all the time.
Nothing I like better than to see a tight pair of buns hanging out of a
satin G-string. Just peel slowly, will you, Tommy? And save the socks for
last, okay? I've got a thing for feet. Oh, gee. I just realized. You're going
"all the way." This'll be even better than Chippendale's. I'll get to see
<u>everything</u>. Can you give me a sneak preview? Wadda ya say, huh? Whip
that puppy out. C'mon, let's take a peek at Tommy Junior.

                                TOM

You're some twisted piece of work, lady. Are you serious?

                                EDNA

I am if you are.

                                TOM

You're crazy. I'm sitting in my kitchen with a sex pervert with a gun!

Edna crosses to the kitchen sink where she washes a glass, dries it and eventually
helps herself to some of his scotch.

                                EDNA

I was just thinking.

TOM
Of what?

EDNA
My father's probably going to ask me how this went.

TOM
Just tell him the truth. You teased and tormented a blind man on the day before Christmas Eve.

EDNA
Have you been blind for long, Thomas?

TOM
You're still not going?

EDNA
Not only am I not going -- I'm going to drink some of your scotch.

TOM
Please. I insist. Take the <u>furniture</u> with you while you're at it!

EDNA
Have you been blind for long?

(no reply)

Have you been blind for long?

(no reply)

It's called conversation. You have the advantage. You can picture anyone you'd like. You like Oriental hookers? Well, I'm poured into a black satin dress split clean up the side. I'm wearing black fingernail polish and a ring on each finger.

(like an Oriental hooker)

"So, American big boy... You like Ting Lu? You been blind for long?"

TOM
Eight years.

EDNA
How did it happen?

TOM
The way I went blind?

EDNA
Yes.

TOM
Don't you have all that in your handy little file from the Lighthouse?

EDNA
Sure, but it's so much more delicious when I hear it first hand.

TOM
If I tell you, will you go?

EDNA

Okay.

TOM

You will?

EDNA

Why not? All I want is a tragic story to share with the girls at tea -- then I'm gone.

TOM

Okay. Deal. Come this February it'll be eight years. I'm at the bar with Lou one night and it's cold, real cold, as cold as it is today, maybe even colder. It's four in the morning. Lou's closed the bar. He's got the door locked, we're inside drinkin'. We're doing some <u>serious</u> drinking. <u>Very</u> serious drinking. We're drunk is what we are.

EDNA

Yes.

TOM

Time to go home, I walk with Lou out to his motorcycle. His cycle has been sitting in sub-zero weather for twelve hours and the battery is dead. I've got my cab, there's a pair of jumper cables in the trunk. Lou says, "Gimme a jump start." I don't want to. I tell him he's too drunk to ride a motorcycle over the Fifty-ninth Street Bridge in two-degree weather, he tells me I'm too drunk to drive a cab, I tell him to go to hell, we have a fist fight. There we are, two drunks on Ninth Avenue at four in the morning having a fist fight to see who's more sober. Lou wins the fight, so I agree to give him a jump start. Is a taxicab battery the same voltage as a motorcycle battery? Can you <u>do</u> such a thing? We don't know. We're drunk out of our minds! I hook up the cables to his battery, take the other end over to the cab's battery, touch the terminals and my battery explodes in my face. I've got battery acid everywhere. My face, my hands, I can taste it in my mouth, my eyes... I'm in shock. I'm running around. Lou's trying to catch me. We're drunk, we're falling down. There's traffic coming down Ninth Avenue. I try and stop a car... I'm waving my arms. "Help me! Help me! God! Help me!" Who's going to stop on Ninth Avenue at four in the morning for someone yelling "Help me!?" Huh? Would you?

(no reply)

By the time I got to the hospital both my corneas had been too damaged for them to... I can't even see silhouettes or blurs or shapes. Just black.

EDNA

I'm sorry.

(pause)

You don't seem to be big on food.

TOM

Huh?

EDNA

Your kitchen. There's not much to eat.

TOM

Yeah, well, I usually just pop out to Smiler's and... Hey, weren't you going to leave?

EDNA
(examining can)
You paid two dollars and fifteen cents for a can of chili?

TOM

I said, weren't you going to leave?

EDNA

Is that what they charge?

TOM

You said you were going to go.

EDNA

I lied. Is this what they charge?

TOM

Yes! That's what they get at Smilers! If it <u>says</u> two dollars and fifteen cents then I <u>paid</u> two dollars and fifteen cents! Now, you said you would —

EDNA
(interrupting)
A dollar five in New Jersey.

TOM

You live in New Jersey?

EDNA

No, Eighty-fifth and Madison.

TOM

Excuse me!

EDNA

But my father drives me out to Newark once a week, sometimes twice. We load up on everything. It's <u>so</u> much cheaper out there it's ridiculous. Know what I could do?

TOM

What? Pick up a few items for me? Do my shopping <u>for</u> me?

EDNA

No, that would be a lot of extra work that I'm not willing to do.

TOM

Oh...

EDNA

What I was about to suggest was you come with us. My father takes the Lincoln Tunnel. We drive right by this building. You could do your weekly shopping and save a lot of money. Do you want to do that?

TOM

Well, uh... there's all kinds of stores on Ninth Avenue, you know. I mean besides Smiler's. There's, uh, well, you know, there's a Puerto Rican deli on Forty-fifth, and uh the Korean grocery store... you know... cheese and milk... fruit... stuff...

EDNA

Is that a "yes" or a "no?"

TOM

Your old man's got a car?

EDNA

Yes. It's his hobby.

TOM

Hobby?

EDNA

Yes. When Daddy retired, he read an article about men who stop working without making plans. The article claimed men who don't plan for their retirement have a life expectancy of only a few years.

TOM

So?

EDNA

So that was my father. He read the article and got scared. Very scared. One day he asked my mother and me to come outside. There, parked at the curb, was this car. A Chevrolet. A four-door, black Chevrolet. The most unimaginative car I'd ever seen. I had no idea a car could come with so little chrome! He parks it on the street. We live in the most competitive parking environment in the world and my father's plan to stay involved with life is to battle for parking spots with this drab automobile. Moving the car once a day would be enough aggravation for anyone, but my father <u>thrives</u> on it. He'll see someone putting on their coat and he's on them like a hawk. "Going somewhere? Need a lift?" "No," we tell him. "Don't give up your parking space. You worked so hard for it." It means nothing to him! He gives up a parking space he got up at six AM to get just to drive you to somewhere where he can circle the block and wait for you so he can drive you back home and circle the block again looking for another parking spot. He's out there right now. Circling the block. Like a shark. Waiting for me to fail. He's not playing the radio because the car doesn't <u>have</u> one. They wanted ninety dollars extra for a radio. So he's circling the block. Silently. Windows fogging up. Round and round.

TOM

This is his retirement?

EDNA

I'm afraid so.

TOM

That's crazy. Now, you take my father. When he retired, he did it right. He retired on a Friday, hung around the house Saturday and Sunday, come Monday, he went to the Terminal Bar and he went there every morning like clockwork for three months. Religiously. That's how I met Lou. The guy you met. Lou works at the Terminal Bar.

EDNA

The "Terminal Bar?"

TOM

Yeah. It's next to the Port Authority Bus Terminal.

EDNA

Oh.

TOM

Yeah. So my old man'd get so wasted, there wasn't no way he could make it home. Lou would call me, say "Come and get your old man." I'd hop down to the Terminal Bar and get him. Lou and I became friends. At least, we were.

EDNA

What happened?

TOM

To me and Lou?

EDNA

No, to your father.

TOM

He died. Right at the bar. One minute he was talking to some guy – next minute he was stone cold dead.

EDNA

How ironic.

TOM

What?

EDNA

Your father. He died at the Terminal Bar.

TOM

Huh?

EDNA

"Terminal." He died at the --

TOM

(getting it)

Oh! Right. Yeah. I never thought of it that way. Right. "Terminal." They keep a shot glass with some whiskey in it on a shelf above the cash register. Sorta like a tribute. There's five or six glasses up there. All the guys who died at the bar over the years.

EDNA

(offering toast)

To your father.

TOM

Huh?

EDNA

I'm making a toast to your father.

TOM

Sure, why not.

They drink.

EDNA

What was he like?

TOM

What was he like... Well, you'd like my father. Everyone did. Liking him was probably the easiest thing a person could ever do. He was the most beloved man in this neighborhood. If they were electing a mayor of Ninth Avenue, he would've won by a landslide. The man's middle name was charm. He had buckets of it. On the street, he was the nicest man you could ever know. To walk with him was like walking with a celebrity or something. I used to wait for him at the bus stop on 42nd Street every night just so I could walk home with him. So I could be seen with him. He was so well liked. On the street. And only on the street. Because at home he was the coldest, most ruthless, black-hearted son-of-a-bitch that ever brought home a paycheck. He spent his time in this apartment like he was serving a prison sentence. This silent, smoldering mountain of a man that you were too afraid to even talk to. He beat me. Beat me so bad I joined the Army the minute they'd take me. Beat my sister. He beat my mother like a dog. See the doorway?

EDNA

Yes.

TOM

There used to be a door there. A French door. With all the panes of glass.

EDNA

No...

TOM

Pushed me through it when I was sixteen. I came at him with a heavy frying pan and he threw me right through the French door. Took forty-eight stitches at Saint Clair's emergency room. Somewhere along the way, between the time my father met my mother and the day he died, somewhere in that space of time someone did something that put a bug up his ass. A great, big, black, creepy-crawly bug got up his ass one day and stayed there. And we, my mother, my sister and me, we were supposed to guess how to get the bug out. With every little thing we did, every single move we made. My mother... I felt the worst for her. Married to a man that has every heart in the neighborhood in his pocket -- he comes home and he doesn't even bother to say hello. Silence. Not so much as a grunt to acknowledge she <u>exists</u>. Just another day of punishing her for something... Sometimes I have this awful thought about the man. Sometimes I think my father was warm and friendly with everyone just so it would hurt my mother all the more. And if that's true, then why was my father not the cruelest, most heartless person who ever existed?

EDNA

Because my father is.

TOM

No way.

EDNA

I'm serious.

TOM

No one was worse than my father.

EDNA

My father would go to the office in the morning and ruin the life of someone like your father just for <u>practice</u>.

TOM

That doesn't count. That's just business.

EDNA

My father is the most heartless, loveless man who ever lived. I'm sure your father was bad, too, but he'll have to take second place.

TOM

For cruelty and not loving -- my father takes second place to <u>no</u> <u>one</u>.

EDNA

He does this time.

TOM

Uh-uh.

EDNA

Oh, yes.

TOM

Sorry.

EDNA

I'm sorry.

TOM

Get away.

EDNA

I can prove it.

TOM

Baloney.

EDNA

I can. I can tell you a story about my father -- it wouldn't even have to be his worst story -- I could tell you about him and you would have no choice but to say, "Yes, you're correct. Your father is the most heartless man who ever lived."

TOM

Never.

EDNA

Want to bet?

TOM

Sure. What're we betting?

EDNA

If I lose -- I go. Get my coat, walk out the door, I'm gone. I win -- I stay. I mean, I get to come back.

TOM

I dunno.

EDNA

You get to judge.

TOM

How do you know I won't say you lose just so you'll go?

EDNA

Because you'd have to lie and that would mean you have no soul, like my father, and I could never read to a man with no soul.

TOM

All right. Go 'head.

EDNA

Very well.

TOM

But I'm warning you, if I feel in my heart your father's not any worse…

you're gone.

            EDNA

Fair enough.

            TOM

Go 'head. Shoot.

            EDNA

Give me a minute. Let me think.

Edna helps herself to some more scotch as she thinks. Finally:

            EDNA *(cont'd)*

I'm just thinking...

            TOM

Take your time.

            EDNA

There are so many tales to choose from. Here, this will do. It's short, yet numbing. We rented a house in the woods one summer. I was twelve. We had never spent any time in the country to speak of. A visit here, a half day there. This would be an entire month and I can't tell you how I was looking forward to it. Our first night in the country, and I was just about to fall asleep when I heard this terrible racket. I got up, looked out my window and there they were. A family of raccoons going through our metal trash cans! I was thrilled beyond words! Live animals, cute ones, no less, at our back porch pawing through our garbage. I watched from my window and simply... giggled. My welcoming committee were these bandits complete with masks and they made all this entertainment from refuse. The next night I couldn't even think about sleeping. I put a pillow on my window sill and waited for the raccoons. I remember one of them had a fondness for orange rinds and I had left some at the top of our garbage for him. I fell asleep waiting. An hour or two must've gone by when suddenly the trash cans rattled. I woke up instantly. The raccoons were back. The biggest one -- he must have been a male -- the leader -- he was on top of a trash can trying to get to the orange rinds when someone... There was a shot. This gunshot rang out and he fell backward off the trash can six or eight feet from the force of the bullet into his back. He flailed his arms and legs in the air for just a moment or two and then he was dead.

            TOM

And your father shot the raccoon. Listen, I'm sorry, but that's not --

            EDNA

        (interrupting)

Apparently you can shoot a raccoon who goes through your garbage, but there's no guarantee the others will stay away. Not unless you do what my father did. Yes, my father shot the poor animal. He stepped out from behind some bushes where he had waited for the raccoons like some great white hunter. This was my father's first official act with nature. To kill something. He had a rope with him. And he tied the rope around the dead animal's hind legs then dragged him out to the edge of the woods and hung him from a tree. Not high. Just a few feet. The other raccoons who had run away -- they came back to the edge of the woods to the tree. They gathered around their dead friend in a circle and mourned him with a grief I did not know existed. They stood in a perfect circle and wailed these shrill cries of anguish until I thought I would go insane from their misery. They flung themselves upon the ground, held and comforted each other and looked to our house as if to say, "Are you <u>insane</u>? Why? Why!" And when they were done they moped off into the woods. We rented that house for the next three summers. The raccoons never came back. My father brags about that to this day. How he protected our coffee grinds and egg shells one night in July.

Tom goes to speak but stops himself. He tries again, then stops. Finally:

TOM
You really wearing a black dress with a slit?

EDNA
Am I what?

TOM
You know what you said before? The Oriental gal and the dress...

EDNA
Oh. No, I'm not.

TOM
Just thought I'd ask.

EDNA
Did you take these photos?

TOM
Yes. Years ago.

EDNA
They're wonderful.

TOM
Thank you. See the camera hanging on the wall? Guy got in my cab and left it in the back seat.

EDNA
Oh my...

TOM
I dropped him off at Grand Central. So much for finding him there. The cab company had a lost and found department: my boss' <u>living room</u>! So I kept the camera.

41

EDNA
Wise choice.

TOM
That's how I got into photography. Someone left a camera in my taxi. You work, Edna?

EDNA
At home, yes. I don't have a regular job as such, but there's so much that needs doing. I nursed my grandfather when he died several years ago. Then my grandmother. People said she would go right after him.

TOM
That happens a lot, yeah.

EDNA
I got to go to Washington last summer. Turns out a grand aunt was dying. I got to see the Washington Monument on the way to the cemetery.

TOM
Oh.

EDNA
My brother Andrew. He died young. I nursed him. Mother is not well. I'm sure she'll be next. I'll nurse her. Then father will die. Then my work will be done.

TOM
Well, it's nice to have things planned.

EDNA
Not very Christmassy conversation, I suppose.

TOM
It's okay. Christmas seems to treat some people better than others. I've always liked Christmas, but somehow Christmas Eve, Christmas Day... I always seemed to be driving a cab. Midtown has no traffic, everyone wants a cab, tips are great. You get what you can out of Christmas.

EDNA
Yes. Is there any last-minute shopping you'd like to do? I have time still.

TOM
Naw, not really.

EDNA
Gift wrapping, Scotch tape, ribbon? We could go get some.

TOM
My gift list was just Lou this year. I got him a lovely bottle of something which we're drinking right now.

EDNA
(offering toast)
To Lou.

TOM
To Lou.

They drink.

TOM *(cont'd)*
I went to Saint Patrick's Cathedral for midnight mass last Christmas. Man, I figured that oughta be something. The choir, the organ, the smell of incense... But I get there and they tell me I need <u>tickets</u>. Tickets! They turn me away from midnight mass because I don't have a <u>ticket</u>!

EDNA
A lot of people want to go.

TOM
Seems that way.

EDNA
It's like a Broadway musical.

TOM
I bet.

EDNA
I have tickets.

TOM
To what?

EDNA
Saint Patrick's, tomorrow night, midnight mass.

TOM
How'd you get them?

EDNA
My father is a big contributor to Saint Patrick's. I have two tickets. Would you like to go?

TOM
You won't need the other ticket?

EDNA
No.

TOM
No one else you want to take?

EDNA
No.

TOM
What about your father?

43

EDNA

His sister is arriving at Newark at eleven at night and he insisted on picking her up.

TOM

Hmm, midnight mass at Saint Patrick's. Sounds mighty tempting. Huh? Yeah, sure. I'll go. Yeah, what the hell. Let's do it.

Edna begins putting on her coat, preparing to leave.

EDNA

Very well. Shall I come by here first?

TOM

Sounds like a plan. Say eleven o'clock?

EDNA

Could we make it ten-thirty? I'd like to get there early.

TOM

Fine.

EDNA

I'd like to light a candle for my brother Andrew.

TOM

I'll light one for my mother.

EDNA

Then we can say a prayer if you'd like. A prayer to Saint Odilia.

TOM

She a patron saint?

EDNA

Yes.

TOM

For who?

EDNA

The blind and hopeless causes.

TOM

I had to ask.

EDNA

Tomorrow then.

TOM

Tomorrow.

Edna goes to exit but stops when:

TOM

Listen, Edna, can I ask you a question?

EDNA

Sure.

                             TOM

Tell me the truth. No bull.

                             EDNA

All right.

                             TOM

Did you really have a gun before?

                             EDNA

Yes... but I was only going to shoot you in the leg.

Edna exits.

                             TOM

Oh...

The lights fade to black.

                   <u>END OF ACT ONE</u>

ACT TWO

It is exactly eight days later -- New Year's Eve morning. Tom's apartment is much improved. Clothes no longer lie about, the floor is shiny clean, the garbage no longer overflows, there are no dirty dishes in evidence, things are neat, orderly and pleasant-looking. Tom's cupboard is fully stocked with neatly arranged groceries. The formerly greasy window is now clean and it even sports a frilly curtain. The dead plant is gone and in its place there is a live, healthy plant.

As we begin the stage is empty. From outside we can hear the occasional faint SOUNDS of New Year's Eve party HORNS. The hot water kettle on the stove begins to WHISTLE.

Tom hurriedly enters from his bedroom. He is just finishing getting dressed. Tom's appearance is much improved, too. He looks neat and clean-shaven, and his clothes are freshly washed and pressed, although not much can be said for his color selection. Tom goes about the task of making a pot of tea. When he is just about done there is a knock at the door.

                TOM

Who is it?

                EDNA *(O.S.)*

It's me.

                TOM

Just a second.

Tom disappears into his bedroom for a moment then returns with a sweater in a bizarre color or pattern. He quickly puts it on, pats his hair, etc. and goes to speak. He stops himself. He sits at his kitchen table and strikes a nonchalant pose.

                TOM *(cont'd)*

It's open.

Edna tries to open the door but the chain has been set.

                EDNA

Tom?

                TOM

Huh?

                EDNA

The chain is on.

                TOM

The what?

EDNA

The chain, Tom. I can't open the door.

TOM

Oh! Wait. Hold on. Lemme get that. Hold it. Just one sec.

Tom crosses to the door and unlatches the chain easily.

EDNA

Sorry.

TOM

Uh-uh. Not your fault. I'm always putting this thing on and forgetting about it. There.

Edna enters. Edna's appearance has changed somewhat, too. She has had her hair done, she's wearing makeup and she also wears a dress that looks closer to spring than winter.

EDNA

Hello.

TOM

Hi. I'm sorry about the door.

EDNA

It's all right.

TOM

I'm always putting up the chain then telling people, "It's open!"
  (laughs nervously)
Heh heh... It used to drive Lou nuts. "The chain! The chain!" Well, you just saw...

EDNA

In a city like New York, it's best to keep your door locked in the first place.

TOM

You're right. All kinds of creeps and weirdos crawling around.

EDNA

Yes.

TOM

Yes.

EDNA

Well...

TOM

Yeah.

EDNA

Sorry I'm late.

TOM

Were you late? I didn't even know.

EDNA

There are people starting to celebrate New Year's Eve already. It's not even noon.

TOM

Can you believe it?

EDNA

The police had some streets closed off of Times Square. My cab driver had to take a detour.

TOM

Aha.

EDNA

Well.

TOM

Well.
    (then)
I made some tea.

EDNA

Really?

TOM

Actually I'm <u>making</u> tea. Just poured the water. It'll be ready in a minute.

EDNA

Oh, good. I'd love some.

TOM

You got it.

They both laugh nervously.

TOM *(cont'd)*

It's your favorite, too. English Breakfast tea.

EDNA

Oh, how nice.

TOM

Even though it's nowhere near breakfast.

They both laugh nervously.

EDNA

And we're nowhere near England.

TOM

Huh?

EDNA

English Breakfast tea. We're nowhere near England.

TOM

(getting it)
Oh! Yeah! Right!

They both laugh nervously, then.

TOM

Funny.

EDNA

Hmm...

TOM

Hmm...

EDNA

Don't you look nice.

TOM

Aw, this? This is just knock-around stuff I wear. Like the sweater?

EDNA

It's interesting.

TOM

Nice, huh?

EDNA

<u>Very</u> interesting.

TOM

Knew you'd like it. I've had it for a while.

EDNA

You bought it when you could see?

TOM

No.

EDNA

Aha.

TOM

But it was a few years ago. I went down to Canal Street. Old geezer who runs the store says, "What're you lookin' for?" I tell him I need a sweater. He says, "What kind of sweater?" Can you imagine that? He took the time to ask me what <u>kind</u> of sweater I was looking for. I say, "I'm looking for a classic Christmas sweater. One that's red mostly and white and a picture on it that looks like it was done in needlepoint. You know, Santa, his sled, people ice skating, like that..." He says, "You're in luck. I just got one of those in today." And he sells me this one.

Tom's sweater is nothing like his description.

EDNA
It's lovely.

TOM
I haven't worn it that much. But this seemed like the time to take it out. My corny Christmas sweater. Tea must be ready by now.

EDNA
Would you like me to...?

TOM
Uh-uh. Let me. You sit. Relax.

Tom goes about the task of serving her tea.

EDNA
Guess what I just saw outside.

TOM
A dead guy?

EDNA
God no. Why on earth would you guess that?

TOM
In this neighborhood it's not that wild a guess.

EDNA
Well, it wasn't a dead person.

TOM
I give up.

EDNA
I saw a white cat. Right outside, in front of the building. He was beautiful... sleeping on a pile of plastic garbage bags. Pure, snow white. Not the slightest smudge on him.

TOM
A pure white cat in this neighborhood?

EDNA
Yes.

TOM
Must've fallen off a truck from Jersey.

EDNA
There's going to be a miracle.

TOM
Hmm?

EDNA
When you see a pure white animal, that means there's going to be a miracle. That's what Sister Mary Sebastian used to tell us. "Before God

performs one of his miracles, he sends down an angel in the form of a white animal. To make sure His miracle goes the way He wants it."

TOM

Who told you that?

EDNA

Sister Mary Sebastian. Fifth grade.

TOM

And where did she come up with that?

EDNA

No idea.

TOM

"There's going to be a miracle." That's rich. How old was Sister Mary what's-her-name?

EDNA

Sebastian.

TOM

How old was she?

EDNA

At the time… in her eighties.

TOM

Well, that's what eighty years of no sex will do. You start making up stories about white cats and miracles.

EDNA

No, this is going to happen. I can feel it in my bones the way you feel the cold sometimes. I've been feeling this way ever since we prayed together in Saint Patrick's. Something really wonderful is going to happen and it's going to happen right here. The cat, it looked at me as if to say, "Don't look so surprised. You know why I'm here. I'm here for the miracle."

TOM

Edna, this neighborhood, Hell's Kitchen, it wasn't built for miracles. It was built for tragedy. That's why all the apartments are too small. So people can bake in the heat of summer, get drunk and kill each other. I've lived here my entire life. The only miracle I've ever seen is when my father left something in the bottle.

EDNA

You just wait. Wait 'til something good happens and you were the only one who didn't believe it was coming.

TOM

If that happens I will personally apologize, buy you lunch, then give the white cat a blow dry.

Tom offers to pour some whiskey in Edna's tea.

TOM *(cont'd)*

Want some?

EDNA

No, I shouldn't.

TOM

It's like Irish coffee except you do it with tea.

EDNA

No.

TOM

I make lousy tea. It'll kill the taste.

EDNA

I don't think so.

TOM

I hate to drink alone.

EDNA

No thanks.

TOM

You sure?

EDNA

I'm sure.

TOM

Just one?

EDNA

No.

TOM

It's New Year's Eve.

EDNA

Okay.

Tom pours whiskey in both of their teas.

EDNA *(cont'd)*

Guess where I went yesterday.

TOM

No idea.

EDNA

The New School.

Tom chokes on his tea.

TOM

The wha...?

EDNA

Are you all right?

TOM

I'm fine, I'm fine... What's this about the New School?

EDNA

It's where I registered to take a class. It's one night a week.

TOM

Ooo, Edna. Edna, Edna, Edna... Don't you know about that place?

EDNA

Know about what?

TOM

What goes on over there? What kind of people go there?

EDNA

What are you talking about?

TOM

There are a lot of -- how can I put this in a nice way -- there are a lot of real smooth, smarmy guys on the make over there who are looking for only one thing and it ain't no education.

EDNA

Where did you hear this?

TOM

It's something everybody knows.

EDNA

I never heard any such thing.

TOM

Then I'm surprised. Because it's a basic, well-known fact about New York City. New York City: it's cold in the winter, the subways smell of urine and the New School's got a lotta horny gigolos in it.

EDNA

Well, I'll just have to be extra careful in my Tuesday night Shakespeare class.

TOM

You do that. I'm not kidding, Edna. That place is like a shark tank. Watch yourself.

EDNA

I will.

TOM

You're taking Shakespeare, huh?

EDNA

To start.

TOM

They cover any of his sonnets?

EDNA

Some. And about six of his plays.

TOM

Maybe we could read some of his stuff one of these days, huh?

EDNA

I'd love to. You like Shakespeare?

TOM

Love 'im! I've read all his plays. Some of them more than once. And those romantic poets. You know, the British guys.

EDNA

Shelley, Byron…

TOM

Yeah. I'm nuts for that stuff. In high school, Mister Kaiser made everyone memorize twenty lines of a sonnet by a romantic poet for an exam. Man, guys were forcing that stuff into their brains like it was poison. Me? I had twenty lines memorized in no time. I aced the exam and a few of the guys got suspicious. Thought I actually <u>liked</u> poetry.

EDNA

Uh-oh.

TOM

You'd better believe it. You don't want to go through high school in New York City known as a "lover of poetry" believe me. It's easier to be known as a drug addict.

EDNA

What did you do?

TOM

I told everyone I cheated. I was a hero. But I held on to my poetry book, bought some others. I keep them on this shelf. Haven't read one in years.

EDNA

Did you ever ask Lou?

TOM

To read me some poems?

EDNA

Yes.

TOM

Lou D'Marco makes a telephone bill sound worse than it is. Can you imagine what he'd do to Robert Browning?

EDNA

Aha.

TOM

Wordsworth. He's my favorite. Here's a guy who hung around, wrote poems about nature, rainbows, life, women...

(from memory)
"She was a PhanTom of delight When first she gleamed upon my sight;
A lovely Apparition, sent To be a moment's ornament;
Her eyes as stars of Twilight fair;
Like Twilight, too, her dusky hair;
But all things else about her drawn
From May-time and the cheerful Dawn;
A dancing Shape, an Image gay,
To haunt, to startle, and waylay.
A perfect Woman, nobly planned, To warn, to comfort, and command;
And yet a Spirit still, and bright
With something of angelic light."

(then)
Could this guy write or what!

EDNA

Beautiful...

TOM

His stuff is terrific.

EDNA

I never pictured you as someone who would like Shakespeare and Wordsworth, Thomas.

TOM

See? People build up these preconceived notions about people based on what? Nothing, really. Like I was watching this movie the other night...

EDNA

Uh-huh.

TOM

There was this blind guy and he's feeling some gal's face, and I guess it was all very tender and sensuous because there was all these violins.

EDNA

Yes.

TOM

And this guy, he's feeling away, and the gal, she's going, "Yes, John, please go ahead. Feel my face." And the guy's going, "I've been wondering what you look like for ever so long." He talked funny, you know, because he was British.

EDNA

Yes.

TOM

And this goes on for a while, I guess he's running his fingers all over her puss 'cause there's more and more violins every second. And he goes, he finally goes, "My word! You're beautiful!" Hah!

EDNA

Not true?

TOM

A total misconception.

EDNA

The girl's not beautiful?

TOM

No. I mean yeah, she's beautiful probably, but you can't tell what somebody looks like just feeling their face. You can't. I sure as hell can't. I can't tell if someone's ugly, beautiful or whatever. It's all baloney. "Blind people are these sensitive human beings that can paint pictures with their fingers." Wrong! I can barely tell my sister's face from a toaster! I don't have the slightest idea what anyone looks like if I feel their face. It's a total misconception created by Hollywood or some other bunch of assholes -- excuse my French.

EDNA

Of course.

TOM

Okay, you can tell some absolute basics, like if someone is a hundred. They're going to have wrinkles. You can tell if someone's really old. Or if someone has a scar or an enormous nose, if they're bald... something like that.

EDNA

Uh-huh.

TOM

You can also tell if someone is really young. Their head is smaller. Aside from that, there's not much I can tell. There are a lot of notions about blind people that just aren't true. There's a lot they don't talk about. There's a lot they don't tell you. I'm starting to forget what certain things look like. My nephew, he's nine, I go to sit on my sister's couch and I feel something. I go, "Matty, is this your toy car?" The kid goes, "It's a bus." See, I was feeling it. I was holding it in my hand and I couldn't tell the difference between a car and a bus. I know they've both got four wheels, there's a lot of steel and glass, but as to the actual shape... It's... I can't really visualize that. What a difference, huh? I'm not going to be driving either but still... I used to know the difference between cars and buses. You know, I can't remember what I look like anymore. It started a few years ago. What I look like got a little fuzzy to me in my mind. Then it got worse. Now I try and picture what I look like and the picture comes out blank. When I shave I still do it in front of the mirror. I put my face before the mirror as though doing that will... My own face has slipped away from me. I try... I try to see myself but... not anymore...

EDNA
You have blue eyes.

TOM
What?

EDNA
Your eyes. They're blue. A light blue that looks almost gray in some light.

TOM
Are they cloudy?

EDNA
No.

TOM
They're not all white and milky?

EDNA
Not a bit.

TOM
For eight years I've wondered. Do my eyes stare in different places?

EDNA
No. They're normal.

TOM
Like a sighted person?

EDNA
Like a sighted person.

TOM
I've never asked Lou.

EDNA
It's not the kind of question one man can ask another.

TOM
I don't make eye-contact with people.

EDNA
You come close.

TOM
But when I talk to you I don't look directly at you.

EDNA
Neither do a lot of sighted people. Your hair is blond and baby fine.

TOM
Is it thinning?

EDNA
No. But you have some gray on the sides.

TOM
The old man. His head turned <u>white</u>.

EDNA
It makes you look distinguished.

TOM
Not old?

EDNA
No. Like a professor or a judge.

TOM
Yeah?

EDNA
Yes. Your skin is clear. A little on the pale side.

TOM
I don't go out enough.

EDNA
Your chin is round. You have high cheekbones. When you smile your eyes are little more than slits.

TOM
Yes.

EDNA
There's a small scar on your forehead.

TOM
I was ten. I got hit by a Coke bottle.

EDNA
You have long eyelashes for a man. They're quite beautiful. Your mouth is overwhelmingly kind. When you smile...

TOM
Edna...

EDNA
Yes, Tom?

TOM
I know we've only known each other for a week and you've probably got plans, tonight being New Year's Eve and all...

EDNA
Yes?

                             TOM
It's not much but it's something I've done every New Year's Eve since I was a kid...

                             EDNA
Yes.

                             TOM
We're just a couple blocks from Times Square. I usually bundle up good, take along a bottle of something to keep me warm... I was wondering...

                             EDNA
Yes, I'd love to.

                             TOM
Really?

                             EDNA
I think it would be wonderful to scream like madmen at midnight.

                             TOM
Well, all right... Great...

                             EDNA
Great...

                             TOM
Yeah, great.

                             EDNA
Great.

There is a moment where Tom would like to kiss Edna, however he has very little idea of how to approach it or if she is willing.. Edna wonders if she should help and initiate the kiss. The moment becomes more and more awkward, yet compelling. Just as it looks like this kiss might actually happen there is a KNOCK at the door.

                             TOM
Who is it?

                             LOU (O.S.)
It's Lou.

                             TOM
Lou?

                             LOU (O.S.)
C'mon, open the door, it's cold out here. I could spit ice cubes, I swear! C'mon, open up!

Tom crosses to the door and unlocks it. Lou enters bundled well from the cold. He carries a piece of luggage, a brown paper bag and a souvenir shopping bag from Vermont. He also sports a warm-looking hunter's hat -- an obvious purchase from his trip.

During the following there is a certain air of insensitivity from Lou regarding the neatness of the apartment. His hat and gloves get tossed in different directions. When Lou misses the trash with the cap to a bottle of beer he makes no effort to pick it up. This does not go unnoticed by Edna.

LOU *(cont'd)*
Thanks, Tommy. Wow. Cold out there...
(to Edna)
Hiya...

EDNA
Hello.

LOU
You know, I almost...
(registers apartment)
Holy shit! What went on in here?!

TOM
(re Edna)
Hey, Lou, watch it with the language, huh?

LOU
Oh, yeah. Hey, I'm sorry. I been livin' with wolves for too long. Man, look at this place! I never seen it so clean.

EDNA
We tidied up a bit.

LOU
What'd you do? Use a rake? I've never seen this place look so good.
(looking out window)
Hey, you've got a fire escape! I never knew you had a fire escape!

TOM
What difference does it make?

LOU
It would make a <u>big</u> difference if there was a fire.
(noticing the well-stocked cupboard)
You got <u>food</u>. Lookit this. Eight, ten years I been comin' here, you ain't never had more than a can of tuna... Look at all the food! And a dishcloth that matches a towel! Whooie!

TOM
I know you're having fun researching your article for <u>House and Garden</u>... but don't you want to hustle on down to U-Haul, rent a truck and get out of town?

LOU
Yeah, well...

EDNA

How was Vermont?

LOU

Cold and white. Here, Tom, I got you some maple syrup. I wish I could tell you I bought it at some folksy little place from an old geezer with a pipe and suspenders, but I didn't. I bought it at a souvenir store when the bus stopped at the Nelson E. Rockefeller Memorial Rest Oasis.

TOM

You took the bus back?

LOU

Yeah.

TOM

I thought you were driving up with Mona.

LOU

Drove up -- took the bus back.

TOM

Uh-oh.

EDNA

Something go wrong?

LOU

I'm not movin' to Vermont, Tommy. I'm not movin' nowhere.

TOM

You're not?

LOU

I'm back to stay.

TOM

Hey, all right!!!

Tom and Lou engage in some macho hugging, back slapping and boxing. Edna manages a weak smile.

TOM *(cont'd)*

That's terrific, man! What happened?

LOU

Aw... I had the Christmas from hell. You're talkin' to a very depressed and disillusioned person. Mona comes to pick me up and the first thing I realize is she drives a Citroen. You know this car? Lays low to the ground until you start it -- then the whole thing lifts up like a vacuum cleaner.

TOM
So?

LOU
So it's the stupidest car ever made. If schmucks had an official car it would be a Citroen. I shoulda known right then. I should never've gotten into that car. We get to Mona's parents' house and the first person I meet is Mona's sister Jane. "Jane has an alternate lifestyle," Mona's been tellin' me. "Jane has an alternate lifestyle." I figured that means she's a vegetarian or she hang glides or somethin'. Jane turns out to be a lesbian. I mean a <u>veteran</u> lesbian. A confirmed, dedicated, card-carrying, short haircut, khaki pants with heavy-duty work shoes lesbian! And Jane's brought her "friend" Bobby. Actually it's Roberta, but nobody's called her that since Eisenhower was President. Then I meet Mona's father. "He was blacklisted," Mona's been tellin' me. Like it was some honor. Fine, he was blacklisted. I never had the nerve to ask, "Blacklisted from <u>what</u>?" I just kept my mouth shut and looked impressed. Mona's mother comes in the room... a woman who doesn't wear a bra but should. You gotta hope to God there's a bra waiting for her under the Christmas tree. Please! Something to hold these things up! Doesn't matter. More exciting things are just around the corner. Mona's mother and father begin the Christmas Eve "festivities." Her father goes, he goes, "Mona, Jane... your mother and I are getting a divorce." Holy mackerel. Did it hit the fan! What went on for the next five hours! There's no way to describe how tense and nervous and weird and painful everything was. If it had been my family, someone woulda got a gun and killed everyone. At least it woulda been over quick. Not Mona's family. They believe in squeezing out every drop of suffering and agony through <u>talking</u>. Mona takes her father into the den, Jane-the-lesbian takes Mom into the kitchen. There's wailin' and cryin'. You hear bits of stuff being said. "She never forgave me!" "His work has been his wife!" "I can't take it anymore." Mona's ex-husband Burton drops by. Burton is dropping off their kid. He's twelve. Weird, sick-looking little weasel who takes forty different pills a day for all the stuff that's wrong with 'im. Mona can't wait to spread the joy. "Sweetheart, grandma and grandpa are getting divorced!" The kid goes into an asthma attack like I never seen! People are screamin' an' cryin', "You did this! This is your fault! Call an ambulance! No, don't!" You know, the TV was on through all this. Here these two old farts are ending a marriage of fifty years on Christmas Eve and there's Clay Aiken singin' "Holy Night" from Hawaii. Mona's ex hasn't left. He just keeps goin', "Anything I can do?" Finally, Mona takes me aside and says, "Lou, Burton and I are going out for coffee." I spent my Christmas Eve playin' checkers with Bobby-the-lesbo listening to two old communists cry upstairs. We played maybe ten games in a row, didn't speak a word, either one of us. Gets to be one in the mornin'. All you can hear is the sound of the clock tickin' and the wind outside. Me an' Bobby ain't said

a word for hours, and all of a sudden Bobby looks up at me an' says... she says, "You know, Lou, I'm a lesbian." And I've got to be polite and act <u>surprised</u>. Go, "Really?" When all I really want to say is, "Oh, I just thought you <u>liked</u> looking like Ernest Borgnine!" Or, "Let's go look under the tree. Maybe Santa's left you a girl's volley ball team!" That was my Christmas in Vermont. I didn't go skiin'. I didn't go tobogganin', or talk with colorful old guys spinnin' yarns. Mona an' me did <u>not</u> look for a house to rent or jobs to get. That plan was abandoned instantly. It was just a stupid pipe dream. I was lookin' to change my life, Tom.

(partially to Edna)

I was lookin' to make myself into somebody new, somebody different. Guys like us, Tom... from this neighborhood, from our backgrounds... nothing changes for us. They don't make miracles in Hell's Kitchen.

EDNA

You'll meet someone else.

LOU

Where? Where's a guy like me goin' to meet a woman at my age, huh? I work five days a week, ten, twelve hours a day at the Terminal Bar and Grill.

EDNA

Women go to taverns.

LOU

Hey, Tom. You hear that? "Women go to taverns."

TOM

Don't make fun. She hasn't seen much of life.

LOU

Edna, the women who crawl into the Terminal Bar and Grill are on the food chain right next to Dobermans.

EDNA

Oh...

TOM

But in any case, you're back to stay, huh?

LOU

I ain't never settin' foot outta Manhattan again.

TOM

All right!

LOU

Yeah.

Tom and Lou high-five.

LOU *(cont'd)*

Hey, Tom, know what I seen?

TOM

What?

LOU

The cops, they were settin' up barriers on Times Square. Gettin' ready for tonight.

TOM

You think the weather's going to cut down the size of the crowd?

LOU

Who cares! We're gonna be screamin' our lungs out! Ahooo!

TOM
(matching Lou)
Ahooo!

EDNA

You know --

LOU
(interrupting)
Ahooo! Hey, look, Tommy. Check out what I got.

Lou rummages through his brown paper bag. He whips out an air horn and gives it a blast.

TOM

All right!

LOU

You believe it?

TOM

Man, that thing is <u>loud</u>!

LOU

Gotta be careful with it. Don't hold it next to your ear.

TOM

That's all I need. To be blind <u>and</u> deaf.

They laugh.

TOM *(cont'd)*

What else you get?

LOU

I got all kinds o' stuff. Noise makers, hats...

Lou takes other New Year's Eve items out of his brown paper bag; hats, horns, noise makers, etc.

TOM

Where'd you get all this?

EDNA

Thomas --

LOU

(interrupts)
Some guy down the street. He's sellin' everything.

TOM

He have any cherry bombs?

LOU

Naw, but I got some at my place from last year.

EDNA

Tom...

TOM

Terrific.

EDNA

Tom.

TOM

(to Edna)
Just a sec.
(to Lou)
Wouldn't be a New Year's Eve without cherry bombs.
(to Edna)
Yeah?

EDNA

Have you forgotten?

TOM

Huh? Oh! Yeah, right. Sorry. Lou, Edna's comin'.

LOU

She's what?

TOM

She's coming with us. I invited her to Times Square.

LOU

Oh.
(operating noise maker)
Hey, Tom, you like this one?

TOM

It's nice but it's nothing like that air horn.

LOU

Naw, this baby's a beaut!

Lou goes to blast the airhorn again but Edna stops him.

EDNA

Please!

Lou puts the airhorn down.

EDNA (cont'd)

Thank you.

LOU

Sorry. It's just that we get so excited over New Year's Eve.

TOM

Man, this is great. I got Edna here to read to me, you're back from this stupid Vermont thing… Hey! We gotta celebrate.

LOU

Huh?

TOM

I don't want to wait 'til tonight. We oughta have a toast right now.

LOU

Sure. You got a bottle in the house?

EDNA

There's some whiskey.

TOM

(getting his coat)

Naw naw... not that. Champagne! We've got to toast the New Year with champagne! Nothing less will do. Lou's my oldest friend. Edna, you're my newest friend. If that's not a celebration I don't know what is! Let me run out to the liquor store. They always got some champagne that's cold.

LOU

Want me to get it, Tom?

TOM

Lou, I've got to do more for myself. Know what I mean? Stay here. I'll be right back. And hey. Don't go putting any moves on my date for New Year's Eve, huh?

Tom laughs. Lou and Edna respond with nervous laughs. Tom exits. There is an uncomfortable silence, finally:

EDNA

So...

LOU

So.

There is another uncomfortable silence. Finally:

LOU *(cont'd)*
You did good.

EDNA
With what?

LOU
With what. With him. With Tom. With his apartment. You did good.

EDNA
Oh. We just tidied up a little.

LOU
No, you did a lot more than "tidy." You did good. I never liked how filthy it was in here. Man, I tried everything. Teasing, shaming... everything. There were times I just wanted to take a bucket with hot water and Lysol and... looks like that's just what you done.

EDNA
Once we got started, it was easy.

LOU
I guess what the place needed was a woman's touch. I mean look what I got done in eight years and look what you done in eight days.

EDNA
We didn't do that much.

LOU
Sure. You, uh... come by here what time generally?

EDNA
Generally?

LOU
Yeah, generally.

EDNA
About ten in the morning. Maybe eleven.

LOU
Ten.

EDNA
Maybe eleven.

LOU
And you stay 'til when?

EDNA
It depends.

LOU
You stay 'til...

EDNA
Four, five.

LOU

All day.

EDNA

Well, not <u>all</u> day. Well, yes.

LOU

And what is that, two days a week? Three?

EDNA

We haven't worked out an exact schedule...

LOU

How many days a week?

EDNA

It's only been one week so far. We haven't formalized any --

LOU

How many days a week?

EDNA

Tom and I haven't...

LOU

How many...

EDNA

Seven! Every. Day. So far, that is. I've been here every... all eight days. There seems to be a lot to do.

LOU

You love 'im?

EDNA

What!

LOU

You love 'im? Are you in love with Tom?

EDNA

I don't see how that's any of your concern.

LOU

He's my best friend.

EDNA

Congratulations.

LOU

He's blind as a bat. I've been lookin' out for 'im almost nine years. He meets a new chick -- I ask.

EDNA

And how many "new chicks" has he met in nine years? I guess they file up here on a regular basis. You perform this service often, do you?

LOU

You... never mind. Do you love Tom?

EDNA

Did you love Mona?

LOU

Seems to me you do.

EDNA

Just stop it.

LOU

If you didn't love 'im, you'd be denyin' it left an' right.

EDNA

Stop it!

LOU

One thing people don't want to be accused of is lovin' someone they don't.

EDNA

It's none of your concern.

LOU

Right. It's none of my concern that you're in love with 'im.

EDNA

You're going to tell him.

LOU

Tell "him?"

EDNA

Tom. You're going to tell him.

LOU

Tell him what?

EDNA

Everything! You're going to tell him everything! About me, about... everything.

LOU

What "everything?"

EDNA

Stop it! Stop toying with me! You're going to tell him, aren't you?!

LOU

He's my best friend. Besides, he's gonna ask me. The second me an' him is alone he's gonna ask me as sure as Christmas, "Hey, Lou. What's Edna look like?"

EDNA

And you're going to tell him.

LOU
He's my best friend.

EDNA
You're going to tell him. Your way. The way men have. That cruel, common way they talk sometimes. That awful way of talking that men think makes them more manly or weary or something. "Tom, I'm sorry I gotta be the one, but this Edna chick is a dog, pal. And there's something wrong with her leg or her hand or something." Won't you feel good then!

LOU
Hey, look, first of all, I'm not gonna tell Tom in no crude manner like you just said. I'll tell 'im with respect. Trust me. If he asks me, I'll tell 'im you don't look good in a <u>nice</u> way. Second of all, if I don't tell him he would just find out anyway.

EDNA
No. That's just it. He wouldn't find out. Not really. Not in the way he'd find out from you.

LOU
You're crazy.

EDNA
In his mind he's built a much kinder image of me. I'm not saying he thinks I'm beautiful, but he sees me as someone special. I know he does.

LOU
Yeah, well...

EDNA
And if you came back six months from now or six weeks from now or even six <u>days</u> from now and you were to tell Tom anything negative about me...

LOU
Yeah?

EDNA
He wouldn't believe you.

LOU
Why?

EDNA
Because he'd be in love with me. You could say whatever you'd like, he wouldn't believe you. He <u>couldn't</u> believe you.

LOU
No way.

EDNA
It's what falling in love does to a person. Have you ever seen a couple in their forties or fifties that's obviously been together for many years?

LOU
Huh?

EDNA
And let's say the woman is still quite attractive but the man has simply let himself go. He's overweight, his belly hangs over his pants, his face is puffy, he's lost his hair, he needs a few trips to the dentist.

LOU
So?

EDNA
So -- do you think he looked like that when his wife met him?

LOU
What?

EDNA
Do you think they were in college and she said to herself, "Wow, look at the fat, sloppy guy with bad teeth and no hair!?"

LOU
Some guys just get like that.

EDNA
Of course! He was probably handsome once.

LOU
So?

EDNA
So if the woman is still attractive, why does she put up with a man who looks like that?

LOU
How should I know!?

EDNA
It's because she doesn't see it! Not what we see. Not all of it. When she looks at him she sees the handsome man she fell in love with. When we fall in love with someone there's a moment when we take a picture of that person, an emotional snapshot, that we carry with us forever. If we're lucky, if we're very, very lucky, the person we fall in love with will always resemble that snapshot.

LOU
What are you talking about?

EDNA
I'm talking about loving someone. Thomas is getting ready to fall in love with me. He hasn't felt like he's worth doing that in a very long time but his self respect is... well, you saw him. He's different now. Thomas

is changing. We'll be in Times Square tonight. We'll both be drinking. He'll kiss me at midnight and sketch a picture in his mind that will last him a lifetime. Nothing will change it. Not even if you wait a day to tell him what you think is so important. I've never been surer of anything. When my father first took my mother out, they went to Coney Island. They rode the carousel six times in a row. They went on some other rides, the Ferris wheel, I believe, the wild mouse... My father bought my mother a bag of peanuts. He tipped the man selling them an extra nickel and she thought he was "devilishly mad" seeing as how it was the height of the Depression. Then my mother didn't feel too well, probably one of the rides. They sat on a bench on the boardwalk. My father listened to every word my mother said that night as though she were the most intelligent, fascinating woman he had ever met. More than that he thought she was funny. Yes. She made him laugh. It made her feel very special. To make a person feel they are bright is one thing. But to make them feel they are witty and clever... They spent the rest of their night sitting on that bench talking. My mother has shown me the bench. I've been to "the bench." The lights danced behind them, music blared from the rides, and in the middle of all that, when the moment was absolutely right, my mother took a snapshot of my father with her heart. She fell in love and this was the man and the moment she would remember until the day she dies. She tucked away her photo in her soul. As the years went by, my father ceased to find my mother funny. He also did not find her interesting or intelligent or any of the other things he found her to be that night. Worse than that, he has let her know it. With every disinterested look, with every silent goodbye. Was it last week or the week before...? I'm not sure but my father was on his way out and my mother, what's <u>left</u> of my mother, came shuffling by and he took one end of his scarf and tossed it over his shoulder and, I suppose, for the briefest moment, he resembled something called dashing to a woman like my mother who still listens to big band music, and he said to my mother, "Adios, sweetie!" and the old woman's eyes filled with colored lights and cotton candy! You could almost hear a calliope playing in the background. Her face! Her expression! The life that flared up in her! "There! That's him! The kind and gentle man who loves me!" She forgave <u>everything</u>! He was the handsome young man on the bench again. It was only for a second but a second was all it took. It didn't make my mother's day -- it made her <u>life</u>! Don't you see? You don't love someone for who they are. You love someone for who you <u>think</u> they are. If Tom thinks I'm pretty what right do you have to take that away from him? What am I going to do with the picture I took of Tom? What will I do with my picture?! He stood there and recited a poem for me. A poem he memorized in high school. Wearing his favorite Christmas sweater. The one he thinks is red and white. You saw him! Running out to buy champagne... What am I to do with my picture? Why would you think...

Edna cannot continue. Neither she or Lou can speak for several beats. Finally the door opens and Tom is standing there. He is speaking to someone down the hall.

LOU

Listen, that's a cute pooch. What's his name? Diablo? I love it!

(pause)

He's a dog! Sometimes he can't help himself. Hey, Diablo... Happy New Year, fella. Hey, maybe I could walk him for you sometimes. Get him used to going <u>outside</u>. You, too. Feliz Navidad.

Tom enters. He carries a bag and happily goes about the task of serving champagne for three.

TOM

Nice guy down the hall. Turns out he's not Puerto Rican. He's from El Salvador. Man, it is cold outside. Must be ten, twelve degrees. Get this, I ran into Herman the German at the liquor store. Lou, you know Herman. Sees me buying champagne and has the nerve to say to me, "Wadda <u>you</u> celebratin'?" As though I've got nothin' to celebrate. The nerve on that guy. "Wadda you celebratin'?" I looked him straight in the eye -- well, I <u>hope</u> I looked him straight in the eye -- I said, "Herman, I'm going home to celebrate the fact that I don't have to stand here and smell your <u>breath</u> anymore." Man, I would've given anything to see the look on his Nazi puss. Here's a guy, stinks like road kill his whole life, has no friends at all and has never bought me a drink. He has the gall to say to me on the morning of New Year's Eve, "What are <u>you</u> celebratin'?" Germans! Why does the word "charming" <u>not</u> come to mind? Lou, you want the glass with Fred or Barney? I can tell which is which, you know. Fred has more paint on the glass. Lou, you usually like Fred, huh?

LOU

Sure.

TOM

Then you get Fred. I get Barney, my personal favorite. Edna, you get Bamm Bamm, because it's the only girl glass I got.

There is a moment when neither Lou or Edna know what to say. The silence seems to go on forever. Finally:

LOU

She's not here.

TOM

What?

LOU

Edna. She went down the hallway to the can. You know, had to powder her nose.

73

TOM
Well, thanks for tellin' me. I'm talking away here like she's in the room.

LOU
Sorry.

TOM
Is she okay?

LOU
Yeah, she's fine. Just had to go to the little girl's room. And not a minute too soon.

TOM
Huh?

LOU
Edna. She didn't get out of here a minute too soon, Tommy.

TOM
What are you talking?

LOU
Leave me alone like that with her. Here, in your place. Don't do that again.

TOM
Huh?

LOU
I'm your best friend so don't go leavin' Edna with me no more.

TOM
Why?

LOU
Why! Because I'm only human is why. The chick is gorgeous. A couple more minutes I woulda been hittin' on her for myself.

TOM
Hey, hey... watch it. Edna's spoken for.

LOU
Well, don't leave her with me like that no more.

TOM
Just keep it in your pants, D'Marco. Understand?

LOU
I understand.

TOM
All right.

LOU
All right.

TOM
She really pretty?

LOU
Trust me. This chick is a fox.

TOM
I had a feeling. You know, when you lose your sense of sight, your other senses sharpen. The way she sounds, the way she moves, little things, the way she picks things up, puts them down, always real lady like... feminine. Sexy. And the way she smells, not all perfumey, but nice, you know? She walks by and for half a moment she's still there. It starts to drive you crazy.

LOU
Yeah.

TOM
I had a feeling she was someone special.

LOU
I'd better duck outta Times Square tonight, Tom. Three's a crowd, huh?

TOM
Thanks, Lou.

Edna opens the door to the apartment, then closes it, pretending she has returned from her trip to the bathroom.

EDNA
Oh, Tom. You're back. That was quick.

TOM
When it comes to toasting the New Year, I don't mess around.

EDNA
You certainly don't.

TOM
You okay? Something wrong?

EDNA
I'm just very cold all of a sudden. It's so chilly in the hallway.

TOM
(re champagne)
Well, this'll get your fire burning.

LOU
Yeah, let's drink up. I still gotta unpack.

They each take a glass.

TOM
Lou, you got any wishes for the New Year?

LOU
No.

EDNA
There must be something.

TOM
Yeah, you're always complaining.

EDNA
Don't you wish for anything?

LOU
I just wish I never see Vermont again.

TOM
A lovely wish, Lou.

LOU
You got a wish, Tommy?

TOM
I wish that the three of us can become good friends.

EDNA
That was going to be my wish.

LOU
Good, we all got a wish, I'm so happy, bottoms up.

TOM
Happy New Year.

They all drink.

LOU
Nice stuff, Tom. What is it?

TOM
(joking)
Dom Perignon. Ninety bucks a bottle.

LOU
(playing along)
Really? The label don't say "Dom Perignon."

TOM
What <u>does</u> it say?

LOU
"Larry's."

TOM

That darn salesman!

Tom, Lou and Edna laugh.

LOU

See ya later, ya potato head, ya.

TOM

Get out of here, you dumb Italian. Happy New Year.

EDNA

Goodbye, Lou.

Edna gives Lou a long, heartfelt hug.

LOU

Happy New Year...

Lou exits.

TOM

Good guy... a real friend.

EDNA

Yes, he is. To real friends.

TOM

You got it.

They drink.

TOM *(cont'd)*

By the way, Lou can't make it tonight.

EDNA

Oh?

TOM

Something he had to do. No big deal. You and I will just have to pick up the slack. Make the noise of three people.

EDNA

And we will!

TOM

Ahoooo!

EDNA

(mildly)
Who-ray!

TOM

It needs work. Wait a minute! Is this your first New Year's in Time Square?

77

EDNA

Yes.

TOM

Then we've got to preserve this event for posterity.

Tom feels around the kitchen table for the items Lou brought with him.

TOM (cont'd)

Where's that stuff Lou brought?

EDNA

Here. What are you...?

TOM

I got it. Here they are.

Tom finds two silly party hats. He puts one on himself and gives the other to Edna.

EDNA

What are these for?

TOM

For New Year's Eve!

Tom goes about the task of retrieving his camera from where it hangs on the wall and making space on a shelf that is eye level.

EDNA

What are you doing?

TOM

I'm going to take a picture.

EDNA

But how... I don't feel like having my picture taken.

TOM

Uh-uh. We've got to do this. It's a sin if we don't. That's what Sister Mary Dominick taught us at Our Lady of Perpetual Pain, Suffering and Agony.

Tom hands the camera to Edna.

TOM (cont'd)

See the red ring on the lens. The F-stop... What's it on?

EDNA

Two point five...

TOM

Perfect. Now focus on the shelf.

EDNA

Hmm?

TOM
Focus on the shelf. You'll see. Move this part here. See?

Tom helps Edna with focusing the camera.

TOM *(cont'd)*
Look through here, move this like so to focus...

EDNA
I see. Yes. Wait. Hold on...

TOM
This is great. I'm inventing blind photography.

EDNA
There. I think that's it.

TOM
Now, don't move.

EDNA
But...

TOM
Don't move.

Tom crosses to the shelf and puts the camera on it. He points it toward Edna.

TOM *(cont'd)*
Is it pointing at you?

EDNA
No, I... it's...

TOM
To the left?

EDNA
Yes, a little.

Tom moves the camera.

TOM
Like so?

EDNA
A little more. Tom, you can't expect to...

TOM
Is that it?

EDNA
Yes. It's pointing at me. I guess.

TOM
Got your hat on?

EDNA
Yes.

                            TOM

Get ready.

                            EDNA

You're not actually going to...

                            TOM

You bet I am!

Tom presses the timer device on the camera. He races over to join Edna. They stand side by side wearing their party hats, holding their drinks.

                            EDNA

This is silly.

                            TOM

Yes, it is, isn't it?! Thank you! You're welcome!

Edna giggles.

                       TOM *(cont'd)*

Edna?

                            EDNA

Yes, Tom?

                            TOM

Happy New Year.

                            EDNA

Happy New Year.

They smile at each other and the camera takes its picture. The LIGHTS FADE TO BLACK.

                          THE END

ONLY KIDDING!

CAST

JACKIE DWAYNE, fifty or sixty, veteran Catskill comic. Rude, impatient, insincere, mean, egotistical, frustrated, bitter yet funny.

SHELDON KELINSKI, twenty to thirty, comedy writer. Shy, insecure, poker-faced, easily frightened and extremely neurotic.

TOM KELLY, mid to late twenties, handsome, likeable, easy going, quick witted.

JERRY GOLDSTEIN, mid to late twenties, handsome, funny, animated, charming and self-destructive.

SAL D'ANGELO, forties to fifties, shy, soft spoken, dim, easily impressed and entertained, warm yet snake-like.

BUDDY KING, the voice only of a popular late night TV host.

ONLY KIDDING! was presented by Bruce Lazarus and Patrick Hogan at the Westside Arts Theatre in New York City on April 14, 1989, with the following cast:

JACKIE DWAYNE	Larry Keith
SHELDON KELINSKI	Howard Spiegel
TOM KELLY	Andrew Hill Newman
JERRY GOLDSTEIN	Paul Provenza
SAL D'ANGELO	Sam Zap
VOICE OF BUDDY KING	Peter Waldren

Directed by Larry Arrick
Scenery by Karen Schultz
Lighting by Debra Dumas
Costumes by Jeffrey L. Ullman
Sound by Paul Garrity
Casting by Rosalie Joseph, C.S.A.
Production Stage Manager, Zane Weiner
Associate Producers, Heather Holmberg and Richard Voss

The play was originally produced at the American Jewish Theater, Stanley Brechner, Artistic Director.

Jim Geoghan and Paul Provenza were both nominated for Drama Desk Awards.

ACT ONE

SCENE 1

A night in July, 1977

Lights up on:

A bungalow in the Catskill Mountains. A depressing little box of a room furnished with an inexpensive table, two unmatched chairs and a torn and stained couch.

JACKIE DWAYNE sits at the table which serves as his "office." On the table he has arranged a typewriter, paper, pens, pencils and a telephone. He is dressed in classic comic garb: tuxedo, patent leather shoes, ruffled shirt and loose bow tie.

He sits at the table for several moments staring at the typewriter woodenly, almost fearfully. Finally, he ceremoniously selects a clean sheet of typing paper, inserts it in the machine and braces himself to begin writing. He cracks his knuckles, flexes his fingers, rubs his chin then lifts one finger high in the air and strikes a key on the typewriter. He instantly realizes he has typed the wrong letter.

        JACKIE

Shit...

He rolls the paper up, grabs an eraser and begins erasing. He becomes dissatisfied with his erasing, rips the paper from the roller, crumples it and tosses it into or near the wastebasket. He waits several beats, inserts another fresh sheet of typing paper and thinks. The phone rings. He answers.

       JACKIE *(cont'd)*
  (annoyed)
Yeah!
  (pause)
Murray!
  (pause)
Yes, you're bothering me. I'm busy writing. I was on a hot streak.
  (pause)
Naw... don't call back later. The mood's gone. You ruined it for me.
  (pause)
No, he's not here yet. I don't go on for a couple of hours still. Are you sure this kid is any good? You know I only work with the best.
  (pause)
Uh huh... uh huh... yeah, great.
  (pause)
I'll <u>have</u> the new material, Murray. I'm busy writing day and night up here. Speaking of which -- did you set it up yet?

(pause)

You have? Thanks a bunch! Why didn't you tell me? Do I have to drag it out of you, you schmuck?

(pause)

Yeah. Uh huh. Hold on.

(he writes in his appointment book)

I'm writing it down. Grossingers on the... I'm writing it down!!! Grossingers on the twenty-second.

(pause)

Hitch? What hitch?

(pause)

A showcase?!! You mean they're not going to pay?!! What are you doing to me?!! Are you trying to kill me?!! With slow torture?!! A showcase! Give me strength! You should rot in hell for what you've done to me! You black-hearted shit! I'll piss on your grave! Your facacta brother... I'll piss on his grave! You blood-sucking bastard! You shit! I'll piss on your whole God damn family!!!

(pause, then calmly)

Yeah... my love to Mildred.

Jackie hangs up the phone, pours himself another scotch, crosses to his typewriter and inserts another sheet of clean typing paper. He is about to begin typing again when there is a knock at the door.

JACKIE *(cont'd)*

What!

SHELDON KELINSKI enters. He is a meek, poker-faced, nervous type and carries a briefcase.

SHELDON

Mister Dwayne?

JACKIE

Yeah?

SHELDON

I'm Sheldon Kelinski.

JACKIE

Sorry to hear that.

SHELDON

Murray said you'd be expecting me.

JACKIE

(realizes)

The kid! Of course! C'mon in. Yeah... drop your stuff anywhere.

Sheldon enters further and stands uncomfortably, taking in the tacky room.

JACKIE *(cont'd)*
Yeah... Murray said you might drop by. Sure. Sure. Can I get you anything? Coffee? Soda? Glass of water?

SHELDON
No thanks.

JACKIE
You sure? Some seltzer? This is the Catskills. Seltzer comes out of the tap.

SHELDON
No thanks, I'm fine.

JACKIE
So, how was the drive?

SHELDON
I took the bus.

JACKIE
Aha. How did the <u>driver</u> drive?

Jackie lights up expecting Sheldon to laugh. Sheldon finally gets the point and responds with a meek but forced smile.

SHELDON
Funny...

JACKIE
You're too kind. So sit down. Relax.

Sheldon sits down, but he doesn't relax.

JACKIE *(cont'd)*
Took the bus, eh?

SHELDON
Yes. I sat next to an old Nazi. According to him, Hitler loved to yodel in the shower.

JACKIE
Yeah. Ah... you hungry? Want something to eat? Huh?

SHELDON
No, that's all right. We stopped on the Thruway at the Helen Keller Memorial Rest Oasis.

JACKIE
Where's that?

SHELDON
I'm not sure. It's the one with the water pump out front.

85

JACKIE
(laughs uneasily)
Aha ha ha... funny... You got a place to stay? Listen, you can stay here with me.
(crosses to phone)
Hotel's booked solid. Happens every time I play here. I'll get Sid to send over a cot.

SHELDON
That won't be necessary.

JACKIE
Huh?

SHELDON
I already checked in at the hotel.

JACKIE
(surprised)
You got a room?

SHELDON
Uh huh.

JACKIE
In the hotel?

SHELDON
Yes. It overlooks Simon Sez.

JACKIE
Great. Sid got a room for you. That's... great. I told Sid you might be dropping by. God bless 'im. Saved a room for you. I don't like staying at the hotel myself. No privacy. I said to Sid, "Sid, put me in a bungalow. I'll be a lot happier." He always says the same thing. "Jackie, for you? Anything!"

Jackie extends his arms and gestures at his room. Sheldon takes it in with a blank expression. Finally...

SHELDON
Yeah...

JACKIE
So, you want to be a joke writer.

SHELDON
Excuse me?

JACKIE
You want to learn about comedy, huh? Well, you came to the right place. I usually don't talk to kids just starting out. Most of 'em won't listen. I said to Murray, "Murray, what do I want to talk to some kid for?" And Murray begged me and said, "Jackie, give the kid some help. Listen to

86

some of his jokes. Please?" How could I turn him down?

SHELDON
Thank you.

JACKIE
How do you know Murray?

SHELDON
He's my agent.

JACKIE
Oh? We're like a two-headed cow.

SHELDON
We share the same asshole.

JACKIE
We share the same assho...
    (realizes)
You've heard the line.

SHELDON
Yeah.

JACKIE
I'm not surprised. My stuff gets around. You happy being with Murray?

SHELDON
I have no complaints.

JACKIE
Wait'll you've been with Murray as long as I have, kid. Wait'll the honeymoon is over.

SHELDON
Murray tells me you need new material for an audition for the Buddy King Show.

JACKIE
Audition! I don't need to audition for Buddy's show. If I want to do the Buddy King Show I'll call Buddy and tell him when.

SHELDON
When are you doing the show?

JACKIE
I haven't called him yet! I'm too busy these days! When my schedule lightens up -- I'll call Buddy!

SHELDON
You mean you'll call Jack Casey.

JACKIE
Who's that?

SHELDON
Buddy's talent coordinator. Has been for years.

JACKIE

Of course, yeah... How come you know so much all of a sudden?

SHELDON

I'm one of Buddy's writers.

JACKIE

You? You write for Buddy King? What're you doing here? Shouldn't you be on the coast?

SHELDON

The show's on hiatus for a few weeks.

JACKIE

"Hiatus?" TV language for "out of work..."

SHELDON

For a few weeks.

JACKIE

You see, when you do real comedy, live comedy, you're never out of work. Fifty, fifty-two weeks a year... twelve, sixteen shows a week! That's how much I work. And why? Because I love it. I fuckin' love it! Have you seen me work? You must've seen me work.

SHELDON

I'm afraid not.

JACKIE

You should see my act. The way I work an audience. Hecklers. My takes. I work harder on my takes than anything else. Have you ever seen my double-take? I got the best double-take in the business!

(he does an awful double-take)

See what I mean?

Jackie waits for Sheldon to gush over his double-take. Sheldon manages another weird smile.

JACKIE *(cont'd)*

(exasperated)

My God...

SHELDON

Have you done any television?

JACKIE

(incredulously)

Have I what?

SHELDON

Have you done any television?

JACKIE

Are you serious? Are you serious?!! Where've you been all your life, kid? In a coma? "Have I done any television?" Try thirty-one Ed Sullivan appearances.

SHELDON
(blankly)
Ah...

JACKIE
Sullivan? <u>Ed</u> Sullivan?

SHELDON
Yeah...

JACKIE
You know who he was?

SHELDON
I've heard the name.

JACKIE
"Heard the name!!!" You never <u>saw</u> the Ed Sullivan Show?

SHELDON
Not really.

JACKIE
Ed Sullivan! Sunday night! Eight o'clock. CBS! Prime time!

Jackie moves in close to Sheldon, eyeball to eyeball. There is a crazed glare on Jackie's face.

JACKIE *(cont'd)*
Thirty million people!

SHELDON
Sounds wonderful.

JACKIE
Wonderful. What do you know? The show gobbled up my material faster than I could come up with it. Singers! They could come back every six weeks and sing the same song. In the fifties no one ever got tired of hearing fuckin' "Volare!" But comics. Comics always had to have a new hunk.

SHELDON
Hunk?

JACKIE
And not just a good new hunk... a great new hunk! Killer hunks! You had to be funny! If you weren't funny you were dead!!! Washed up! Through! Banished to obscurity! Worse yet -- the Catskills!

After a long silence, Sheldon finally manages to speak.

SHELDON
Foot...

JACKIE
Foot?

89

SHELDON
You're standing on my foot.

JACKIE
   (realizes)
Oh.

Jackie steps off Sheldon's foot but stays close.

SHELDON
Could you... back away from me? Please?

JACKIE
Why?

SHELDON
You smell of... alcohol...

JACKIE
I smell of Johnny Walker Black. There's a big difference.

SHELDON
My... my father used to smell exactly like you do now.

JACKIE
I like 'im already.

SHELDON
He would smell of alcohol and yell at me. Close. Like you are now. Full of drunken hate... calling me stupid idiot. I was always positive he was going to kill me. With his bare hands.

JACKIE
I'm not going to kill you.

SHELDON
I understand that. Intellectually...

JACKIE
Good.

SHELDON
But emotionally...

JACKIE
Yeah?

SHELDON
I'm on the verge of a severe anxiety attack.

JACKIE
Yeah, you look a little knotted up.

SHELDON
I know. Could you...
   (pointing)
... stand over there, please? Just... stand over there?

JACKIE
Could I...

SHELDON
Stand over there!!!

Jackie stands where Sheldon has pointed. He feigns a pleasant expression.

JACKIE
This better?

SHELDON
Much. I'm sorry. I'm sorry I never saw Ed Sullivan.

JACKIE
Just you and all of Red China.

SHELDON
I preferred reading as a child. We had a television, but I never watched very much of it. Shall we get started?

Sheldon opens his case. He withdraws a handkerchief and covers an area of the coffee table with it. He then withdraws note pads, file cards, pens, pencils, paper clips, a stapler, several rubber bands, a small dictionary, world atlas, thesaurus, and a portable electric pencil sharpener. He carefully sets up shop on the coffee table.

Jackie watches all this in uneasy and silent amazement.

JACKIE
Ready?

Sheldon sharpens pencils. Jackie watches on exasperated. Finally.

JACKIE *(cont'd)*
So, you write for Buddy King, eh?

SHELDON
Yes.

JACKIE
You like your work? Being a joke slave?

SHELDON
We all get new shovels every Christmas.

JACKIE
Good, good. You live in L.A.?

SHELDON
Sort of.

JACKIE
"Sort of"... What's sort of?

SHELDON
The show is six weeks on, four weeks off. I commute.

JACKIE
Between New York and L.A.?

SHELDON
Uh huh.

JACKIE
Wadda ya take? The "A" train?

SHELDON
United Airlines usually.

JACKIE
Jesus! I'm only tryin' to joke around with you. You don't have to take everything I say <u>literally</u>.

SHELDON
Sorry...

JACKIE
Just trying to get the funny juices worked up is all. Look, kid... if we're gonna work together...

SHELDON
Yeah?

JACKIE
You gonna use that face?

SHELDON
What?

JACKIE
That... <u>puss</u>. That sad, worried expression like a beagle that just shit on the rug. Can't you... smile or something? Like you're having <u>fun</u>?

SHELDON
Writing jokes isn't fun. It's work.

JACKIE
Maybe to you it's work. But to me it's fun. It's hysterical. Like right now. I'm having so much fun I can't believe it! I hope I don't bust a gut or have a heart attack! Whoa shit! This must be illegal in Texas! Hot damn! Am I ever havin' me some <u>fun</u>! <u>Ha</u>! <u>Ha</u>! <u>Ha</u>! <u>Har</u> <u>dee</u> <u>har</u> <u>har</u> <u>har</u>!!!

SHELDON
You're frightening me.

JACKIE
What? I remind you of your father again?

SHELDON
No.

JACKIE
Good.

SHELDON
My <u>mother</u>. She used to go like that.

JACKIE
Like what?

SHELDON
Like you just did. Har dee... har har har...

JACKIE
There's help for people like your mother.

SHELDON
I know. It's called Valium.

JACKIE
Wow, a mother who's a junkie. Your old man's a wino. No wonder you've got a puss like that.

SHELDON
Please, stop!

JACKIE
Stop what?

SHELDON
Making personal comments. I find criticism about my physical appearance very painful to take. I'm not big on... smiling.

JACKIE
I noticed that. You don't want to smile, don't. You don't have to. You're a nice-looking boy. Got a good job, nice clothes. Chicks probably fall all over you.

SHELDON
Stop!

JACKIE
What! What'd I say <u>now</u>?

SHELDON
I find praise more difficult to accept than criticism!

JACKIE
All right, no praise!

SHELDON
Okay, can we get back to work?

JACKIE
I'd love to. Just tell me how you like to work... "Sparky." You like to riff? Wanna riff a little?

SHELDON
Riff?

JACKIE
Yeah, riff. Riff some jokes back and forth.

SHELDON
I'm not very good at "riffing."

JACKIE
So we won't riff. We'll bounce.

SHELDON
Bounce?

JACKIE
Yeah. I'll bounce some of my new material off you. See what you think. How's that?

SHELDON
Okay, I guess.

JACKIE
If I can make <u>you</u> laugh, I can make anyone...

SHELDON
Please! I asked you not to make personal comments!

JACKIE
Sorry...

Jackie looks at some of his notes on the table.

JACKIE *(cont'd)*
Been working on some stuff here. Lemme see... I was on a roll just before you came...

Jackie sifts through the papers.

JACKIE *(cont'd)*
My secretary just quit...

He feels uncomfortable and leaves the papers where they are.

JACKIE *(cont'd)*
I don't need to look at them. Got 'em all locked up here in my head. Mind like a file drawer.
    (thinks; then)
Got a great one-liner about two gay judges. They tried each other!

Jackie smiles and waits for a response. There is none out of Sheldon.

JACKIE *(cont'd)*
Wadda ya think?

SHELDON
    (woodenly)
About what?

JACKIE
The joke.

SHELDON

Boffo.

JACKIE

Boffo?

SHELDON

Screams, boffo.

JACKIE

You don't look like it was screams, boffo.

SHELDON

No, I enjoyed it.

JACKIE

You didn't laugh, though.

SHELDON

I laughed. In my own way.

JACKIE

What way is that? You don't move a muscle in your whole fuckin' body? <u>That's</u> the way you laugh?

SHELDON

Please. I asked you not to…

JACKIE

Sorry.

SHELDON

It doesn't matter anyway. Mister King would never let you do that joke on his show.

JACKIE

Why not?

SHELDON

He doesn't permit homosexual jokes.

JACKIE

It's not a "homosexual" joke. It's a judge joke.

SHELDON

It's a homosexual judge joke. Same thing. Buddy won't permit any joke that even mentions the word "homosexual" or "gay."

JACKIE

Why not?

SHELDON

He doesn't want to do jokes that would belittle and persecute a minority that's struggling desperately for help and understanding as it battles a grotesque and incurable disease.

JACKIE

Okay. Besides that.

SHELDON
Isn't that <u>enough</u>?

JACKIE
Okay, fine. Be picky. Still, when I tell a joke it would help if you laughed a little. Something. A joke's like good sex. It's got to be good for the both of us. If I'm bustin' my back in the sack I wanna hear some moans. Get me?

SHELDON
Please. I don't appreciate the metaphor.

JACKIE
I didn't think you would. Okay. I'll try another joke. This time, please, don't embarrass me by laughing so hard. I <u>hate</u> it when people go overboard. Old woman in Miami is on the beach with her grandson. Wave comes along and sweeps the kid away. She prays to God on her knees… "Dear God, please! My one joy in life! Give him back, dear God! Please!" Another wave comes along and plops the kid right on the beach. She hugs and kisses her grandson, looks up to God and says…

SHELDON
"He had a hat."

JACKIE
Okay. You know the punch line. You must've heard my act.

SHELDON
Actually, I heard it on a Myron Cohen album. He's one of my favorite ethnic comedians.

JACKIE
"Ethnic?" What ethnic?

SHELDON
Ethnic in that most of the people in his jokes and stories are from the old country. There's a sociology book that covers emigrant humor quite well. In the fifties most of America was trying to deny its ethnic heritage while feeling a deep sense of shame and guilt.

JACKIE
This is great stuff. I can use it in my act.

SHELDON
Jokes about simple-minded, elderly people who clung to old world values were very popular. They helped people rationalize and reinforce their new identities and eased the pain of betraying their ethnic roots.

JACKIE
I have absolutely no fuckin' idea of what you just said!!!

SHELDON
It's not important.

JACKIE
But you broke one of the most important unwritten rules of comedy.

SHELDON
I did?

JACKIE
You did. You blew my punch line.

SHELDON
But I recognized the joke. Right away.

JACKIE
Still. You're supposed to shut up and listen. Smile like you never heard it before. When I tell you the snapper, you laugh. If for nothing else... as a courtesy.

SHELDON
Where does that get us? I mean, my sitting here pretending to laugh? Pretending I never heard old jokes? Where does it get us?

JACKIE
Not all my jokes are "old," kid. I've been working hard on new material. Got a great, offbeat impression of Alan Ladd.

SHELDON
Who?

JACKIE
Alan Ladd.
(exasperated)
God! Give me strength! Alan Ladd! Ask me if I'm a tough guy.

SHELDON
Huh?

JACKIE
I'm gonna do my Alan Ladd impression, but you gotta feed me the straight line.

SHELDON
I'm not an actor.

JACKIE
Just say it!

SHELDON
I can't!

JACKIE
Why not?!

SHELDON
I've never done anything like that before!

JACKIE

So do it now! Explore new horizons! Tell your grandchildren, "I once fed a straight line to Jackie Dwayne!!!"

SHELDON

Please...

Jackie grabs Sheldon and makes him stand up.

JACKIE

Stand up.

SHELDON

Don't wanna...

JACKIE

Stand up, and gimme my straight line like a man.

SHELDON

You're hurting me!

JACKIE

I'll fuckin' kill ya like ya always thought your father would if you don't do this for me!!!

SHELDON

Do what! Do what!

JACKIE

Give me my straight line!

SHELDON

I'll do it! What do I say?

JACKIE

"Are you a tough guy?" Remember, I'm Alan Ladd.

SHELDON

(calming himself)
I think I'm ready. Are you ready?

JACKIE

(almost screaming)
I've been ready over here since Labor Day!!!
(calmer)
Remember. I'm Alan Ladd.

SHELDON

Ahem... How big are you?

Jackie reels in disbelief.

JACKIE

Holy shit!!! Can you <u>believe</u> this kid!!!

SHELDON

I did it wrong?

JACKIE

You had one line. One stinking line, and you got it wrong!

SHELDON

Maybe we should've rehearsed first.

JACKIE

(exasperated)
"Rehearsed." Okay. "Are you a tough guy?"

SHELDON

No, I'm not.

JACKIE

(explodes)
That's your line!!!

SHELDON

Don't hit me!!!

JACKIE

I won't. Remember. "Are you a tough guy?"

SHELDON

"Are you a tough guy?"...

JACKIE

Perfect.

SHELDON

That was just a rehearsal.

JACKIE

(patronizing)
And a very good one.

SHELDON

Now we'll do it for real.

JACKIE

This one's a keeper.

SHELDON

Then you'll leave me alone.

JACKIE

I promise.

SHELDON

Okay. I'm ready again. Ready?

JACKIE

Ready.

SHELDON

Are you a tough guy?

JACKIE
(like Alan Ladd)
Toughenuf.
  (after a beat; as himself)
Well?

SHELDON
(after a long pause)
Who's Alan Ladd?

JACKIE
The movie star! The guy who played Shane!!!

SHELDON
Oh.

JACKIE
"Oh!"

SHELDON
Isn't he dead?

JACKIE
So?

SHELDON
So why do you want to do impressions of dead people?

JACKIE
Because I do them so well! Know what? <u>All</u> the people I do impressions of are fuckin' dead. They couldn't <u>wait</u> to die on me. Couldn't die <u>soon</u> enough. Make my act look dated.

SHELDON
Please. Don't talk so much about dead people.

JACKIE
Why, you got a sister who runs around the house dead now?

SHELDON
Buddy King doesn't care for impressions much anyway.

JACKIE
Are you sure?

SHELDON
Positive. He hates them.

JACKIE
Ah, shit! And I had the perfect segue gag to get from the impression to the jokes.

SHELDON
How's it go?

JACKIE
Well, after I do my Alan Ladd impression just to warm up the audience,

I say "Alan Ladd... he was a really great actor. But Hollywood had some not-so-great actors. Like this one actor I know who went home to his mother and said, 'Mom, I got a part in a play.' She said, 'Really, what kind of part?' He says, 'I'm going to play a Jewish husband.' And she says, 'What's the matter...'"

SHELDON

"Couldn't you get a speaking role?"

JACKIE

Damn you! You did it again!

SHELDON

But it was so obvious.

JACKIE

Obvious?!! That was my best joke!

SHELDON

I saw it coming a mile away.

JACKIE

But the construction was <u>perfect</u>. I've been working that joke every night for weeks. Getting it to where it shines! Sparkles! I take it out of the box, and you throw shit all over it.

SHELDON

You're being a little extreme.

JACKIE

You might know the business, kid. But you don't know the art. The craft of comedy. The punch line means nothing if you don't construct the joke properly. Guy walks into a bar with a dog.

SHELDON

And the dog says, "DiMaggio?"

JACKIE

This one's different. Guy walks into a bar with a dog.

SHELDON

"I wanted him to be a doctor."

JACKIE

(angrily)

Guy walks into a bar with a dog.

SHELDON

"I never had the five bucks before."

JACKIE

(shouting)

Guy walks into a bar with a dog!

SHELDON

"Yeah, but now I can't stop him!"

JACKIE
You tryin' to piss me off?

SHELDON
These jokes are old. They're boring.

JACKIE
They're not old! They're mine! Old man gets on a trolley car.

SHELDON
Trolley car?

JACKIE
Old man gets on a <u>bus</u>. An energy-efficient, solar-powered, organic <u>bus</u>! Driven by an equal-opportunity civil service worker!

SHELDON
Danny Thomas does this joke.

JACKIE
I gave my wife a thousand bucks in cash.

SHELDON
"She blew it on the rent." Dangerfield's been doing that one for years.

JACKIE
Two Pollacks walkin' down the street. A bird craps on one guy's head. His friend says, "I'd better get some toilet paper." First guy says, "That's okay..."

SHELDON
"The bird's probably miles away by now."

JACKIE
Pollack finds his wife in bed with the butcher.

SHELDON
"Don't laugh. You're next."

JACKIE
Pollack buys a zebra for his kid.

SHELDON
Easy! Named him "Spot."

JACKIE
Christ could never've been born in Poland.

SHELDON
Couldn't find three wise men and a virgin.

JACKIE
My house was burglarized by a Pollack.

SHELDON
The garbage is gone, and the cat is pregnant.

JACKIE
I took a flight on a Polish airplane.

SHELDON

There was hair under the wingpits. Buddy hates Polish jokes.

JACKIE

Fuck 'em! The Italian army's out in the desert for three months when everyone gets an order to change underwear.

SHELDON

"Mario, you change with Vito. Vito, you change with Antonio..." Mister King hates Italian jokes, too. He would never let you do them.

JACKIE

Why? Does his paycheck come from an olive oil company in Brooklyn?

SHELDON

No. He just has better taste than that.

JACKIE

Fuck taste!

SHELDON

This is not what I would call a "productive writing session."

JACKIE

It <u>could</u> be if you kept your mouth shut. You might <u>learn</u> something.

SHELDON

I'm not here to learn.

JACKIE

There's plenty you could learn. I know more about comedy in my little pinky than you know in your whole fuckin' body!

SHELDON

I doubt that. You know, I came all the way up here to help you, and...

JACKIE

<u>You</u> help <u>me</u>? Now that's rich! Little college prick like <u>you</u> helping me?!! Hah! Well, I never went to college, kid!

SHELDON

Neither did I.

JACKIE

I went to the school of hard knocks. Hard Knocks U. I started in <u>toilets</u>! <u>Toilets</u>!!! Hear me? Scummy little clubs full of tough guys, hit men, whores, pimps, you name it. All of 'em with faces that'd stop a freight train!!! If you weren't funny, they'd break ya fuckin' thumbs!!!

SHELDON

You're yelling again.

JACKIE

You're damn right I'm yelling!!! You! You sit behind your safe little typewriter. If a joke sucks, you file it away under "S." You writers. You don't know what it's like under battle conditions. What it's like to take your lumps. To stand there with nothing but a microphone. No props.

No scenery. No furniture. Just you. Barefaced. Eyeball to eyeball with two, three hundred people. You know what flop sweat feels like? How could you? You punch out at five. You tell a joke. A good joke. You tell it... perfectly... "My mother-in-law is living proof that the American Indian once fucked buffalo!" Two, three, four... The silence falls on you like an avalanche. All those faces with this collective expression that says, "So...?" If God was merciful, He'd strike you dead on the spot, but no!!! He leaves you there to tell more jokes! Their expression changes from, "So...?" to "What kind of waste of time is this." You're dying. Traveling down the long black tunnel of no return. Vaseline starts oozing out of your skin. This cold, clammy sweat baptizing you as a born-again asshole. You wonder why you're fifty-two and still doing this. Selling aluminum storm windows doesn't sound so bad.

SHELDON
Why do you still do it?

JACKIE
Do what?

SHELDON
Perform? Do comedy?

JACKIE
Did I say "good night" yet?

SHELDON
Huh?

JACKIE
Did I say, "You're a great audience! Enjoy the rest of the show! Good night!" Did I?

SHELDON
I don't understand.

JACKIE
You will. I'll make you understand. I... am the comedian! King shit of turd mountain! The guy they came to see! I own them! They belong to me! I'll get them! I'll make something happen. The fat, ugly woman in the front row sucking chopped liver off her diamond ring. I hate her. They hate her, too, only they don't know it yet. Talk with her. Get to know her better.

(to an imaginary woman)
Excuse me... but are you in show business?

(pause)
No? Then get your feet off the fuckin' stage! Do I go to where you work and knock the broom out of your hands? Only kidding... only kidding... Where you from?

(pause)
Jersey? That's a great place to live. If you're a garbage can! Only kidding.

What's your zip code, dear? E-I-E-I-O? What are you doing here tonight? K-Mart close early? What do you do in Jersey? Fuck bowling balls? Only kidding... only kidding... It's working. The audience is starting to laugh.

    (to imaginary woman)

Better stop eating, dear. You get any bigger and the phone company will have to give you your own area code. Did you go swimming today? Were you the one who left a ring around the pool? You look very nice. I like the way you put your makeup on with staples. And that's a very pretty pattern you're wearing on your stockings. Oh? You're not wearing stockings. She don't like this. She didn't pay ten-fifty to be made fun of. She wants to say something <u>back</u> and "put me in my place..." Please do! Open your fat, common mouth and show us where you come from, baby! You're a gift from God!!! Now it's me and the audience against the fat lady. No <u>way</u> I can lose. I'm doing their dirty work for them. Their trashman cometh! I found the one emotion that binds us all together as human beings. <u>Hate</u>!!! "Thank you, Jackie. We love you, Jackie." You're a great audience. Enjoy the rest of the show. Good night.

SHELDON

That makes you happy?

JACKIE

What?

SHELDON

Making fun of fat ladies?

JACKIE

Getting laughs makes me happy. Nothing else matters. How could <u>you</u> understand? You're just some Hollywood hack with dollar signs for a soul. Writes for Buddy King. Big fuckin' deal!!! Know what the difference is between me and Buddy King?

Sheldon begins packing his briefcase to leave.

SHELDON

About four million dollars a year.

JACKIE

Luck! He was just luckier than me, that's all! And what makes you think you're so good? Huh? Got anything better in...

    (gestures at briefcase)

... your little <u>fagbag</u>?

SHELDON

I don't think there would be much point to it now.

JACKIE

What's the matter? Afraid you're in for some "personal criticism?" Let's see what you got, kid. Whip it out.

Jackie waits for a beat, then grabs Sheldon's briefcase and papers. They struggle over it.

JACKIE *(cont'd)*
Lemme see! Maybe there's some boffo stuff in here!

SHELDON
Don't! Don't!

JACKIE
"Don't! Don't!" You sound like my second wife. C'mon, lemme see!

SHELDON
Stop! Leave them alone!

JACKIE
"Leave them alone!" Now you <u>really</u> sound like my second wife.

SHELDON
Leave my stuff alone!

JACKIE
Lemme see! C'mon! I'm a joke junkie looking for a <u>fix</u>!

Jackie manages to reach inside the briefcase and withdraw some papers damaging them in the process.

SHELDON
My papers!!! My papers!!!

JACKIE
My papers!!! My papers!!!
    (reading aloud)
"Never buy a used car from an old man who has to jump start the engine with his pacemaker?"

SHELDON
Please! Stop!

JACKIE
    (reading aloud)
"Never buy a used car from someone in New Jersey if the inside of the trunk has scratch marks on it?"

SHELDON
No one's supposed to see those! They're my own private notes!

JACKIE
Ooooo...
    (covers groin)
I'm peeking at your private notes.
    (reading aloud)
"Never buy a used car that's on fire?" This stuff is crap!

SHELDON

Stop!

JACKIE

You've got some set of balls writing crap like this, kid.
　(reading aloud)
"Never buy a used car that has a herpes blister?"

Jackie grabs Sheldon's briefcase and clutches it to his chest protectively in a sarcastic manner.

JACKIE (cont'd)

Why, I've run into a <u>gold mine</u>!!!

SHELDON

Gimme! You have no right!

JACKIE

I have every right. I <u>know</u> what's funny, kid.

SHELDON

What're you going to do with my stuff?

JACKIE

Set a match to it. I'll probably win a Pulitzer Prize.

SHELDON

Gimme!

JACKIE

No!!! This stuff is too funny to give up!!! Har dee har har har!!!

SHELDON

I've put up with a lot of shit in my life, but no one does that to me. No one -- but no one -- laughs at my jokes!!!

JACKIE

Some straight lines are too good to be true.

SHELDON

Now gimme!

JACKIE

Eat shit and live.

SHELDON

I'm tellin'! I'm tellin' Murray what you did!

Jackie rips a small piece of paper, crumples it and throws it at Sheldon.

JACKIE

Here's his ten percent.

SHELDON

I'll tell Buddy. Yeah! I'll tell him you saw his jokes!

JACKIE

While you're at it, tell 'im to go fuck himself!

SHELDON
You dirty... fuck!!!

JACKIE
Ooooo... you said the "effy" word! I'm tellin'!

Jackie hands the briefcase back to Sheldon.

JACKIE (cont'd)
(laughs)
Stupid idiot.

Sheldon becomes enraged and raises the briefcase high in the air and strikes Jackie on the head. Jackie is sent to the floor semi-conscious. He tries to get up but can't. He slowly props himself up against some furniture and rubs his head. Sheldon is shocked and curiously impressed with himself over what he has done.

SHELDON
I've never hit anyone in my whole life.

JACKIE
Could've fooled me.

SHELDON
You shouldn't have made me mad.

JACKIE
You Hell's Angels are all alike.

SHELDON
Are you all right?

JACKIE
Fine. Think I'll go jogging. Where are my running shoes?

SHELDON
I'm sorry it didn't work out.

JACKIE
No big deal. It was just hate at first sight, that's all.

SHELDON
I don't hate you. I kinda... feel sorry for you.

JACKIE
Please. I'd rather you hate me.

SHELDON
Do you want me to tell Murray everything went okay?

JACKIE
What I want is for you to leave.

Sheldon looks to exit but feels guilty. He thinks for several beats, then:

SHELDON
Ah... you know the one about the comedian who does a show in the

Catskills one Saturday night? Well, for some reason, he has no idea why, but for some reason he does, without a doubt, the best show of his entire life. He can't believe it. The audience laughs at anything he says. They're roaring with laughter, falling off their chairs, tears pouring down their faces, pounding on tables, stamping their feet, gasping for air, begging for more. He has to do fifteen encores before they let him off the stage. The second show is a different audience, and it goes okay for the comedian. Not great, just okay. Nothing like that first show. He goes back to his cabin, and there's a knock at the door.

Sheldon knocks on his briefcase.

SHELDON *(cont'd)*

Like that. He opens the door and there, standing in the moonlight, is the most beautiful woman he has ever seen. Stark naked! She says, "I saw your show tonight. You are the funniest man I have ever seen. I want to spend the night with you. Make wild passionate love to you." The comic looks at this gorgeous naked woman glistening in the moonlight...

(beat)

Want to tell the snapper? Sorta... get back at me.

JACKIE

If I knew it I would.

SHELDON

The comic looks at this gorgeous naked woman glistening in the moonlight, and says, "Which show did you see? The first or the second?"

JACKIE

Ach!

SHELDON

It's an old joke.

Sheldon looks at Jackie sadly for a few beats, then exits. Jackie thinks for a few moments, then.

JACKIE

"Which show did you see?" Hump. With my luck? She probably saw the <u>second</u>.

Lights slowly fade to black.

ACT ONE

SCENE 2

A night in July, 1977

Lights up on:

A niteclub basement somewhere in Brooklyn. The room is nothing more than a cold, dark cellar that serves as a dressing room for the performers who appear at the nightclub. It is stacked with cases of liquor, beer, wine and soda. There is a collection of dusty, broken chairs and tables stacked high in one corner. Various articles one might find in a niteclub lie about. There is an ancient office chair on wheels among the junk; something Jerry will use to great affect later on. A pay phone is mounted on the wall. There is a doorway leading to the niteclub. There is also a doorway leading to a bathroom.

We hear audience applause and whistles from offstage as TOM and JERRY enter. Jerry carries a cassette tape recorder in one hand and a glass of cola in the other. They are all keyed up and excited having done a good show at the club. The applause and whistles slowly fade off.

TOM

Good show.

JERRY

Good? It was terrific!

TOM

You see the guy in the front row? How hard he laughed?

JERRY

The fat guy?

TOM

Yeah, him.

JERRY

He laughed so hard he almost dropped his gun. The bartender loved the show, too.

TOM

Tony.

JERRY

Watched every bit we did.

TOM

He had such a good time he forgot to steal from the cash register.

Jerry has put down his glass of cola and tape recorder. The two continue to talk as Jerry crosses to the pay phone, inserts coins and dials.

TOM *(cont'd)*

You messed up, though.

JERRY

What do you mean I messed up?

TOM

You dropped some lines. A whole section.

JERRY

Hey, we're a <u>team</u>, remember? We don't mess up individually. If something goes wrong, it's because of <u>us</u>. Together.

TOM

Okay, so "we" messed up tonight.

JERRY

That's it.

TOM

Because <u>you</u> dropped some lines.

JERRY

Cute.

(into phone like a stereotypical homosexual)

Yes, this is Jerry Goldstein.

TOM

What are you doing?

JERRY

(sotto to Tom as himself)

Calling my answering service. You talk like a fag, they don't put you on hold.

(into the phone gay again)

Hmm? She did? When did that come in?

(pause)

Oh, fabulous! Ciao.

Jerry hangs up the phone and searches through pieces of scrap paper for a phone number.

TOM

Did we get the whole show on the machine?

JERRY

We sure did. Listen.

Jerry presses the "play" button, and we hear the same audience applause and whistles. As it plays…

TOM
That's not the part I want to hear.

JERRY
It's the part I want to hear.

TOM
I want to go back to the beginning. Where "we" mess up.

JERRY
What for?

Tom shuts off the tape recorder.

TOM
Jerry, do you realize we haven't done a new bit in over eight months?

JERRY
Bullshit. We do new stuff all the time.

TOM
Bits and pieces. A line here, a line there. Hunks. Hunks. I want to do new hunks.

JERRY
Why's it so important?

TOM
Because I am bored to shit with our old stuff. I'm daydreaming on stage. Right in the middle of bits, I'm saying the words, I'm making the moves, but my mind is wondering if the blonde waitress has big sloppy nipples or teeny-tiny ones.

JERRY
(praying)
Oh, please let them be big and sloppy.

TOM
We had a hunk to do tonight. We wrote it on the Belt Parkway. We rehearsed it on the Brooklyn/Queens Expressway. We forgot to do it on stage. I want to listen to the tape and find out why.

JERRY
Later. I've got to do this now. I got a message from my agent.

Jerry crosses to the pay phone, inserts coins and dials.

TOM
It's ten-thirty. She's not in her office now.

JERRY
I'm calling her at home. The two best-kept secrets in New York are my agent's home phone number and the combination to her chastity belt.

TOM
I'll bet.

                          JERRY
Funny thing is... one's worth a fortune. The other's not worth shit.
          (into phone ultra sweet and phony)
Barbara? Jer here. I got your message. Am I calling too late?
                           TOM
          (imitating Barbara)
"Oh, it's never too late for you, Jerry..."

Jerry laughs too loud and too long. Tom silently mimics Jerry's phony laugh.

                          JERRY
What are you doing? Hmm? Something dirty? Hmm?
          (pause)
Aha ha ha ha ha!!!

Again, Jerry laughs too loud and too long. Tom mimics the phony laugh again.

                     JERRY *(cont'd)*
I did? I got it? The commercial? Really? The Yippie National? Oh, marvey! Simply, absolutely marvey!

Tom silently mouths the word "marvey" in disbelief.

                     JERRY *(cont'd)*
I'm not surprised. The director said I was the only actor who auditioned who could give him exactly what he wanted.

Tom mimes a blowjob.

                     JERRY *(cont'd)*
You're a doll, you know that? A complete and absolute <u>doll</u>.
          (pause)
Yes, I'll talk with you in the morning. Now you go back to what you were doing, okay? But be careful. You'll go blind. Aha ha ha ha!!!
          (hangs up phone)
Chee! What a bitch.
                           TOM
Must be a lot of work in the morning.
                          JERRY
What?
                           TOM
Shaving two faces.
                          JERRY
Cute. Very cute.
                           TOM
You got another commercial?

JERRY

Yeah. Yippie dog food. It's a national, too. I film it next week. Guess who the director is?

TOM

No idea.

JERRY

Sam Peckinpaw. Get it? Paw... Peckin-paw.

TOM

I got it.

JERRY

This dog won't eat the dog food.

TOM

I'll bite.

JERRY

So I shoot 'im.

TOM

Kids oughta love it.

JERRY

It's great. It's in slow motion and everything.

Tom takes a drink from Jerry's glass.

TOM

Cough! Whoa... what the... what is this?

JERRY

A little something to keep the cords oiled.

TOM

You were drinking this? On stage?

JERRY

Yeah, my voice was a little tight.

TOM

This is not for drinking.

JERRY

It's not?

TOM

It's for stripping wax off of kitchen floors.

JERRY

C'mon, it's just a little rum and Coke.

TOM

(imitating electronic penalty buzzer)
Wrong, this is a lot of rum and very little Coke.

114

JERRY

Aw, get off my back.

TOM

You never did that before. Drink on stage. During a show.

JERRY

Yeah, well I also never had five commercial auditions in one day. That's how many I had today. Five auditions. My voice was almost shot.

TOM

Aw, what horseshit!

JERRY

Each audition was worse than the one before. I'm sitting in some casting director's outer office, trying to learn my commercial copy, and who walks in but some <u>face</u>.

TOM

Face?

JERRY

Face! Some face I've seen eighteen billion times on TV doing this commercial, that commercial. Cool, confident, ready to score another commercial. Then there's another face. And another.

TOM

Wait a minute. Who are these guys?

JERRY

That's just it. I don't know. They're good. Real good. They work all the time. They get commercials one after the other. And I'm reading for the same part. The pressure is incredible, man. You have no idea.

TOM

(indicates glass)
So you have to drink <u>that</u> on stage to loosen up?!

JERRY

I already told you! It's for my cords. My voice was shot.

TOM

That's why you forgot the new lines tonight. Isn't it?

JERRY

I said <u>back off</u>!!! Jeez, Kelly! A guy has a little drink, you gotta make it sound like mass murder. C'mon, man. Lighten up. We did a good show tonight. Now it's time to cruise the bar for chicks. Bring them down here into our deluxe dressing room.

TOM

Yeah, sure.

JERRY

Let them perform oral sex upon our organs.

TOM

Aw, don't start that again.

JERRY

Hey, you never know, man. You never know.

TOM

Jerry, how long have you been a comedian?

JERRY

As long as we've been together. Five years.

TOM

And in those five years, how many times have you gotten laid as a result of your being a comedian?

JERRY

As a <u>direct</u> result?

TOM

Direct, indirect, whatever.

JERRY

(thinks, then)
Approximately... none.

TOM

I keep telling you -- we're comedians. Bass players and drummers... <u>they</u> get blowjobs in their dressing room.

They look at each other for a beat then are struck by the same thought. They improvise a jazz riff -- Tom playing bass, Jerry playing drums. When they are done, they laugh, then:

JERRY

Still, there's hope. Hope that out there in this world there's a young and beautiful girl with a very low I.Q. and equally low self-esteem... looking to get back at her parents in her own peculiar way... by having sex with complete strangers... who don't give a shit about her.

TOM

That's a beautiful dream, Jer.

JERRY

I know. I'm a hopeless romantic.

TOM

Hold on to that dream. Hold on to it.

JERRY

Yeah, I'll hold on to the dream. I just want to find some chick to hold on to this.

(grabs crotch)

Known in Latin American countries as "El Diablo."

TOM

El what?

JERRY

It's a new name I came up with for my peenie. Like it? It was a toss-up between that and "The Punisher." "El Diablo" won for its foreign flair.

TOM

You want "foreign flair," why don't you call it what it really is. "El Tacquito!" I've seen you naked at the health club, my man. You've got some nerve calling it that.

JERRY

Aw, there you go spoiling everything for me again. What are you happy now?

TOM

Is that what you do all day? When you're not out on commercial calls? Think up names for your dick?

JERRY

I know it doesn't sound like an elegant pastime, but it gives me something to do.

Jerry has helped himself to a bottle of Southern Comfort from one of the boxes.

JERRY *(cont'd)*

Wanna hit?

TOM

No, thanks.

JERRY

You call yourself Irish?

TOM

I'm fighting the stereotype.

JERRY

(takes a swig)

So am I.

Jerry drinks hard and often throughout. He reaches into a pocket and takes out some pills.

JERRY *(cont'd)*

Want one?

TOM
What are they?

JERRY
White Crosses. They make the brain sharp. You could use some, Kelly.

TOM
Where'd you get those?

JERRY
From Sal.
   (as Tom reacts)
C'mon, don't look so surprised. You think Sal drives a Porsche like the one he's got from selling beer and Seven-Ups in this shit hole?

Jerry takes some pills and washes them down with a slug from the bottle.

TOM
Phew... White Crosses and Southern Comfort...

JERRY
Yeah, the cocktail o' rock stars.

TOM
You're crazy, man! You know that!

JERRY
Think I'll stay up all night tonight.

TOM
Like you've got a choice, Elvis.

JERRY
Couldn't sleep if I wanted to. I've got a nine AM audition tomorrow. I'm gonna nail that one, too. You just watch.

TOM
Why do you bother with that shit, Jerry?

JERRY
Why? For the <u>money</u> is why. It's going to help me overcome the three things I've got going against me. I'm poor, ugly and Jewish. It's a fuckin' hat trick.

TOM
You make it sound like it's some sort of disease or something. Like...
   (as a solemn doctor)
I'm sorry, sir. Your test results are in and I'm afraid you're suffering from poor, ugly, Jewish.

JERRY
   (as an old Jewish man)
Ach! Doctor, is there any cure?

TOM
Money. Big piles of money.

JERRY

Ach! Never say "big piles" to an old Jew!

TOM

Sir, about my bill. If you're poor, how are you going to pay me?

JERRY

Oh, great! Now my hearing's shot, too!

TOM

My bill, sir.

JERRY

Can't hear a thing.

TOM

You owe me...

JERRY

Deaf like a stone. Hello?

TOM

Hello.

JERRY

Hello.

Tom segues his "hello" into an impression of Jerry Lewis emceeing a telethon. Jerry sits in the office chair near Tom looking old and decrepit.

TOM

Hello! And welcome to the seventeenth hour of our telethon coming to you from our studio of love in Los Angeles.

JERRY

It's lovely here. We come every year.

TOM

With us now is this year's poster child for poor, ugly, Jewish... Mister Jerry Goldstein.

Jerry moves forward using the office chair like a wheelchair.

JERRY

Hello!

TOM

Hello!

JERRY

Hello!

TOM

Jerry is ugly.

JERRY

It hasn't been a good year.

TOM
Boy, is he ugly.

JERRY
Enough.

TOM
Real ugly.

JERRY
All right already.

TOM
He's so ugly the mice walk hunchback!

JERRY
Enough with the fuckin' ugly!!!

TOM
Jerry can't get into a country club.

JERRY
They won't let me in, those Nazi bastards!

TOM
But someday, with your help...

JERRY
Thank you, MacDonald's Corporation!

TOM
... Jerry will be rich, handsome and gentile!

JERRY
Think so?

TOM
It could happen.

JERRY
It would take a miracle.

Jerry rises to his feet and feels his body tingle as Tom sings his own Christian hymn.

TOM
(singing)
"Miracle oh miracle, that's what this must be! Miracle oh miracle, found its way to me!"

Jerry's Yiddish accent disappears.

JERRY
What's going on? I feel the power! Oh my God! I'm breaking out in argyle! Quick! Someone get me a pipe!
(as Ward Cleaver)
June! Wally! Beaver! I'm home. Come on. Let's hop in the Volvo and drive back to Connecticut. These kids! Where do they get the energy?

Meanwhile, we'll try and figure out what I do for a living. Oh, what the heck. Let's buy <u>retail</u>!

Tom and Jerry laugh from the fun they've had and Tom jots down some notes as Jerry watches on.

JERRY *(cont'd)*

Volvo... hop in the Volvo...

TOM

I got it...

JERRY

You know what? We're too damn good for toilets like this. Look at this dump. And we're working for chump change.

TOM

Yeah, but I take that chump change and pay my chump landlord with it.

JERRY

I've been thinking. We ought to cut this dump loose. Work the showcase clubs in the city. That's where all the big agents go.

TOM

But you <u>have</u> an agent.

JERRY

I have a commercial agent. I want a <u>real</u> one. And they don't come out here to Brooklyn.

TOM

But the <u>money</u> is here.

JERRY

The money here is crap.

TOM

True. But the money at the showcase clubs is <u>less</u> than crap.

JERRY

Aw, what are you worried for? You're still writing gags for what's-his-face, aren't you?

TOM

Steven Maclain?

JERRY

Yeah, him. That no-talent, polyester scum wad who goes on talk shows and talks about his fuckin' <u>feet</u>!

(off Tom's reaction)
Oh, no! You didn't write <u>that</u>, did you?

TOM

He told it wrong.

JERRY

How could you do that, Tom? I mean, write for some guy like that?

TOM

Well, artistically speaking, I know it doesn't rank up there with Yippie dog food commercials.

JERRY

I just think we're better than toilets like this. And Sal... he treats stupidity like it's some kind of career goal. Tommy, I swear, if his I.Q. was one point lower, he'd be a crustacean.

TOM

Sal's been good to us, Jer. He pays on time and in cash.

SAL enters holding a bottle of champagne and stands there listening. Jerry doesn't see Sal yet. Tom does.

JERRY

He's a dumb, stupid, ignorant asshole who doesn't pay us <u>half</u> of what we're worth...

TOM

Ahem.

JERRY

(instantly catches on; covering)

... and I don't ever wanna work for that guy in Boston ever again. And that's that. Oh, look. It's Sal.

TOM

Hey, Sal!

JERRY

Sal! Baby!

(to Tom)

C'mon, Tommy. Let's get 'im.

Tom and Jerry rush over to Sal. Tom stands behind Sal holding his arms as Jerry gives Sal the third degree. This is obviously a game they play often, and Sal loves it.

TOM

Had the nerve to show up, eh?

JERRY

Okay, Sal... where's our dough?

SAL

(playing along)

I ain't got it.

JERRY

Ya hear that, Noodles? He says he ain't got it.

TOM

He's lyin'!

JERRY

C'mon, fish face. Where's the dough?

SAL

I swear, I ain't got it.

JERRY

Listen up, you piece o' spit. We can do this the hard way... or we can do this the hard way.

SAL

Oh, my God... please don't hurt me...

TOM

Break his legs, Jer.

Jerry digs through Sal's pockets and withdraws some money.

JERRY

So! Ya ain't got it, eh?

TOM

He was holdin' out on us!

Jerry slaps Sal in the face with the money.

JERRY

We don't like guys that hold out on us, ya unnerstan?

SAL

I swear. I don't know how that money got there.

JERRY

You asked for it, porcupine.

Tom lets go of Sal. The two stand before Sal and run an assortment of *Three Stooges* noises and gestures at him.

TOM & JERRY

Wu wu wu wu wu wu!!! Na na na na na!!! La dee dah!!! Ruff!!! Ruff!!!

Sal is reduced to a helpless puddle of laughter.

SAL

Aw, shit... Oh! That's funny! You guys is demented, you know that? You're demented.

JERRY

Thank you.

Jerry counts the money and gives Tom his half.

SAL

You did a real good show tonight. We're very pleased.

123

TOM
Thanks.

SAL
I swear, I can watch you guys do them bits over an' over an' over...

TOM
You do. Every week.

SAL
I even know some of your stuff by heart, I swear.

JERRY
Yeah?

SAL
Yeah. I could repeat some of your bits <u>every single word</u>.

TOM
Wish I could say the same about Jerry.

SAL
Every time you come out here, I see them same bits, I figure I'll get tired of 'em, but I don't.

JERRY
Uh... we were going to do some new bits tonight, but, uh... Tom fucked up. He forgot.

SAL
Really? How's it go?

JERRY
Well, remember when you were a kid... the way kids used to insult each other's mother?

TOM
Like your mother's so low she could play handball against a curb.

SAL
Right, right.

JERRY
Or your mother wears combat boots.

SAL
Yeah, sure. I remember. Or like, uh...
   (trying to remember)
... hold it... uh... ya mother eats shit!

Tom and Jerry react. There is a pregnant silence. Finally:

JERRY
Right. Sure.

TOM

Actually, we hadn't thought of that one ourselves. Anyway, do you think kids in other countries do the same thing?

SAL

I dunno.

TOM

Two kids in England insulting each other's mother. Right? Two English kids... insulting each other's mother.

Tom and Jerry assume the mannerisms of two ultra-cultured and prissy upper-class English children.

TOM *(cont'd)*

I say!

JERRY

Yes?

TOM

Your mother...

JERRY

Lady Wickshire, Grand Duchess of Kingsbridge?

TOM

Yes. I find her to be... inappropriate.

JERRY

How dare you. You take that back.

TOM

I shan't.

JERRY

You shat.

TOM

I shan't.

JERRY

You shat. Because your mother...

TOM

Yes?

JERRY

Your mother is... ostentatious.

TOM

You despicable lout!

JERRY

Watch your mouth, dear boy.

TOM

You're dashing for a thrashing.

JERRY

I shall be forced to give you the finger.

TOM

You leave me no choice but to respond in like kind.

JERRY

Very well, the finger.

TOM

The finger.

Tom and Jerry take their index fingers and make a "shame shame" gesture at each other.

SAL

Aw, shit! The finger! That's great!

TOM

(as himself)
Okay. Two Polish kids doing the same thing.

JERRY

Two kids in Poland.

Tom and Jerry muss their hair, pull their shirt-tails out, whatever makes them look "stupid." They almost scream at each other in thick Polish accents.

TOM

Hey, you person!

JERRY

What? Him?

TOM

No. Them.

JERRY

Oh.

TOM

Your mother.

JERRY

That lady at breakfast?

TOM

Yes. She is sleeping with... your father!!!

JERRY

Noooooooo!!!

TOM

Yes!!!

JERRY

Then your mother... she is good cook!!!

                              TOM
Nooooo!!!

                             JERRY
Aha ha ha!!!

                              TOM
Your mother... pretty!!!

                             JERRY
Why you!!!

They playfully slap each other and Sal loves every minute of it.

                              SAL
    (laughing)
Aw, shit! I love you fuckin' guys, you know that?

                             JERRY
You love us enough to bring your silver bullet, Lone Ranger?

                              SAL
Right here, Tonto.

Sal reaches into his pocket and hands Jerry a cocaine bullet. Jerry takes a huge hit up each nostril.

                             JERRY
Knnn! All right! Knnn! Jeez!

Jerry hands the bullet back to Sal.

                              SAL
    (to Tom)
Wanna hit?

                              TOM
No, thanks. I'm driving our space craft back to the city.

Jerry struts about feeling terrific from the coke.

                             JERRY
Mmm, yeah. Man, I feel good.

                              TOM
Must be those whole grain breads at breakfast.

                             JERRY
    (registers bottle)
Champagne? Special occasion, Sal?

                              SAL
Guess you might say that.

                             JERRY
    (lifts bottle to examine)
Expensive stuff. What is it? Jimmy Hoffa's birthday.

SAL

Naw, nothin' like that.

TOM

You look like you know a secret, Sal.

SAL

Guess I do. An' it's a biggie.

JERRY

Well, give! Give!

SAL

Okay, but gimme time. I wanna tell this thing in my own way, ya know?

JERRY

Your way can take <u>months</u>.

SAL

Well, it's the only way I know. I got some news for yas.

TOM

Good news?

SAL

Could be. You remember a couple of weeks ago I had my cousin Carmine come down here with his video tape shit and make a cassette thing of you guys?

JERRY

Sal, you ever think about teaching linguistics at Harvard?

SAL

Huh?

TOM

Jerry!

JERRY

Sorry. Go ahead.

SAL

You remember. I told you guys it was for Carmine. The tape thing. You know, he likes comedians and likes to make tapes and shit.

TOM

Yeah.

SAL

Well, that was sorta like a lie. I didn't wanna get ya hopes up or nothin', but the tape wasn't for Carmine.

JERRY

Who was it for?

SAL

Well, I got some friends who know some people and them people... they know Buddy King.

TOM

Buddy King?

JERRY

The Buddy King?

SAL

I sent the tape to Buddy King. Through my friends. He's always lookin' for funny, young comedians for his show, right?

TOM

And?

SAL

And he fuckin' loved you guys. He saw the tape. He wants yas to do his show.

JERRY

He... he...

TOM

He what?

SAL

Buddy King says you guys can do his show any time you want!

TOM

My God...

JERRY

Oh! Oh! Oh, my God!!!

Tom and Jerry pace the floor in wild excitement, jumping up and down, hugging each other, etc.

JERRY (cont'd)

My God!!! Holy shit!!! Yeah!!! The Buddy King Show!!! I don't believe it!!!

SAL

You guys don't have to say yes or no right away.

JERRY

Buddy fuckin' King!!!

SAL

You can take time to think it over.

JERRY

Hah!!! Yeah!!! Ho boy!!!

SAL

(to Tom)
What's he doin'?

TOM

That's Jerry "thinking it over."

Jerry crosses to the champagne bottle, pops the cork, gives the bottle a shake and sprays everyone and everything in sight.

JERRY
Holy shit!!! This is terrific!!! The Buddy King Show!!! Who-<u>eee</u>!!!

TOM
Jerry! Watch it!

SAL
Be careful. You'll get the contract wet.

TOM
What contract?

JERRY
They sent a contract already?

SAL
No. I thought it would be good if we put some stuff in writing sorta.

TOM
What kind of stuff?

SAL
To be honest with ya, I wanna manage you guys. Help your careers. Be there for things ya need.
(withdraws contract)
It's just a standard kinda management contract here. Just... standard.
(withdraws pens)
Got a fifty-dollar Parker Pen for yas. Got one for each of yas. You can keep the pens.

JERRY
(grabbing pen)
Terrific. Where do we sign?

SAL
On the last page where it says...

TOM
(snatching contract)
Maybe we should <u>read</u> it first? Huh, Jerry?

JERRY
What's to read? We're going to be on the Buddy King Show! Oh, baby! I can't believe it.

TOM
Is this like a package deal, Sal?

SAL
Huh?

TOM
I mean if we don't sign the contract, do we still get to do the Buddy

King Show?

                    SAL
Boy, you really put me on the spot there, Tommy.

                    JERRY
Tom, what are you putting Sal on the spot for, huh?

                    TOM
I just want to know, that's all.

                    SAL
There's a lot of interest up at the Buddy King Show over you guys. But that interest has come from me. Ya understand that? Comes time for them to send a contract... I'm not your manager... I'm out of a deal. I'm gonna look real stupid to them. I got a reputation to protect. They'll say, "Eh, Sal... are we dealin' with you or no?" I'll have to say, "No." I'm gonna look like a real asshole. I don't know if I can keep the deal alive if I'm not in on it.

                    JERRY
So we'll sign! We'll sign!

                    TOM
Jerry, don't you want to see what we're getting into?

                    JERRY
We're gettin' "into" the Buddy King Show! That's all I need to know. Five years we've been trying to get on that show. Five years! Didn't I tell you I felt good tonight? Didn't I? You feel good... good things happen. You make them happen. You draw them to you. Like Sal. My pizanne!

Jerry hugs Sal and helps himself to his silver bullet. He snorts up both nostrils.

                    JERRY (cont'd)
Knnn! Yeah! Damn, I feel good. Feelin' even better! Knnn!

Jerry tosses the bullet back to Sal.

                    TOM
If you were our manager, we'd still need a booking agent, wouldn't we?

                    SAL
Got some lined up. No problem gettin' you guys with someone.

                    TOM
So, we'd pay our commission to you...
        (looking through contract)
What is it... Ten percent? Fifteen?

                    SAL
Thirty.

                    TOM
Thirty percent!

JERRY
And he's worth every God damn penny.

SAL
I'll be losin' money the first three years, believe me.

TOM
Thirty percent to you, another ten to the agent... it means we'd each be working for thirty cents on the dollar.

SAL
If you wanna look at it <u>that</u> way.

JERRY
(singing in a world of his own)
"Here's my Buddy, my buddy... our buddy boy..."

SAL
There's a lotta work we could pick up for you guys. Vegas, Reno, Atlantic City... Miami.

JERRY
Miami! I can visit my grandmother!

TOM
The main rooms?

SAL
Not right away. Mostly lounges to start.

JERRY
(singing)
"When you need a friend, who's the living end, who could do most anything..."

TOM
Jerry, I'm trying to talk over here.

JERRY
(singing right at Tom)
"Call buddy... your buddy... here's Buddy King!!!"

Jerry suddenly dashes to the bathroom where he hear him vomit.

JERRY (O.S.) (cont'd)
<u>Arrrrrrrrrf!</u>

SAL
There goes two hundred bucks right into the toilet.

TOM
So, we would work the lounges, huh?

SAL
Yeah, opening for singers, guys like that. The people I know got a whole bunch of singers you could open for. Joey Vee... ever hear of him?

TOM

No.

SAL

You will. He's the next Vic Damone. Believe me. Tommy Ventura. You musta heard of him.

TOM

No.

JERRY (O.S.)

Arrrrrrf!

SAL

He's terrific. He's the next Beatles. There's a lotta guys you could work with. A lotta guys.

TOM

And no contract... no Buddy King Show... right?

SAL

C'mon, you're not a baby. They call it "show business" not "show friendship." It's just a standard contract, Tommy. You know, I get some singers in here, some rock and roll groups... they've heard I'm lookin' to get into management and stuff. They go, "Eh, Sal! Why don't you manage us?" And I go, "Maybe in another lifetime..." Because they all got one thing in common.

TOM

What's that?

SAL

They're stupid. All the singers and shit... they're stupid is what they are. The people I know, my friends, my bartenders, my waitresses... don't get me wrong... they're all nice people... but they're stupid, too. Everyone I know is stupid. Everyone who works here wears the same clothes, drives the same fuckin' Trans Am... nobody ever says anything that's clever, stuff like that. The most clever thing anyone ever says around here is "fuckin' A." That's it. Sometimes I think I'm gonna drown in stupid people. Sometimes I think I'm kinda stupid myself.

TOM

Aw, Sal... c'mon.

SAL

Naw, that's all right. I know I'm not that smart. But you guys... I watch yas talk, perform on stage. You make up jokes left an' right... You're so clever and shit I can't believe what I'm seein' sometimes. I get angry inside. "How come you can't make up shit like that!" I tell myself "How come you can't make up shit like that!" In my circle of friends, guys like you...

TOM

Yeah?

SAL

You're from another planet. I don't wanna do what everybody else here does. There's somethin' inside me that's very restless. You know what I'm talking about? You know that feeling?

TOM

Yeah.

SAL

I knew you would. I wanna manage a comedy team. The best comedy team there is in the world. You guys. I would work very hard for you, Tommy. Try and think what your lives would be like if I could manage you guys.

JERRY *(O.S.)*

Arrrrrf!!!

SAL

Think it over.

Sal exits. After a few beats Jerry enters from the bathroom wiping his hands on a paper towel.

JERRY

Where's Sal?

TOM

He just left. How do you feel?

JERRY

Terrific! I swear, I never felt better in my whole life. Where's the contract? You didn't give it back to Sal, did you?

TOM

No, it's right here.

JERRY
(takes pen and readies to sign)
Good, good... I didn't sign it yet.

TOM

Jerry...

JERRY
(looking at contract)
You didn't sign it either.

TOM

I know. I thought we should talk about it first.

JERRY

What's to talk about? We're going to do the Buddy King Show. Oh, man! We're gonna be rich, you know that? Rich! Tommy, I'm gonna buy you your own set of Korean twins.

TOM
Jerry…

JERRY
Uh uh uh uh uh… I insist.

TOM
Jerry!

JERRY
Yeah?

TOM
I think signing a management contract with Sal could be the worst mistake of our entire lives.

JERRY
I think it's the best thing that ever happened to us.

TOM
Well, at least we don't disagree by much.

JERRY
Tom, Sal's got us our shot. All we have to do is sign.

TOM
All we have to do is <u>not</u> sign… keep doing good shows, get better and better as an act. We'll get on the Buddy King Show <u>without</u> getting involved with Sal.

JERRY
Aw, Sal's a pussycat. So what if he's a little mobbed up?

TOM
A "little mobbed up!" He named his first-born daughter Jimmy the Weasel! It's not worth it, Jerry. You should see this contract. It's for seven years. Seven <u>years</u>, Jerry.

JERRY
Seven's my lucky number.

TOM
Sal wants thirty percent <u>before</u> an agent takes his ten. He wants to put us in lounges… <u>lounges</u>! Opening for guys who sing "Feelings" and play the accordion.

JERRY
The Buddy King Show, Tommy.

TOM
Lounges don't pay more than a thousand a week. Our take-home after taxes will be less than three hundred each. Then you've got to pay living expenses…

JERRY
I don't want to hear this!

TOM
And you get paid in chips, man. Casino chips. Sure, you can cash them in, but it's a <u>long</u> walk through the casino to the cashier's window, and I know you, Jerry. You'd never make it past the blackjack tables.

JERRY
Oh, you know me real good, don't you? So good you can fuck up the best chance of my life. Well, you don't know <u>shit</u> about me, Kelly. You don't know the way my gut aches to get on the Buddy King Show. "Another young comedian, and another young comedian, and a bright and funny young comedian..." but never <u>us</u>! <u>Me</u>! Twenty million people!

TOM
Jerry...

JERRY
Shut up! I've waited for that night all of my life it seems. Because sitting out there in America in some perfectly pathetic domestic situation... sitting in their ugly, drunken, fat... is every motherfuckin' sonofabitch who ever shit on me! They're all out there! Married to each other drowning in hopelessness. Watching me! On televisions that aren't even paid for yet! Watching <u>me</u>!!! The ones who tormented and teased and humiliated me. The bitches who giggled behind my back! Their boyfriends who stole my lunch money! The fuckheads who called me Jew boy! You know what's going on with them now?! Their lives add up to <u>zip</u>! There's Jerry Goldstein on the Buddy King Show... Their lives add up to <u>less</u> than zip. It's Jerry Goldstein.

TOM
Boy, will <u>they</u> be sorry.

JERRY
Damn right. Wonder what they'll all do.

TOM
They'll probably kill themselves.

JERRY
I could dig that. I want to do that show, Tom.

TOM
I know. And we will someday.

JERRY
I want to do it... <u>now</u>!

TOM
The price is too high.

JERRY
Don't stand in my way.

TOM
I'm right beside you. You just can't see me.

JERRY

I want you to sign this, and I want you to sign it right now.

TOM

Who are you? Have we met? You look a lot like my partner.

JERRY

Sign this.

TOM

No way.

JERRY

Your last chance. Sign it or else.

TOM

Is being pathetic an Olympic sport yet? If it is, you should try out for the team.

JERRY

You signing?

TOM

Read my lips -- no fucking way!

JERRY

Get out.

TOM

What?

JERRY

I said get out.

TOM

Get out of where?

Jerry throws a childish tantrum and begins throwing Tom's personal articles toward the door. Tom's hat, coat, briefcase all go flying at the door.

JERRY

Get out of <u>here</u>! My dressing room! Get out of my dressing room!

TOM

You're crazy.

JERRY

We're through. I'm sick and tired of this shit! You're holding me back! We're through! Get out of here!

TOM

What are you doing?

JERRY

<u>Out</u>!!! <u>Get outta here</u>!!! <u>Get</u>... <u>out</u>!!!

TOM

Stop!!!

JERRY

Do this to me?!! Do a thing like this to me?!! Who the fuck you think you are?!! You are no one!!!

Tom lunges at Jerry and pins him against the wall. Jerry loses none of his rage.

TOM

Stop it!!!

JERRY

Get out!!!

TOM

Stop!!!

JERRY

Ain't shit!!!

TOM

Stop!!!

JERRY

Hate your fuckin' GUTS!!!

Tom slaps Jerry hard across the face. It stops Jerry cold.

TOM

What are you, crazy? Who sat up with you in Atlanta when you thought you were going to die? Who? You so coked up you can't remember? You remember a hundred and five fever? Who stayed up with you for two days and nights? Was it Buddy King? Was it Sal? Who got his jaw broke in Pittsburgh? You thought it'd be funny to call some guy a "dumb fuckin' Pollack!" Turns out he was! Who got his jaw broke?!! Who was it!!! A few minutes ago you were ready to burn Sal forever! Work the city, find a new agent, burn the old one! Now you want to burn me? Just like that? Is it that easy? Is it? Is it?!! Are you in there? Are you in there somewhere?

Tom waits for a reply. There is none. After several beats he lets go of Jerry. Jerry gathers himself and crosses to the table where he takes a drink and sits down. He takes one of the pens and finds a napkin on the floor, picks it up and prepares to make notes on the napkin.

JERRY

Okay. No problem here. I'm going to do the Buddy King Show on my own. That's what I'll do. I'm going to take all the bits I thought up... do 'em on my own. Make a list here. Write them down just like you do. "Tom's a writer... the brains of the team..." Hah! You don't write. You type! Make a list... all our bits. Work solo and do the bits I thought up. I'm takin' my bits, Kelly. And I'm writing new ones. Brand new bits... make a list... yeah.

TOM

You didn't forget.

JERRY

What?

TOM

On stage tonight. You didn't forget the new material?

JERRY

I'll write funnier stuff than <u>that</u>.

TOM

You were scared. I saw it in your eyes, Jerry. It was time to launch into the new material on stage. You took a beat, stammered around, then jumped into the old material. The safe stuff. The stuff we've done a million times. And I said to myself, "Holy shit! He's scared..." It was all over your face, man. You had the same expression you have right now.

JERRY

I'm going to send you a color TV, Kelly. A great big one. You can watch me kill on the Buddy King Show. Alone. Without you.

TOM

Yeah, sure. You do that.

JERRY

I will.

TOM

Looks like you've got everything you need. Your paper, your pencil, yourself...

(indicates bottle)

Your inspiration. Oops, almost forgot. Your reason. Gotta have a reason, Jer.

Tom finds the cassette recorder and brings it to the table where he sets it down in front of Jerry.

TOM *(cont'd)*

Can't do comedy without a good, solid, realistic reason. Here.

Tom presses the play button on the recorder. We hear the same wild audience applause and whistles we heard before. Jerry listens to the machine, expressionless. Tom surveys Jerry for a few beats, then sadly exits.

The lights slowly fade to black.

<u>END OF ACT ONE</u>

ACT TWO

A night in July, 1980

Lights up on:

The Green Room of the Buddy King Show. A modern, comfortable room giving off industrial warmth. A couch, some chairs, a state-of-the-art coffee table covered with trade journals. Perhaps some nicely framed portraits of various network stars and a logo featuring the initials "B.K." There is a monitor hung from the ceiling. The audience can only see the back of the monitor as the screen faces upstage. There is a bar.

Sheldon Kelinski enters. He is dressed in a suit which should suggest he has matured over the last three years -- at least in dress. He carries a plastic ice bucket and a clipboard. He seems anxious.

Sheldon crosses to the bar and dispenses the ice cubes from the bucket into the state-of-the-art ice bucket on the bar. He deals with the ice cubes clumsily -- dropping some and washing them off, etc.

After a few beats Tom Kelly enters. He looks angry and sullen. Tom is dressed nicely but not in a suit. He holds a script binder with the logo of the Buddy King Show printed on the cover.

SHELDON
Hi.

TOM
Hiya.

SHELDON
What are you doing here? Never mind. Listen, how many ice cubes does the average person use in the course of an evening?

TOM
Six point four.

SHELDON
You sound so sure.

TOM
I'm from an Irish family. The ice cube is my birthstone.

SHELDON
Great. What a night. God. Get this. My friend just called me. The one who works at Teletron.

TOM
The ratings company?

SHELDON
Right. Looks like tonight's final episode of Yellow Rose is getting even bigger numbers than they expected.

TOM

Sure. The whole country wants to see who raped Clem.

SHELDON

My friend says our lead-in from Yellow Rose on the East Coast is going to be a seventy share.

TOM

Wow...

SHELDON

And we're not going to lose any audience. Not with Crystal Starr on the show. God, is she gorgeous or what?

TOM

Yeah.

SHELDON

Think she'll come in here?

TOM

Crystal Starr? The high priestess of rock? A woman who won't hang out with Cher because she isn't "trendy" enough? Hang out in here? With us? Dah... gee... I sure do hope so!

SHELDON

I'm sorry I asked. I'm scum. I should die.

TOM

So, who else is on the show tonight?

SHELDON

Couple of comics I hear.

TOM

Anyone we know?

SHELDON

I haven't even looked at the contracts yet. I haven't had time. I've been all day with Crystal Starr's arranger. God, Woodstock had less equipment.

TOM

Well, she puts on quite a show.

SHELDON

"Miss Starr needs this like so and that like so... Miss Starr only uses such-and-such a microphone. Two floor monitors for Miss Starr. Where do we put the smoke bombs? The follow-spot is the wrong shade of lavender. The band won't drink diet cola. No one can touch the audio mix once it's set. No one can touch or speak to Miss Starr." And I have to hear all that from a man with a swastika tattooed on his forehead. A swastika! If my grandmother ever found out! I fail to see the humor in that. Do you see any humor in that?

TOM

No.

SHELDON
Neither do I. What are you doing here, anyway? It's after seven. All the writers are usually home by seven. They don't want to miss Rocky and Bullwinkle.

TOM
Yeah, well, uh... Buddy sorta wants me to do this thing kinda.

SHELDON
Huh?

TOM
I mean in addition to my writing chores.

SHELDON
What are you talking about?

TOM
Well, remember the guy we had on last night? The author who wrote that book? The British guy? Told that terrible, off-color story about Helen Hayes.

SHELDON
What an asshole.

TOM
Turns out he came alone. No agent, no manager... He sat here for two hours scared out of his wits. Evidently Sir Charles hit the sauce a little -- then he hit it a <u>lot</u>. Wasn't anyone here to watch him.

SHELDON
I'm in and out all night. I can't possibly --

TOM
(interrupts)
Don't worry. Your name never came up with Buddy. <u>Mine</u> did.
(ala Buddy)
"Tom, you're an engaging, young lad... I want you to stay in the Green Room. Keep an eye on our guests..."

SHELDON
What are you saying?

TOM
Buddy made me responsible for the Green Room.

SHELDON
He what?

TOM
He made me the goddamn Green Room Monitor, okay?

SHELDON
But I'm responsible for the Green Room.

TOM
I know. That's what I told Buddy.

SHELDON
I have to run between here and the control room, show people where hair and make-up is, deal with --

TOM
(interrupts)
Would you calm down? What do you think? I <u>want</u> this? If anything goes wrong now it's gonna be <u>my</u> fault.

SHELDON
Do you want my job?

TOM
Are you nuts?

SHELDON
You want my job? Is that it? Just say it. Go ahead. If you want my job just say so. Say, "Sheldon, I want your job."

TOM
Sheldon…

SHELDON
Yes?

TOM
I don't want your job.

SHELDON
I knew it! I knew it! You want my job!

TOM
Would you stop. I do <u>not</u> want your job. You've got the worst job in the world.

SHELDON
Semantics. Everyone who works on this show already has the worst job in the world.

TOM
True. But of all those jobs, yours is -- without a doubt -- the <u>worst</u>. It's beyond bad. Your job is in the Twilight Zone of awful.

SHELDON
Tom, I like my job. I want to keep it.

TOM
You can <u>have</u> it!

SHELDON
This job is all I have. I'm not like you. I don't have lots of friends and family and people who like me. I have this job and the clothes on my back and that's it! Okay, and the clothes I have at home. I have some nice sports jackets and Italian shoes but that's it.

TOM
Sheldon...

SHELDON
And my car. But you really can't count that. In Los Angeles a car is a necessity instead of a luxury. It's just a two-year-old Supra and it doesn't even have a phone.

TOM
Sheldon...

SHELDON
Count the car! And my house because I made a large down to keep the payments low. But that's all I have in this world, Tom. This job, my clothes, my car, the house, some sensible stocks, a few bonds and my IRA accounts but that's it. That's all I have in this whole world. That's everything.

TOM
Sheldon!

SHELDON
My stereo maybe, but it's old now. I couldn't get much for it.

TOM
Sheldon!

SHELDON
What?

TOM
Thank you for the list of everything you own, but I don't want your job.

SHELDON
You slick barracudas are all alike. I'm warning you, Tom. I'll ruin you so bad you'll become one of those people who sleeps in their car and smells bad.

TOM
Fine.

SHELDON
I'll...

Jackie Dwayne enters. He carries a garment bag slung over his shoulder.

TOM
(to Jackie)
Hi.

JACKIE
Hiya.

SHELDON
(to Tom)
I'll make your life so miserable you'll...

(realizing)
Oh, God...

JACKIE
I'm looking for the associate producer of the Buddy King Show.

TOM
He's right here and doing one helluva job.

JACKIE
Sheldon?

SHELDON
Oh God...

JACKIE
Sheldon Kelinski?

TOM
You guys know each other?

JACKIE
We sure do.

SHELDON
God...

JACKIE
Sheldon!

Jackie looks at Sheldon with intense sincerity, puts down his garment bag then deliberately crosses to Sheldon and puts his hands on Sheldon's shoulders looking him dead in the eyes. Sheldon quivers expecting the worst.

JACKIE *(cont'd)*
It's so good to see you.

Jackie gives Sheldon a great, big bear hug. A warm, friendly hug. Sheldon's body language is that of a stone. He's completely uncomfortable.

TOM
Boy, you two really <u>do</u> know each other...

Jackie lets go of Sheldon.

JACKIE
And who's your friend?

SHELDON
(still recovering from the hug)
Tom Kelly and he's no friend.

JACKIE
Hello, Tom. I'm Jackie Dwayne.

TOM
Of course. Pleasure to meet you. I thought you looked familiar when you—

Tom is interrupted by one of Jackie's warm and friendly bear hugs.

> TOM (cont'd)
> (as he's being hugged)
> Oh... I get one, too...

Jackie lets go of Tom.

> TOM (cont'd)
> Thank you. That was... very nice...

> JACKIE
> And what do you do on the show, Tom?

> TOM
> I'm one of Buddy's writers.

> JACKIE
> Aha. I have always been in awe of the comedy writer.

> SHELDON
> What is he talking about?

> JACKIE
> You writers don't have it easy and you can never be thanked enough for what you do.

Jackie gives Tom another hug.

> TOM
> (to Sheldon)
> A very intuitive and intelligent friend you have here.

> SHELDON
> This is all a trick. Some massively clever trick to lull us into a false sense of security before he verbally hacks us up like a chainsaw through rice pudding.

> TOM
> What are you talking about?

> JACKIE
> Oh, this's no trick. This is me... for <u>real</u>. I've managed to turn my life around.

> TOM
> How'd you do that?

> JACKIE
> I was fortunate enough to have had a massive heart attack.

> SHELDON
> My God...

> TOM
> Lucky guy.

JACKIE

I was. Very lucky. I had a triple by-pass... the works. Want to see the scar?

TOM

No.

SHELDON

Uh uh!

JACKIE

Talk about being "at death's door?" I was one step into the vestibule. I almost didn't make it. Maybe God was testing me. Maybe he gave me another lifetime to correct my mistakes.

SHELDON

You'd need eight lifetimes to do that.

JACKIE

(laughs heartily)

Aha ha ha... I like that. That's funny. I'm sorry about what happened the last time we met, Sheldon.

Jackie crosses to Sheldon and gives him another sincere hug.

SHELDON

You seem different...

JACKIE

I am. I'm telling you I'm a changed man. My act has changed, too. The kinds of jokes I used to do... well, they lacked... sensitivity. Did you notice?

SHELDON

Sorta...

JACKIE

Joke-joke-joke... blah-blah-blah... one-dimensional, superficial presentation... no real connection with the audience as a person... no vulnerability. Lemme tell ya... you want to know what vulnerable feels like? You should have a heart attack.

TOM

I'll pass.

SHELDON

Me, too.

JACKIE

I wouldn't wish it on anyone. But my life is different because of it. So is my act. I talk about real things. Like my heart attack.

SHELDON

You talk about that in your act?

JACKIE

Why not? It's true. It happened to me. Actually I had it in this coffee shop on Columbus Avenue. Run by this Greek family named Fletnokos. That's Greek for "Open Twenty-four Hours." I was always giving the waiter a hard time about how bad the food was. I would say things like, "With food this bad, your daily special should be the Heimlich Maneuver." Or, "You should put a sign in your window that says, 'Sorry. We're open.'" Anyway, I take a bite of this omelet I ordered and -- wouldn't you know it -- I have my heart attack right there and then. I'm clutching my chest, gasping for air and this waiter's telling me...

(thick Greek accent)

"That's not funny, mister..." I'm going...

(gasping in pain)

"Eee eee..." He's going, "You no like the food you go somewhere else..." Pretty soon I'm on the floor and all seven Fletnokos brothers are standing around me wondering if I need mouth-to-mouth. Me? I'm looking up at the seven ugliest mouths on Columbus Avenue! Fourteen lips only a mother could love. Well, thirteen actually, but you don't want to hear that. Not a pretty story. I'm hoping I die before I get a mouthful of Fletnokos breath! Meanwhile, the father is seating people. They made their father the "host" because you know how charming Greek men get when they're ninety. The father is seating people asking them... "You want a table with a view of the heart attack or no view of the heart attack..." A New York City ambulance finally shows up... They're triple-parked outside with two gunshot victims in the back... so help me God they're putting me in a stretcher and I hear one of them ask for two coffees to go!

TOM

That's funny.

SHELDON

Boffo.

JACKIE

I knew you liked it, Sheldon, by the way you laughed. Sheldon has a very high-pitched laugh. Only <u>dogs</u> hear him. I'm getting booked into <u>colleges</u> now. The kids love me. I'm playing the "hipper" nightclubs. It's like a whole new career for me.

SHELDON

How'd you swing a shot on the show?

JACKIE

The hard way.

TOM

They didn't make you audition?

JACKIE

Like I was some kid, a beginner. But I wanted to do the Buddy King Show so I auditioned. I did real well. I maintained a calm, positive attitude... I wore my best tuxedo and I had my wife blow Buddy in the men's room. Only kidding. Only kidding. Actually...

TOM, JACKIE & SHELDON

It wasn't my best tuxedo.

JACKIE

I'm really sorry about what happened the last time we met, Sheldon.

SHELDON

Well, maybe I was a little difficult to get along with. I had just donated a kidney against my will.

JACKIE

Pals?

SHELDON

No more hugging?

JACKIE

Promise.

SHELDON

Pals.

Jackie offers his hand to Sheldon but Sheldon turns it into a hug of his own.

TOM

Did you find your dressing room?

JACKIE

No. They told me the associate producer would show me where to go.

SHELDON

That's me. That's my job. I do that. I didn't even know you were on the show until you walked in. Let me check with the stage manager. You'll have a dressing room in one minute. That's what I do and I do it quite well.

(indicating Tom)
Listen to nothing he says. He's nobody.

Sheldon exits.

TOM

You know when you walked in I sorta recognized you right away.

JACKIE

You did?

TOM

Sure. Jackie Dwayne... the Ed Sullivan Show...

JACKIE
You saw me do Sullivan?

TOM
Sure. At the Museum of Broadcasting.

JACKIE
The what!

TOM
It's in New York.

JACKIE
I know where it is.

TOM
I was back there a few months ago. They had black and white kinescopes from the late forties, early fifties...

JACKIE
(feigns being impressed)
That far back?

TOM
Shecky White, Bernie Stone, Joey Fagan... Sheldon Biber...

JACKIE
I'll stop you when you get to somebody <u>living</u>.

TOM
I'll tell you something. Watching you and those other comics on those tapes... It brought back a whole part of my life. I remember how excited my family would get when a comic came on a variety show. The TV would be on... well, the TV was <u>always</u> on... no one paid much attention to it. But the comedian would come on and everything would <u>stop</u>. Mama would stop washing dishes, call my dad up from the basement, wake up grandpa... it was time for... "the comedian." We'd sit and watch and pay attention. Laugh like crazy. Some of these guys we'd know their name... others we didn't -- but we always knew which one was which from his jokes. You know... the one who goes "Wadda ya crazy" or the one who does the bit about drive-in movies.... My family... we'd sit around the dinner table talking about comedians. We'd do their jokes at the table. Just sit... doing our favorite jokes like they were songs or something. I miss those days.

JACKIE
Well, I'm about to bring them back.

Jerry Goldstein enters.

TOM
Holy shit...

JERRY
This where they keep the broads?

TOM

Jerry?

JERRY

(ala old Italian woman)
Tomaso?

TOM

Jerry!

Tom crosses to Jerry and they hug.

JERRY

My Tomaso!

TOM

Ya nut! Haa! I can't believe it!

JERRY

Tomaso! Tomaso!

Jerry grabs Tom's face and kisses it. He double-talks Italian. An impassioned speech of a mother reunited with her long lost son.

TOM

Screwball!

JERRY

Tomaso... You smell... <u>terrible</u>!

TOM

What're you doing here?

JERRY

I'm doing the show tonight, dickbrain. <u>That's</u> what I'm doing here.

TOM

You're kidding.

JERRY

What. You didn't know?

TOM

I swear to God. I had no idea.

JERRY

Well, I'm doing the show.

TOM

Hah! That's terrific! You couldn't've picked a better night.

JERRY

I heard. It's up and down the hallways. Something about Yellow Rose and Crystal Starr.

TOM

It's a big night on the show. You'll do great.

JERRY

I'd <u>better</u> do great.

TOM

Jackie, I want you to meet my partner...
    (catches himself)
My <u>ex</u>-partner...
    (to Jerry)
That sounds awful, doesn't it?

JERRY

Divorce is never pretty.

TOM

My <u>ex</u>-partner... Jerry Goldstein.

JACKIE

You use "Goldstein?"

JERRY

Yeah. No one changes their name for show biz anymore.

TOM

Jerry, this is Jackie Dwayne.

JERRY

"Dwayne?"

JACKIE

My generation -- we <u>all</u> changed our names. Glad to meet you, Jerry.

Jerry goes to shake Jackie's hand. Jackie surprises Jerry by giving him a hug. As he hugs Jerry…

TOM

He's into hugging.

JERRY

No shit.

Jackie stops hugging Jerry.

JACKIE

I'm sorry. Some people get uncomfortable. They don't know what to make out of it.

JERRY

Hey, it's fine by me.
    (suddenly)
My wallet!

Tom and Jackie laugh.

JACKIE

That's good.

TOM
(to Jackie)
He's always been quick.

JERRY
Quick is a thing you get from confidence. Confidence you get from experience.

JACKIE
Could be.

JERRY
(indicating Jackie)
Here's a man with experience. I think I've seen you work.

JACKIE
The Museum of Natural History? I do a thing with a woolly mammoth... it's terrific.

JERRY
No. A club somewhere. Maybe a college thing. Whatever. You were great.

JACKIE
Thanks.

JERRY
You on the show? Going on first?

TOM
We don't know yet.

JERRY
I hope you go on first. I want to watch. Really, man. Guys like me... when we watch guys like you... all we can do is learn.

JACKIE
C'mon.

JERRY
No, I mean it. A guy spends five, six thousand hours on a nightclub stage -- he learns a few things.

JACKIE
(to Tom)
I think I love him.

Sheldon enters.

SHELDON
Mister Dwayne, I've got your dressing room for you.

JACKIE
Oh, great.

SHELDON
It's neat and clean. There's a fresh supply of towels and complimentary toilet articles for your personal use. There's soda, juice and a plate of fresh fruit and cheese and should you need anything else, please be sure to see <u>me</u> and no one else.

JACKIE
You got it.

Jackie gets his clothing bag and pauses to talk to Jerry.

JACKIE *(cont'd)*
Good luck tonight.

JERRY
You, too. Chip a tooth.

SHELDON
Jerry Goldstein?

JERRY
Yeah.

SHELDON
Sheldon Kelinski, associate producer. I'll have your dressing room as quickly as I got Mister Dwayne's.

Sheldon and Jackie exit.

JERRY
There's <u>two</u> comics on tonight?

TOM
Sure. It happens every now and then. You'll both destroy. Believe me.

JERRY
You look good. California agrees with you.

TOM
I'm getting to like it. I moved out here, rented a car, rented an apartment, rented some plants and furniture. I'm thinking of putting down roots and renting a family.

JERRY
C'mon, make a commitment in life. Lease a family with an option to buy.

TOM
I will. Hey, I'm living with a woman now.

JERRY
Terrific. How'd your inflatable woman take it?

TOM
Not good. The last thing she said to me was "Thupppp!" Man, it's good to see you again.

JERRY

Ditto.

Sal D'Angelo enters.

TOM

Sal?

SAL

Eh, Tommy!

TOM

Sal D'Angelo?

SAL

Eh!

Sal crosses to Tom and gives him a hug.

TOM

Sal...

SAL

How ya doin'. I missed ya face ya fuckin' potato head ya.
(to Jerry)
How's it goin'? You two kiss and make up or what?

JERRY

Yeah. Tom even slipped me some tongue. It was terrific.

SAL

So, Tommy, you write now for Buddy King now, huh?

TOM

Yeah.

SAL

And you're ready to make my boy a star tonight?

TOM

Your boy?

SAL

I'm Jerry's manager. Have been for a while. Since yas broke up. I know you'll do your best here for the number one client of my management company... "Pisces Management."

TOM

Pisces...?

SAL

You like the name? We named it after my wife.

TOM

Your wife's name is Pisces?

SAL

No, Anna. She's a Pisces. March eighteen. Me, I don't know shit or nothin' about that shit. I needed a name, she said, "Hey, name it after my birthday!" What the fuck do I care? Done. We're growin' like fuckin' crazy, too. Got a whole list of rock n' roll groups we book an' shit. Very exciting things are happening at Pisces Management. An' someday we might even be looking to handle people who can write...

JERRY

As soon as they hire some people who can read.

SAL

Wha?

JERRY

Nothing. Just interjecting a thought.

SAL

You happy with your present representation?

TOM

(can't answer fast enough)
Very! It's working out really well.

SAL

If you ever become unhappy, you know where to come, eh?

TOM

Right to you, Sal. Immediately. I swear... first call I make is to Pisces Management.

SAL

So, my boy is as good as a star, right, Tommy?

TOM

Piece of cake. There's going to be a gigantic audience tonight.

JERRY

Hey, Sal. Crystal Starr's on the show tonight.

SAL

I heard. Is she some piece or what? I mean forget about her body. Just put that aside for a second. Concentrate on that face. Man, wadda face! I'd like to spend a year of my life just suckin' on that thing, ya know? I'd like to take her face, hold it in my two hands like it was a cantaloupe or somethin' an' just suck on it. Mornin', noon and night... I swear I wouldn't leave the house or nothin'. I'd just be suckin' away on Crystal Starr's face.

JERRY

It'd probably get all white and wrinkly...

SAL

And that body? Holy shit wadda bod. Them tits, that ass... God damn! She's probably all white an' soft an' pink underneath. Man, I'd love to jump on her bod... Slam it in there. Slam it in an' out, in an' out... You think she screams when she <u>sings</u>, eh? In an' out, in an' out... bingo-bongo up in the Congo... all the while I'm suckin' an' fuckin'... lickin' an' kissin' her ass, them tits... every square inch she's got for hours an' hours... in an' out, in an' out... bing-bang-bing-bang... until she's wet an' limp like a dish rag an' my salami's shot for a fuckin' week.

TOM

Then you find her attractive?

JERRY

I don't know about anyone else, but I sure could go for a cigarette right now.

Sheldon enters.

SHELDON

Excuse me. Jerry, we've got your dressing room ready. Mister D'Angelo? Is he here? Are you Mister D'Angelo?

SAL

Is 7-11 lookin' for night managers?

SHELDON

I have Jerry's contract for you to look over. If anyone else has told you they have Jerry's contract, they were lying because I'm the only person who has it.

SAL

Right... right... gotta take a look.

Sal goes to exit.

SAL *(cont'd)*
    (to Sheldon)
See them two guys?

SHELDON

Yes.

SAL

Them two guys was the funniest fuckin' guys you ever saw once.

JERRY

Once.

TOM

Before talkies came along.

SAL

    (laughs)
Funny. You're still demented. You know that? You're demented.

Sal, Sheldon and Jerry exit. A beat.

Jackie enters.

JACKIE

I just saw Crystal Starr!

TOM

Please! I don't want to hear!

JACKIE

I was at the water fountain and this group of people goes by.

TOM

Her entourage.

JACKIE

Yeah. They moved in complete unison. Like they were welded together.

TOM

And you saw Crystal Starr?

JACKIE

Yeah. For a couple of seconds, too. Wow she is gorgeous. She was wearing one of those gowns must've weighed all of three ounces! When I think of what I want to do to that lady, I disgust even myself. There oughta be a law against me. She's... she's...

TOM

Easy, guy.

JACKIE

Thanks. After a heart attack, you have to be very <u>careful</u> about becoming stimulated. That's why when I just got married I made sure it was to a Jewish girl.

TOM

You just got married?

JACKIE

Uh huh. Six months ago.

TOM

A newlywed, huh?

JACKIE

Don't get excited. It's my fifth, her third. Or was it her fifth and my third? Ah, who remembers? Thank God they were all named Shirley. That way you never make any mistakes.

TOM

Where'd you meet her?

JACKIE

In yoga class.

TOM

<u>Yoga</u> class?

JACKIE

I'm a different kinda guy. I'm a specialist in relaxation. Stand me next to Perry Como and people would say, "There's Jackie Dwayne and that nervous guy."

Sheldon enters.

TOM

Sheldon, Jackie just got married a few months ago.

SHELDON

I knew that!

TOM

Met his wife in yoga class. Makes good panel, huh?

SHELDON

I was just about to suggest that.

Sheldon goes to his clipboard and gets a bright blue file card. He hands it to Jackie.

JACKIE

What's that?

SHELDON

This is for panel material.

JACKIE

I don't understand.

TOM

It's for Buddy. It goes on his desk.

SHELDON

I'll explain. It's for Buddy. It goes on his desk.

TOM

See, in case you do a killer set... Buddy might signal you to come over and talk with him.

SHELDON

And just in case that happens, we give Buddy some information on you. Little facts and things for Buddy to use. It's something I do for Buddy every night and he's very pleased with how I do it.

JACKIE

(indicating card)
So you give him that.

TOM

Right. He glances down and says, "I've heard you just got married..."

SHELDON

You say, "Yes," start talking about it and to all of America it looks like you're having a conversation.

Sal enters. He seems upset.

SAL
I am shocked! Shocked to find out my contract with this show has been violated.

TOM
What's the matter, Sal?

SAL
I gotta problem but there don't seem to be no way to get to your executive producer.

SHELDON
He's got his hands full with Crystal Starr.

TOM
He <u>wishes</u> he had his hands full with Crystal Starr.

SAL
Well, the Buddy King Show lied to me.

TOM
What?

SHELDON
Lied? How?

Sal looks at Jackie. He makes it clear that he will not speak any further with Jackie in the room. After a few silent beats, Jackie catches on.

JACKIE
I think I left the oven running in my dressing room.

Jackie exits.

SAL
It was my understanding that my client would be the only comedian on the show.

SHELDON
We never make promises like that.

SAL
In a private and confidential phone conversation, I was promised my client would not do his shot on a night when there was another comedian.

SHELDON
Arnie agreed to that?

SAL
Yes.

SHELDON
(crossing to phone)
Wait, let me call him. I've never heard of such an agreement on this show.

SAL

I don't wanna get into no discussion about who said what, when and how... He'll deny it, say he thought I meant somethin' else when he said whatever to me... That kinda talk ain't gonna get none of us nowhere.

TOM

Sal, this show has two comedians on the same night all the time.

SHELDON

It's nothing unusual.

SAL

Maybe not to you. But it's unusual to have my promise broken. That don't happen very often to me. I am shocked. Very shocked.

TOM

Sal, there's nothing to worry about. It's all gonna be fine.

SAL

No, no... there's something very wrong about tonight. I have very bad feelings about this whole thing. I want the old guy off the show.

SHELDON

What?

SAL

You heard me. I want the old guy <u>off</u> the show.

SHELDON

If we let every manager or agent who felt like it control our line-up of guests...

SAL

Look, I don't have time to fart around, so let me say this... Crystal Starr happens to cut records on the Tiffany label. She's very grateful to Tiffany Records. She would never make them unhappy.

TOM

Yeah?

SAL

The president of Tiffany Records has a great deal of admiration and respect for my uncle in Weehawken... a businessman...

TOM

Shit...

SAL

I call my uncle... I tell him how unhappy I am about my comic being mistreated like this. My uncle feels so bad for me...

TOM

He calls the president of Tiffany Records.

SAL

See? You're still sharp. These unhappiness calls continue until they reach Crystal Starr who gets so upset over all this unhappiness...

TOM

She gets laryngitis.

SAL

Or herpes, or upset stomach or whatever... fuck it... she don't have to get nothin'. She just has to leave and I take Jerry with me. You like the old comic? Great. You're...

(gestures)

... that close to having sixty minutes of just him.

(looking at watch)

There ain't much time. I want an answer an' I want it now.

Jackie pops his head through the door. He registers the complete silence curiously for a beat or two then:

JACKIE

I interrupt anything?

TOM

Hmm?

SHELDON

No.

SAL

Uh uh.

JACKIE

Talking about me?

TOM

(laughs)

Ha!

SHELDON

Funny.

JACKIE

Sheldon, I just wanted to know if you'd like to have some chow after the show.

SHELDON

Love to.

JACKIE

Great. How 'bout you, Tom. A little dinner?

TOM

Sure... yeah. Sounds good.

JACKIE

Terrific. We'll do macrobiotic.

Jackie exits. Tom and Sheldon seem relieved.

TOM

Jeez...

SHELDON

God...

SAL

Fuck 'im.

SHELDON

I need to speak with our executive producer for a moment. I'm sure you know why.

SAL

We got less than thirty minutes. Don't take too long.

SHELDON

I won't.

Sheldon exits.

TOM

Sal, you don't have to do this.

SAL

Don't try an' tell me what I have an' don't have to do.

TOM

But.

SAL

I'm protecting the interests of my client. Jerry Goldstein. Remember him?

TOM

But this isn't going to help. Okay, sure... maybe you'll get Jerry on the show alone but you're just creating so much negativity.

SAL

Aw, shit. There's California talkin' now.

TOM

No, this is just a basic, fundamental theory of <u>life</u>, Sal. Whether you're religious or not... believe in an after-life or whatever... The point is, Sal, whatever you put into life... sooner or later it's going to come <u>back</u> to you. If you make good, it will come back to you. If you do something selfish or evil or bad... it'll come back to you, too. Sooner or later everything balances out. Like an equation. Ultimately you get out of life what you put into it whether you like it or not. Don't you believe that, Sal? Haven't you seen it happen to too many other people to deny it? Don't you believe we're all gonna pay for the shit we do one way or another? Huh?

Sal has listened intently. He seems moved. He thinks for several long beats, then...

SAL

No.

Sheldon enters.

TOM

Well?

SHELDON

(to Sal)
You win.

TOM

Aw, fuck...

SHELDON

We are to keep Miss Starr at "<u>any</u> cost."

SAL

You can have the old guy on some other time.

TOM

We're going to New York for a month, Sal. We're all booked.

SAL

After that.

SHELDON

After that we go into summer reruns for nine weeks.

TOM

It could be three, four months before we get around to Jackie again.

SAL

It's not my problem.

TOM

You could change your mind.

SAL

Please, don't start in on me.

TOM

It's not too late.

Sal begins to exit. Tom follows after him.

TOM *(cont'd)*

Call back upstairs and tell them you've changed your mind.

SAL

Tommy, stop...

Sal and Tom exit. The door has barely closed when Jackie enters. He wears his tux ready for his shot.

JACKIE

I put on my tux. I couldn't wait. I just had to put it on.

SHELDON

Hmm...

JACKIE

Besides, show time is getting close. It's not good to put on your tux at the last minute. You tend to stiffen up. You want to give yourself a chance to grow into the outfit. Let it become part of your body.

SHELDON

Yeah.

JACKIE

Give your body a chance to get used to formal clothes. I learned that in one of my body awareness classes.

Sheldon has been half listening. He has poured himself a drink.

JACKIE *(cont'd)*

What's the matter?

SHELDON

Nothing.

JACKIE

Drinking on the job?

SHELDON

I don't drink.

JACKIE

Then what's that for?

SHELDON

I was thinking of starting.

Jackie crosses to Sheldon and takes his drink and puts it down. He leads him to the middle of the floor.

JACKIE

Stop that. Put that down. Look at you. You're a wreck. In ten years, you'll be in worse shape than I was.

SHELDON

I'm okay. Listen --

JACKIE

(interrupts)

It's this job... working in television... the pressure, the deadlines... Just standing next to you I can sense your whole body is a knot.

SHELDON

A girl once told me the same thing. And we had just had sex.

JACKIE

Boy should get into yoga, it's you.

SHELDON
No, please. I tried yoga once. I got to see parts of my body I wish I hadn't. Mister Dwayne, I have to tell you --

JACKIE
(interrupts)
Did you know you can relax just by <u>breathing</u> properly?

SHELDON
Please, Mister Dwayne --

JACKIE
Jackie… my name's Jackie. "Mister Dwayne"… no wonder you're tense. Stand like so…

Jackie adjusts Sheldon's standing position. Sheldon follows Jackie's instructions.

JACKIE *(cont'd)*
Now just for me… for a few seconds… close your eyes, take a deep breath and hold it. Keep holding it for a few seconds… Now slowly exhale. That's it. Let it out slowly. Now take another breath… here… I'll do it with you… this is so relaxing…

Jackie stands next to Sheldon. They both have their eyes closed as they deep breathe together.

JACKIE *(cont'd)*
Inhale… holding it in… exhale slowly…

SHELDON
This is sort of nice.

JACKIE
It's terrific. I do a few of these deep breathing things… I'm so calm you could balance a dime on me.

SHELDON
Well, that's good. That you can be calm and relaxed when you need to because I think it's going to come in <u>real</u> handy.

JACKIE
Uh hmm.

SHELDON
The show tonight… with the big audience and Crystal Starr and all…

JACKIE
Yeah.

SHELDON
You're not going on. You've been bumped off the show.

Jackie comes out of his deep-breathing trance.

JACKIE

I've been what?

SHELDON

Bumped off. You're not doing the show. Inhale...

JACKIE

I'm not doing the show?

SHELDON

Uh huh.

JACKIE

What do you mean I'm not doing the show?!!

Sheldon comes out of his deep-breathing trance.

SHELDON

My breathing. I was trying to --

JACKIE

Fuck your breathing!
    (grabbing Sheldon by the throat)
What do you mean I'm not doing the show tonight?

SHELDON

It was a scheduling mistake. We only have room for one comic.

JACKIE

Well, wadda ya know!! I'm a comic, shithead!!!

SHELDON

They decided to go with the other comedian.

JACKIE

And what dickface made that decision?!!

SHELDON

The executive dickface did. Mister Dwayne, please... you're getting all upset.

JACKIE

You bet your ass I'm upset!

SHELDON

Try your exercise. Inhale...

JACKIE

Fuck relaxation!!! I... want... to do... this... show!!!

SHELDON

I know. It must be very disappointing.

JACKIE

Disappointing?!! I've waited eighteen years to do this show!!! I've told myself for eighteen years, "You belong on the Buddy King Show. You deserve a shot on that show. You're better than those other comics on that show." I've spent eighteen years defining my whole life by this show. "I wonder if Buddy would like that joke? I wonder how this routine might go over on Buddy's show...?" I wasted three perfectly good wives getting to this show. I pissed away a heart valve getting to this show. I've spent half a lifetime working toilets, telling myself it was all gonna change when I did the Buddy fucking King Show! I can't think of <u>one thing</u> I've done in the last eighteen years that wasn't somehow related to getting on the Buddy fucking King Show!!! And now... twenty-five minutes before I go on... you have the nerve to tell me I'm not going on the Buddy fucking King Show?!! Give me one good reason why I shouldn't <u>kill</u> the motherfucker who bumped me off this show!!!

Jackie exits. Sheldon runs after him.

SHELDON

No, wait! Mister Dwayne!

The Green Room is empty for a beat.

Jerry enters nicely dressed for his shot. He takes out a cocaine bullet, makes sure the coast is clear, then takes a big hit up each nostril from the bullet. He puts the bullet away.

The monitor catches his eye. Jerry crosses to the monitor, reaches up and turns up the volume. We hear first the sound of the live studio audience laughing loud and strong. Buddy King is obviously doing his monologue and killing with it to a hot house.

BUDDY *(V.O.)*

Okay, we know the president is emotional, but when Congress adjourns does he have to cry?

We hear the studio audience laugh loud and hard.

Tom enters. He is angry and upset.

TOM

Man...

JERRY

(indicating monitor)
Shhhh...

BUDDY *(V.O.)*

At least the president signed the new education bill and I think we need it, too. When he signed the bill, he wrote his name in crayon.

Again we hear the studio audience laugh loud and hard. Jerry turns the monitor OFF.

JERRY
Man, great audience.

TOM
Hmm? Yeah. It's smokin' out there.

JERRY
And that last joke wasn't that good.

TOM
Thanks. I wrote it.

JERRY
Like I said. It wasn't that good.

Jerry begins to study his jokes which are written on dog-eared slips of paper.

TOM
Sal's got some thick head, you know that?

JERRY
What'd he do?

TOM
You don't know?

JERRY
I spend as little time around Sal as possible.

TOM
You really don't know.

JERRY
Know what?

TOM
Nothing. Forget it. It's not important.

JERRY
Your brain's turning to oatmeal, Kelly.

TOM
Sure.
(registers Jerry's slips of paper)
Jokes for your shot?

JERRY
Hmm? Yeah.

TOM
Cocktail napkins... matchbooks...

JERRY
Yeah, well I'm not caught up in status possessions like...
(a direct dig at Tom)
... <u>some</u> people I know.

TOM
"Status possessions" meaning clean pieces of paper.

JERRY
Whatever.

TOM
Some things never change.

JERRY
What's that?

TOM
I said some things never change.

JERRY
What's your job here, Kelly? You write bad jokes <u>and</u> annoy the guests?

TOM
Sorry.

JERRY
You tryin' to blow my concentration? It's not bad enough I'm nervous out of my mind? I gotta take abuse from you, too?

TOM
I'm sorry.

JERRY
Do me a favor, will ya? Just leave me the fuck alone. I'm trying to concentrate, okay? Please? I'm askin' ya fuckin' <u>nice</u>, Kelly. All right?

TOM
Fine.

Sheldon enters. Tom and Sheldon have a sotto conversation, careful not to disturb Jerry.

SHELDON
God...

TOM
You told him?

SHELDON
Yes.

TOM
He took it bad?

SHELDON
He's in his dressing room screaming into a pillow.

TOM
Christ.

SHELDON
Tom... he cried. He actually cried. I've never seen that before. A grown

man cry. Not like that. No, never. He wept like a baby.

TOM

Jeez... What about another guest?

SHELDON

It doesn't look good. Buddy's almost done with his monologue. Arnie said he'd call around the building. See if he can nab a sit-com actor, somebody...

TOM

(indicating Jerry)
He'll have to panel.

SHELDON

What a break for him.

The phone rings. Sheldon answers.

SHELDON *(cont'd)*

Green Room.
   (pause)
Uh huh. All right.

Sheldon hangs up the phone.

SHELDON *(cont'd)*

(indicating Jerry)
He goes on in fifteen minutes.

TOM

You do a card on him?

SHELDON

God, no. Thanks.

Sheldon finds another blue index card.

SHELDON *(cont'd)*

A night like this... why'd it have to happen... I can't live through another one of these.

Sheldon crosses to Jerry.

SHELDON *(cont'd)*

Jerry is it?

JERRY

Yeah?

SHELDON

There's a high probability you'll be paneling with Buddy tonight in addition to your stand-up routine. What we usually do is jot down some items you might want to --

JERRY

Here.

Jerry reaches into his pocket and takes out the identical blue card and hands it to Sheldon.

SHELDON

Oh... look at this...
    (studies it -- then)
Thank you.

JERRY

Yeah.

Tom crosses to Sheldon, takes the card and looks at it.

TOM

    (to Sheldon)
Jerry just give you this?

SHELDON

Yeah.

TOM

Neatly printed and everything. Nice printing, Jer. All printed up and ready to go. It's as though...
    (looks at Sheldon)
...what.

SHELDON

As though... he knew he was going to panel...? Did your manager tell you that you were going to panel?

TOM

He couldn't. I've been with Sal until a few minutes ago.

SHELDON

    (realizing)
My God...

TOM

Of course. Makes perfect sense...

SHELDON

Did you do that?

JERRY

What?

SHELDON

Did you make your manager do that?

JERRY
Do what?

TOM
The old comic, Jer. Did you make Sal do what he did?

JERRY
Do you mind? I'm trying to study my routine here.

TOM
The card, Jerry.

JERRY
What card?

TOM
(waving card)
This card. Neatly printed... ready to give to Sheldon...

SHELDON
Who told you to prepare a card?

JERRY
What is this? Tag team ball-busting?

SHELDON
You knew you were going to panel?

JERRY
So what if I did?

SHELDON
Then it means you manipulated this whole thing. It means you got your manager to bump Mister Dwayne off tonight's show. A show everyone knows is going to be one of our highest-rated, most talked about shows since...

JERRY
Holy shit! Get off my back will ya! So what if I did! What of it! What'd the old fart ever do for you? Huh? What! I'll tell you what he's done for me. Nothing! I don't even know who he is. I don't even know his name.

SHELDON
It's --

JERRY
I don't want to know! It's not important! So I bumped him off your show! What difference does it make? Who's gonna care in a million years? Who's really gonna give a shit! In the great scheme of things... what fuckin' difference does it make? It's not like it's the first little trick that's been pulled in show biz! Is it? Tommy, you and me... we pulled a few tricks of our own, eh? Where was it? Newark or some shithole like that? Some mealy-mouth comic who lived at home with his mother. We kept pulling out his mike jack. He'd have no sound. Had no idea what the fuck to do. Kept going "Mister Frazzo... Mister Frazzo... my

microphone isn't working..." We were laughing our guts out in the john. We played plenty of tricks on people like that. Plenty of times. It was fun, eh? Tommy? Wasn't it fun? For a goof?

TOM

It had nothing to do with...

JERRY

It's got everything to do with... everything! Down deep -- neither one of yas give a shit. You don't give a shit and he don't give a shit... the old fart don't give a shit about all of us put together! He would've gone out there... gone down the tubes... bummed out the whole audience... Turned the whole night into some kinda depressed pile of shit. I would have to follow that! I would have to take the punishment for something someone else did. We followed some bad acts, Tommy, huh? Guys who did so bad there wasn't shit we could do 'cept jump in the toilet after 'em. I would have to die in front of forty million people because some pathetic, washed up, Catskill piece of horseshit did a Kamikaze on your show. Me! In front of the whole fuckin' country. Following him!!!

SHELDON

You could have gone first.

JERRY

It's not the point! Don't you hear me! Don't you fuckin' understand! Point is he would've done so fuckin' bad it's all people would remember about the show tonight! I can't afford to take a chance like that! I've got a career riding on tonight! I'm putting it all on the line! You guys gotta see that... You've got to understand what I mean. What the fuck do either one of you ever risk?! Huh? Nothing. Nothing! You... risk... nothing! I risk everything! Every time I step on a stage I risk everything! My entire being... my whole entire life gets put on the line every time I step on a stage! You risk shit! Both of yas! You risk shit! Kelly, I've listened to all our old tapes. I've got news for ya. You were never funny. You sucked, man! Christ were you for shit. Why I ever carried you for so long I'll never know. Fuck, it's amazing how a little time puts things in order. I hope you're writing better than you performed because you were for shit. So the old fart got bumped off the show tonight. No sweat off me. I don't even know who the fuck he is. What difference does it make?

Sal enters.

SAL

Jerry, you wanna meet Crystal Starr?

JERRY

You go ahead. I've got jokes to look over.

SAL

Better you should do that.

Sal exits.

JERRY

Asswipe. Ignorant, stupid asswipe... He don't even know what fuckin' time it is on the East Coast. He's so fuckin' stupid he can't figure out if it's earlier or later. Calls his wife and wakes her the fuck up every single time. "Eh, sorry... I didn't know it was five AM in Jersey. Sorry, Anna Maria Fungini Spumoni... Go back to sleep... Kiss Antny for me..." What are you two still doing here? Didn't I hear Buddy sneeze or something? Don't he need cigarettes or coffee or something? Isn't it time for his nightly ball licking? You both make me sick! There ain't an ounce of guts between yas! Kelly, on stage you ate shit!

Jerry sits back down to study his jokes.

SHELDON
(sotto to Tom)
This was your partner?

TOM
Yeah.

SHELDON
You performed together? Traveled and ate food together? What does he do for an encore? Shoot the orchestra?

The phone rings. Sheldon answers.

SHELDON *(cont'd)*
Green Room.
(pause)
Right.

Sheldon hangs up the phone.

SHELDON *(cont'd)*
Five minutes, Mister Goldstein.

Jackie Dwayne enters.

JACKIE
Tom, Sheldon... I'm going now. I uh... didn't mean to get outta hand...

SHELDON
It's okay.

TOM
Jackie...

JACKIE
I'm... I'm sorry... It's... It's just that it's been so many years.

SHELDON
We know.

JACKIE
To come this close... Watch all the pieces fall into place except the very last one... I just kinda... Well, see you around.

Jackie goes to exit but Tom and Sheldon force him to stay.

SHELDON
No, stay.

JACKIE
I can't.

TOM
C'mon. I <u>love</u> macrobiotic.

JACKIE
I wanna get out of here.

TOM
Please. You have to stay.

Jackie reluctantly gives in and sits.

SHELDON
Jerry, you'd better get backstage... you have five minutes... more like four actually.

JERRY
Great.

Jerry goes to exit, then suddenly stops.

JERRY (cont'd)
Damn! Kelly, I promised you a great, big color TV, didn't I? You thought I forgot about that, huh? I promised you a great, big color TV... So you can watch me kill on the Buddy King Show... Tell you what...
   (indicates chair)
Why don't you park it right here? Put your big, Irish butt in this big, cushy chair, put your feet up, sit back, relax. Watch me become what you'll never be.
   (indicates Jackie)
What <u>he'll</u> never be.

TOM
You son of a bitch!

Tom lunges at Jerry and grabs him by the shirt. They struggle for a beat.

SHELDON
Dirty fuck!

Sheldon grabs the ice bucket from the bar and knocks Jerry on the head good and hard. Jerry tumbles to the floor unconscious.

JACKIE

What the...! Sheldon! Are you crazy? What did you do that for?

SHELDON

He pissed me off!

JACKIE

You're nuts!

TOM

Jackie, quick... get backstage.

JACKIE

But I'm not supposed to...

SHELDON

Get backstage, damn it!

Sheldon hands Jackie his index card.

SHELDON *(cont'd)*

Here, slip this to Buddy during commercial.

Sheldon picks up the phone and dials four digits.

JACKIE

(to Tom)
What's going on? Why'd he do that?

TOM

It's a long story. Jackie, just get out there... do your shot, knock 'em dead. C'mon, you can do it. Calm, positive attitude.

SHELDON

Deep breath, c'mon... Inhale.

Sheldon takes a deep breath. Jackie does, too.

JACKIE

Shit!!!

Jackie exits.

SHELDON

(into phone)
Arnie? Sheldon... Green Room. The Goldstein guy... We don't know... he uh... he was drinking a lot. Got wild and real weird... Fell and hit his head.

(pause)
No, he's still here. He's on his way backstage. Dwayne. Jackie Dwayne.

Sheldon slams down the phone.

SHELDON *(cont'd)*

God.

TOM
Terrific!

SHELDON
I don't believe I did that.

TOM
I don't either but I'm glad you did.

SHELDON
I'm glad. I don't care. I'm just glad.
(to the unconscious Jerry)
You deserved it!!!

TOM
(handing Sheldon a beer)
Now comes Miller time.

They open their beers and they each take a swig.

SHELDON
Yuck!

TOM
Know what we oughta do?

SHELDON
You mean after we get fired?

TOM
Yeah. Go to Hawaii. Wanna go to Hawaii with me?

SHELDON
I'm allergic.

TOM
To what?

SHELDON
Anything west of Los Angeles.

TOM
When Sal finds out what you did to Jerry he might want to have a little chat with you.

SHELDON
There's a flight at midnight.

TOM
We're on it.

Tom sees Jackie on the monitor.

TOM *(cont'd)*
Quick. Jackie.

Tom turns up the volume.

JACKIE *(V.O.)*
... run by this Greek family named Fletnokos. That's Greek for open twenty-four hours.

We hear the studio audience laugh loud and hard.

JACKIE *(CONT'D, V.O.)*
I would tell the waiter, "With food this bad, your daily special should be the Heimlich Maneuver."

The studio audience laughs loud and hard. Tom and Sheldon smile at each other, take swigs of their beers and continue to watch Jackie on the monitor as the stage lights slowly:

Fade to Black.

THE END

TWO GENTLEMEN OF CORONA

CAST

JOEY BROCCO, low-level member of a New York crime family. Twenties, handsome, clever, resourceful, street wise, heart of a poet, a romantic, excellent dancer.

CARMINE FABIANO, equally low-level member of a New York crime family. Twenties, lifelong friend of Joey's, not nearly as smart or good-looking but good-hearted.

JOHN ESPOSITO, high ranking under boss of a New York crime family. Late forties, fifties, dresses well, wealthy, powerful, elegant, pompous.

ANGELINA FRATIANO, twenties, John Esposito's mistress, working class, beautiful, smart and getting smarter. Excellent dancer.

PHIL WILLIAMS, African-American, forties or fifties. Hard working, blue collar, quiet and level headed.

LENNY GREEN, forties or fifties, overweight, fussy, mild mannered, sweet natured.

TWO GENTLEMEN OF CORONA was first produced by Dana Reynolds and Richard Israel, West Coast Ensemble at the Lyric-Hyperion Theatre in Los Angeles on June 24, 2005, The cast was as follows:

> JOEY BROCCO . . . . Adrian R'Mante
> PHIL WILLIAMS . . . . Phillip C. Curry
> CARMINE FABIANO . . . . Chris Damiano
> JOHN ESPOSITO . . . . Sam Ingraffia
> ANGELINA FRATIANO . . . . C.B. Spencer
> LENNY GREEN . . . . Michael Zemenick

Directed by Henry Polic II
Scenery by Tim Farmer
Lighting by Lisa D. Katz
Costumes by Shon LeBlanc
Sound by Bryce Ryness
Choreography by Cate Caplin
Production Stage Manager, J.T. Dewart

ACT ONE

The set is a classic diner from the early nineteen sixties somewhere in Corona, Queens.

The diner is a perfect time capsule of working-class New York forty years ago. It has a counter with stools, tables and chairs or booths, a period jukebox, cigarette machine, gum ball machine, cash register, doors that lead to bathrooms, a phone booth, placards that offer a steak dinner for two dollars, ads for Balantine Beer and Pall Mall Cigarettes, a poster of "Miss Reingold" for 1963 and a door that leads to the parking lot.

The neon sign tells us this diner is "CLOSED." It will always be closed.

It's also Christmas Eve and period Christmas decorations accent the diner.

It's 2 AM. JOEY BROCCO (aka Joey Nickles) twenties, and a small time soldier in one of New York's organized crime families, has been loading new records into the open jukebox. *Calendar Girl* by Neil Sedaka begins to play.

Joey can't help but dance to the song. He dances quite well. He is remarkable, in fact, for someone who is not a dancer by profession.

Meanwhile PHIL WILLIAMS, an African-American in his fifties, the diner's night cook, leans on the counter reading that day's Daily News. He watches Joey dance for several beats and smiles.

                        PHIL
Yeah.

                        JOEY
You like?

                        PHIL
Very nice.

                        JOEY
Watch this.

Joey does a particularly nice move.

                        JOEY *(cont'd)*
Huh?

                        PHIL
You dance like a colored man.

                        JOEY
That's high praise, Phil. High praise.

Phil steps out from behind the counter.

                        PHIL
Step aside, young blood. Lemme show you a few things.

Phil shows Joey a dance step or two, more soul than rock 'n roll. Joey likes what he sees and copies it. They dance like this for several beats.

                        PHIL *(cont'd)*
Huh? See? First you make the move... then you keep it smooth...
                        JOEY
Love that. I got it... I got...
                        PHIL
Now these are secret Negro steps. Don't tell no one where you got 'em.
                        JOEY
No one finds out, Phil. How am I doin'? Any pointers?
                        PHIL
Just one. When you dance...
                        JOEY
Yeah?
                        PHIL
Try and find the black man inside you.
                        JOEY
How the hell do I do that?
                        PHIL
Pretend you make love to noisy women and live in a bad neighborhood.
                        JOEY
I'll do that. Just like you said.

Phil goes back behind the counter as Joey continues to dance. CARMINE FABIANO (aka Carmine the Camel) enters. He watches Joey dance for a beat or two.

                        CARMINE
    What are you doin'?
                        JOEY
    What's it look like?
                        CARMINE
    Stop that!
                        JOEY
    I can't help it. I'm happy.
                        CARMINE
    This is Queens! Nobody's happy!
                        JOEY
    Aw, c'mon!
                        CARMINE
    What if John saw you dance like that?

183

JOEY

John's gonna get mad just because I'm dancin'?

CARMINE

No, not because you're dancin'. Because you're dancin' <u>alone</u>! People don't dance alone! They do it <u>with</u> someone! C'mon, stop that before people start talkin'! They'll think you're turnin' homo or somethin'.

Joey stops dancing. Somewhere during the following the music will fade out.

JOEY

Don't you ever do that? You hear a song so good you just gotta dance to it? Even if you're alone?

CARMINE

Two things I don't do alone. I don't dance alone, I don't fuck alone.

JOEY

That's not what I hear. I hear you been goin' steady with your right hand since high school.

CARMINE

You gafone!

They playfully box with each other.

JOEY

I hope you were gentle when you broke the news to your <u>left</u> hand!

CARMINE

I'll show ya my left hand.

JOEY

"Sorry, left hand but my right hand does a better job. Let's just be friends from now on, okay?"

CARMINE

Fuckin' guy!

JOEY

Douche bag!

CARMINE

Asshole!

JOEY

Jerk off!

CARMINE

You're demented, you know that! Demented!

JOEY

I oughta...

CARMINE

You oughta what! I got moves, baby!

JOEY
The only move you got left is shufflin' off to the toilet!

Carmine breaks out laughing.

CARMINE
Hah! That's funny! The toilet! Love this guy!
    (beat)
Hey, Phil you hear what Joey said?

PHIL
    (not looking up)
I didn't hear nothin'.

CARMINE
    (re Phil)
I love this guy! If I'm ever on trial I want him on the witness stand!

JOEY
How was your trip? How was South Carolina?

CARMINE
Aw, please! Wall to wall hicks an' hillbillies! You should come with me someday. See for yourself. Everyone down there marries their own sister and has kids.

JOEY
It can't be that bad.

CARMINE
Picture an entire state where everyone owns one pair of pants and has a bad haircut. And those are the <u>women</u>.

JOEY
C'mon!

CARMINE
And the food they eat! Okra, you ever hear of okra?

JOEY
No.

CARMINE
I think it's a vegetable.

PHIL
It's a fish.

CARMINE
Okra's a fish?

PHIL
Nasty ass, bad smellin' fish.

CARMINE
No wonder I hate it so much. But they eat okra by the ton. And greasy meat that's still on the bone. You could <u>die</u> before you find a restaurant

that serves veal Parmesan or lasagna! And the music they listen to. Holy shit! I got a dog, I got a truck, you left him for me so I'm leavin' her for you!

PHIL

(joking)
I love that song.

CARMINE

Half these people can't even read or write their own name but it works out seein' as how most of them are named "Goober." And stupid? Jesus! One of them told me he thought daylight savings was a <u>bank</u>! Christ, these hillbillies are dumber than a block of provolone. But not your family, Phil. I'm talkin' about white people here.

PHIL

I figured that out. My family's been called a lot of things but "hillbilly" ain't one of them.

CARMINE

Before I forget... Phil, your family says hello and wishes you a merry Christmas.

PHIL

Thanks. You give 'em the presents and the money?

CARMINE

Yeah. And your sister's lookin' better an' better every time I see her.

PHIL

Careful, youngblood. Once you go black...

CARMINE

I know. I mean, I've heard. And she can cook, too. Better than you at least. She makes this thing with biscuits and gravy. What's that called?

PHIL

Biscuits and gravy.

CARMINE

Figures.

Carmine hands Phil a wrapped present.

CARMINE *(cont'd)*

Here, almost forgot. Your sister said she knitted this for you. Feels like gloves.

PHIL

Scarf. It's always a scarf.

Phil puts the present away.

PHIL *(cont'd)*

Thanks for doing that, Carmine. You hungry? Want something to eat?

CARMINE
Naw. I had pizza in Baltimore. Tell you what, a cup of coffee.

PHIL
Coffee.

CARMINE
And give it a little bah-boom.

JOEY
Make mine a bah-boom, hold the coffee.

Phil pours and serves the drinks in coffee cups, then returns to his newspaper during the following.

CARMINE
Listen, Joey, I hope you don't mind I dropped by your house, unloaded forty cases of Tennessee whiskey.

JOEY
Did my mother see?

CARMINE
Of course she did. She had to open the garage for me.

JOEY
Aw, Jesus. What'd she say?

CARMINE
She said she wanted a case of whiskey for herself. I tried to get her to take less but she wouldn't budge.

JOEY
She's sweet but ruthless.

CARMINE
I told her I thought she was bein' a little greedy and she hit me in the nuts with her cane so hard, I swear I'll never have children.

JOEY
If it was so much trouble why didn't you just leave them on the truck?

CARMINE
Are you kiddin'? What if John swung by and saw I was runnin' hootch on the side!

JOEY
So instead it's in my garage now?

CARMINE
It'll be there a day, maybe two.

JOEY
Man, you gotta be careful with that, Carmine. If John ever found out.

CARMINE
John's not going to find out.

JOEY
But if he did...

CARMINE
He won't! I was in and out of your garage in five minutes! Nobody saw nothin'.

JOEY
Dominick help you?

CARMINE
Hmm?

JOEY
Dominick, did he help you unload the cases of whiskey?

CARMINE
(uncomfortable)
Dominick, uh... No.

JOEY
He went with you, didn't he?

CARMINE
Dominick?

JOEY
No, the Queen of frikkin' England! Yes, Dominick. He went along on this trip, didn't he?

CARMINE
Yeah, Dom came along. Part of the trip.

JOEY
What do you mean "part of the trip?"

CARMINE
Well, Dominick went down to South Carolina... but...

JOEY
But what.

CARMINE
Let's just say Dominick is still in South Carolina.

JOEY
How much longer is he gonna be there?

No reply.

JOEY *(cont'd)*
How much longer?

No reply.

JOEY *(cont'd)*
A few days?

No reply.

                    JOEY (cont'd)
Longer?

                    CARMINE
Yeah. Longer.

                    JOEY
No...
    (beat)
Really?

Carmine nods.

                    JOEY (cont'd)
Damn! Not Dominick! No! Not Dominick! We grew up together! We were in first grade together! I've known him my whole life! No, no, not Dominick! No! Not him! Not Dominick!

                    CARMINE
Had to be done.

                    JOEY
Dominick! No!

                    CARMINE
Nothin' I could do.

                    JOEY
But... Aw for Christ sake!

                    CARMINE
It's done, Joey.

                    JOEY
Dominick?!

                    CARMINE
It's done.

                    JOEY
His mother! God! What about his mother!

                    CARMINE
I didn't have to kill her. Only Dominick.

                    JOEY
She'll be heart broken. Totally shocked.

                    CARMINE
Shocked? Her son sleeps with two handguns and uses her Tupperware to mix heroine at her kitchen table and she's gonna be shocked?

                    JOEY
Is that what it was? The drug stuff?

CARMINE

I told him to stop. You told him to stop. I'll bet you Phil told him to stop, too.

PHIL

I didn't tell him nothin'.

CARMINE

Still, we all know the rule. Dominick knew the rule, too. C'mon. No way John was gonna turn a blind eye to that.

JOEY

Then the order came from John?

CARMINE

Even higher. Vincent.

JOEY

Vincent? Jeez! The capo di tutti capi?

CARMINE

Boss of bosses. John had a sit down with Vincent at Vincent's favorite steak house. Very elegant setting. Very formal. Table cloth, cloth napkins... If you're drinkin' red wine and switch to white they put it in another glass. This was very high level stuff. Wasn't nothin' I could do.

JOEY

So you went down to South Carolina with Dominick knowing...

CARMINE

Yeah. And it wasn't an easy trip, lemme tell yuh. Having Dominick in the truck with you is like drivin' with a 10-year-old. "Are we there yet? Are we there yet?" And we're still in New Jersey! I hate that. Takin' a long drive with someone knowin' you're comin' back alone. It almost ruined my whole trip.

JOEY

Where'd you do it? Out in the middle of nowhere?

CARMINE

Pretty much. The great thing about South Carolina is you're never more than five minutes away from the middle of nowhere. "C'mon, Dominick. There's these three sisters. They live in a cabin, way in the woods. They're eighteen and gorgeous. Long legs, tits out to here. And they're nymphos. Yeah, they <u>like</u> it! They can't get enough of it! C'mon, just a little bit more. They live right down here in a cabin. C'mon, this way." Dom walks deeper and deeper into the woods, then he goes, he goes, "Wait! I think I can see 'em! Yeah, I think I can see 'em! Holy shit, I see the nymphos!" Bang!

JOEY

Then he died happy.

CARMINE

Big smile on his face.

JOEY

That was nice of you.

CARMINE

It was the least I could do.

Phil crosses to Carmine and Joey to refill their cups with more whiskey.

PHIL

Dominick?

JOEY

Yeah...

CARMINE

Had to be done, Phil. Wasn't nothin' I could do.

JOEY

You feel bad, Phil?

PHIL

Of course. The part of me that liked Dominick feels <u>real</u> bad. But...

JOEY

But what?

PHIL

The part of me that owed Dominick a hundred dollars don't feel bad at all. It's the money you gave my sister. Damn!

JOEY

What?

PHIL

I should've borrowed more.

JOEY

The family's not gonna get anywhere if we keep this up. You make one mistake, then you pay for it with your life.

CARMINE

(shrugs)
It's our tradition.

JOEY

Well, it's a bad one.

PHIL

The Yakuza.

CARMINE

The whoza?

PHIL

The Yakuza. When I was a supply sergeant stationed in Japan you couldn't move anything that was black market without dealing with the Yakuza. They're what you guys are.

CARMINE

You mean wise guys?

PHIL

Exactly. But they're Japanese.

CARMINE

Holy shit.

JOEY

Japanese wiseguys?

PHIL

And they go way back, too. Centuries. Secret ceremonies, tattoos, the works. But if someone screws up in the Yakuza, they don't get a bullet in the head. They've got this whole "I'm sorry I screwed up" ceremony.

JOEY

No way.

CARMINE

You're kiddin'.

PHIL

They go to their boss and <u>beg</u> for his mercy. They go "I'm sorry I screwed up. I really screwed up. I promise I won't screw up no more." Then they take out a knife and, as a gesture of how serious they are about this thing...

JOEY

Yeah?

PHIL

They chop off a finger.

CARMINE

Holy shit!

JOEY

Oh my God!

PHIL

Or just part of a finger. It depends on how much they fucked up. You know, a little fuck up - just the tip. A big fuck up - the whole thing. Then they all drink some sake and go bang some geisha girls. Everyone's happy, the boss is happy, the guy is happy.

CARMINE

He's happy with nine fingers.

PHIL
Some of the older guys are down to being happy with four or five fingers. It comes from years and years of saying "I'm sorry."

CARMINE
Man, the Japanese are so fucked up.

PHIL
Think about it. A man's got ten fingers but only one life.

Phil crosses back behind the counter and resumes reading his newspaper.

JOEY
At least they don't wind up dead in the middle of nowhere.
> (beat)

It's funny. When your time comes in this family, it usually comes from your best friend.

CARMINE
Dominick wasn't my best friend.

JOEY
I hate to tell you, Carmine… You were his.

CARMINE
Aw, shit. What'd you tell me that for? Now you make me feel bad. I feel very bad now.

JOEY
The person you love and trust the most is the person who leaves you dead in the woods.

CARMINE
It's our way.

JOEY
When it's time for me to go, Carmine.

CARMINE
Yeah?

JOEY
I hope it comes from you.

CARMINE
Jesus, what a thing to say.

JOEY
It's how I feel. I'd like to see your face last. Not some stranger.

CARMINE
In that case, when it's time for me to go, I hope it comes from you.

JOEY
Really?

CARMINE

Yeah.

PHIL

That's beautiful. Just beautiful. Two best friends promising to kill each other on Christmas Eve. Hallmark ought to make that it's next Christmas card. "Merry Christmas, I'll kill you if you kill me. And, if you live another week, Happy New Year." Just beautiful.

CARMINE

Phil's right. C'mon, this is not a time for this! It's fuckin' Christmas. It's time for hope and joy and religion. Shit like that.

Carmine puts a nickel in the jukebox, presses a button and a rock Christmas song begins to play.

CARMINE *(cont'd)*

Good things happen at Christmas! Yeah! We need to cheer this place up. C'mon. It's like a funeral in here. Love this song!

Carmine begins to dance to the song. He's a terrible dancer.

CARMINE *(cont'd)*

Love it! And it's great to dance to.

JOEY

You dance like a printing press.

PHIL

When you went to South Carolina...

CARMINE

Yeah?

PHIL

Did a possum crawl in your pants?

CARMINE

Very funny. You watch, I'll get better.

Phil watches Carmine dances for a few beats, then.

PHIL

If you plan on getting better...

CARMINE

Yeah?

PHIL

You gonna use that body?

CARMINE

Huh?

PHIL

Step aside. Let me show you a few things. Damn, watchin' white people dance is painful. Hurts like a son of a bitch.

Phil steps out behind the counter and shows Carmine some dance moves.

                    PHIL *(cont'd)*
See what I'm doing? This is how it goes.

                    CARMINE
Nice.

                    PHIL
See my face while I'm dancing?

                    CARMINE
What about it?

                    PHIL
See any look of pain or fear?

                    CARMINE
No.

                    PHIL
Try doin' the same thing.

Phil continues to show Carmine some dance steps. Joey joins in, then Carmine. Phil and Joey are doing a great job. Carmine's dancing is still terrible. The three men continue to dance in unison for several beats when...

Joey and Phil see John about to enter. They exchange looks of warning and stop dancing. They don't warn Carmine, however, and Carmine continues to dance.

                    CARMINE
Uh huh... yeah... I got it now... yeah, okay...

JOHN ESPOSITO enters. John is a powerful underboss in this crime family. He doesn't bother to hold the door open for...

ANGELINA FRANTIANO, his mistress, more than thirty years his junior. Angelina, attractive despite big hair, too much makeup, jewelry and a fur coat, has to struggle to push the door open and enter after John.

                    JOHN
Carmine! What are you doin'?

Carmine stops dancing. The song fades out during the following.

                    CARMINE
John! I was just dancin' is all.

                    JOHN
Alone? You don't dance alone. You dance <u>with</u> someone.

                    JOEY
That's what we've been tellin' him, John.

                                PHIL
Maybe he'll listen to you.

Joey and Phil exchange furtive smirks.

                                JOHN
Stop doin' shit like that. That's not right. People will talk. They'll say you're homo or somethin'. You're not turnin' homo on us, are you?

Carmine grabs his crotch.

                              CARMINE
Are you kiddin'? Hey, c'mon. The crack of dawn ain't safe!
                                JOEY
We didn't expect to see you. Merry Christmas, John.
                              CARMINE
Yeah, merry Christmas.
                                JOHN
Yeah. Yeah.

John exchanges hugs and wiseguy kisses with Carmine and Joey. Meanwhile Angelina stands nearby holding some envelopes.

                           JOHN (cont'd)
Carmine, you seein' your mother tomorrow?
                              CARMINE
Seeing my mother? Are you serious? I'd rather have a rusty nail jammed up my eye.
        (off John's look)
Uh... yeah, John. Of course. It's Christmas Day. I'll do that. I'll go visit my mother.
                                JOHN
You be sure and see her now.
                              CARMINE
I will.
                                JOHN
I'm going to call her. I'm going to ask if you were there.
                              CARMINE
You'll do it, too!
                                JOHN
You'd better believe. Angelina!

Angelina flips through the envelopes, finds the one she's looking for, crosses to Carmine and hands it to him.

                           JOHN (cont'd)
This is for you, Carmine.

ANGELINA

John Esposito wishes you a very merry Christmas and a New Year that is both healthy and prosperous.

CARMINE

John, I don't know what to say!

JOHN

Don't say nothin'.

John puts his arm around Carmine and takes him aside.

JOHN (cont'd)

Just tell me about your trip to North Carolina.

CARMINE

South Carolina.

JOHN

What?

CARMINE

It's where I go. Twice a week. Not North Carolina, South Carolina.

JOHN

There's a difference?

CARMINE

I guess not.

JOHN

You had a good trip?

CARMINE

Yeah.

JOHN

I mean, everything worked out?

CARMINE

Yeah.

JOHN

The thing I asked you to take care of?

CARMINE

It was taken care of.

JOHN

Nothin' the cops could come at us with someday?

CARMINE

Naw, the gun I used is in twelve pieces in five states. And there's no blood in the truck. I did it out in the woods. Way out in the woods.

John looks like he might become sick during the following.

JOHN

Good.

CARMINE

Two in the heart, two in the head.

JOHN

Fine.

CARMINE

I mean there was blood. Lots of blood. But none of it's on the truck.

John turns away and covers his mouth. Phil prepares a stomach powder for John and serves it to him.

CARMINE *(cont'd)*

There was this ditch nearby. I rolled him into that. They won't find what's left of him until the spring.

JOHN

Okay!

CARMINE

By then there won't be much left of his body. It'll be shrunk up and -

JOHN

(interrupts)
Enough!

CARMINE

Huh?

JOHN

That's enough!

ANGELINA

You okay, John?

JOHN

Yeah, I'm... yeah... Every time I hear about blood or... I'm okay...

John takes some deep breaths to recover, then forces a smile.

JOHN *(cont'd)*

Joey, you going to Jersey tomorrow?

JOEY

Yeah, my brother's house. I'm taking my mother.

JOHN

I love your mother. Lovely woman. I just dropped by to say merry Christmas to her, she gives me three cases of Tennessee whiskey! Can you believe that?

CARMINE

How many cases?

JOHN

Three. The woman knows how to show respect.

JOEY

No!

JOHN

I swear. Very generous woman. Very generous. I love your mother, Joey.

JOEY

She loves you too, John.

JOHN

Jersey, huh?

John takes out a huge wad of bills, peels off a few and hands them to Joey.

JOHN (cont'd)

This is for your brother's kids. Tell them it's from their Uncle John.

JOEY

I will. And thank you, John. My brother and his family thank you. Mille grazie.

JOHN

And I got a little Christmas gift for you.
    (to Angelina)
Give 'em the thing.

ANGELINA

Hold on.

JOHN

Give 'em the thing!

Angelina struggles with the envelopes.

ANGELINA

I'm lookin'! Okay?

JOHN

Oh, come on!

ANGELINA

Wait!

They both lose control and yell at each other at the same time.

JOHN

Oh, come on, for Christ's sake! How long does it take! I asked you to do one thing for me! One thing! You can't even do that! Hand out some fuckin' envelopes! How difficult can that be! Look at you! Look at you! A fuckin' monkey could do this better! A fuckin' monkey! I say "Here, hold these envelopes and say the thing for me" and you can't even do that! You're helpless! One simple thing and you fuck it up! A monkey could do this!

ANGELINA

Don't start with me, John! Don't start! I'm in no mood! Aw, go to hell! You got a million fuckin' envelopes here! Who the hell can read your writing? Who the hell can read this scribble? They're not even in alphabetical order! Fuck you, John! Fuck you! Blow it out your ass! There's a thousand envelopes here and half of them are made out to someone named "Tony!" Get cancer and die! You smell like a monkey! And you write like one, too!

Angelina finds the right envelope then hands it to Joey.

ANGELINA *(cont'd)*

Here!

(calmly)

John Esposito wishes you a very merry Christmas and a New Year that is both healthy and prosperous.

JOEY

Thank you, John. Thank you very, very much.

JOHN

(shrugs)

What the fuck. It's Christmas. We gotta celebrate the birth of Jesus H. Christ with love.

John sits at a table where he's joined by Carmine and Joey.

ANGELINA

What do you want me to do now, John?

JOHN

Go sit down. Keep yourself busy or somethin'. Go do your little puzzle books or whatever it is you do.

ANGELINA

They're not puzzle books.

JOHN

Whatever!

ANGELINA

I'm increasing my word power in ninety days.

JOHN

Who the fuck cares!

ANGELINA

It wouldn't kill you to increase your word power a little.

JOHN

Get sick and die, will yuh!

ANGELINA

"Fuckin' A" is all I ever hear from you. "John, you having the steak?" "Fuckin' A!" "John, lookit the sunset!" "Fuckin' A!" "Fuckin' A! Fuckin'

A! Fuckin' A!" Not everything in life is "Fuckin' A!" John.

JOHN

Fuckin' A shut up!

ANGELINA

John, you are so arbitrary it ain't even funny!

JOHN

Crazy bitch.

Angelina sits at another table, opens a paperback and studies it silently.

JOEY

You're out late tonight, John.

JOHN

It's Christmas. There's lots of Christmas-y stuff to do. Gifts to buy, parties to go to, cops to pay off.

John holds his thumb and index finger an inch apart indicating he'd like a drink.

PHIL

Comin' up.

Phil pours a better brand of scotch into a coffee cup.

JOHN

Then, in the middle of all this Christmas shit, Vincent calls a meeting tonight.

JOEY

Vincent?

CARMINE

On Christmas Eve?

JOHN

Fuckin' A!

CARMINE

Someone else goin' to South Carolina?

JOHN

Not this time. This time the meeting was business. Important business. Vincent called in all the heads of the family. You know what's comin' to Queens this summer.

JOEY

Of course.

CARMINE

Everyone knows.

JOEY

The World's Fair.

201

JOHN
That's right. It's a fair but it's for the whole world.

JOEY
I like the way you explain that, John.

CARMINE
It's a fair...

JOEY
But it's for the whole world.

CARMINE
Yeah.

JOEY
Nice.

CARMINE
I like that.

JOEY
Sounds good.

JOHN
Vincent carved up the World's Fair tonight and we got ourselves one helluva slice. Here's how it breaks down: hookers, that's all gonna be Tony the Wheel.

JOEY
That's all he does.

CARMINE
Nothin' else.

JOEY
He's great with hookers.

CARMINE
He'll do great.

JOHN
Let's hope so because there's people comin' here from all over the world.

JOEY
So?

JOHN
So these girls, they gotta fuck in different languages.

JOEY/CARMINE
Yeah... Right... Of course... Gotta...

JOEY
Never thought of that.

JOHN
Gamblin' and loan sharkin' goes to Pauley.

JOEY
Pauley's very good at that.

CARMINE
Very good.

JOHN
That's why he got picked. Garbage is Freddy Fat Ass.

JOEY
He can kiss my balls.

CARMINE
Dipshit.

JOEY
Asshole.

CARMINE
Douche bag.

JOEY
Fuck head.

CARMINE
Jerk off.

JOHN
He can have it. And most of the construction goes to the Rosatto Brothers. But the concrete, that's ours.

JOEY
All right!

CARMINE
Yeah!

JOHN
And we also get all of the food service, linens, parking, and souvenirs.

JOEY
Woa!

CARMINE
Marone! We're gettin' all that?

JOHN
Yeah.

JOEY
A World's Fair.

JOHN
It's a fair but it's for the whole world.

Phil crosses to John and serves him his scotch.

PHIL
Doesn't the city award these things to the lowest bidder? You know, with, what is it, sealed bids, something like that?

JOHN
They do. But when they open them sealed bids...

JOEY
Uh huh.

JOHN
Something tells me we're gonna get all kinds of lucky and win.

They all share a menacing chuckle.

JOEY
Good.

CARMINE
Yeah.

PHIL
I don't know why I bothered to ask.

JOHN
(mock surprise)
"Ooo! I get all the food and restaurants? Wadda surprise!"
(then)
Vincent says this fair will draw more than twenty million people.

JOEY
Marone!

PHIL
Damn!

CARMINE
Mama mia! Will Queens even <u>hold</u> twenty million people?

JOHN
They're not all comin' on the same day, you fuckin' idiot! It's spread out over two summers!

CARMINE
Oh. Well, that's what I mean.

JOHN
Vincent is already buyin' up some of the slums around here to turn it into parking.

PHIL
There go my friends.

JOHN
It's not personal, Phil. It's progress.

PHIL

Every time a colored man moves away it's progress.

Phil crosses back behind the counter.

JOHN

(re: Phil)
Love that guy.

JOEY

Man, we've been waiting on this World's Fair thing for a long time.

CARMINE

Long time now.

JOHN

Well, it'll be here before you know it. This summer Queens will be neck deep in people from all over the world. Krauts, Frogs, Spics, Micks, Beaners, Polacks, Camel Jockeys, Ricans, Ruskies, Hayseeds, Bohunks, Towel Heads, Canucks, Spades, Limeys, Gooks, Chinks, Japs, Italians...

CARMINE

Foreign scum. Except for the Italians.

JOHN

Except for them. Everyone else...

CARMINE

Foreign scum.

JOHN

Foreign scum with money. They're gonna buy food, soda, beer, candy...

JOEY

You bet.

JOHN

That's gonna be us. They might be foreign scum but they're gonna get hungry.

JOEY

You bet!

CARMINE

And how!

JOHN

They want to buy a hotdog but it costs a dollar!

JOEY

A buck twenty-five!

CARMINE

A buck and a half!

JOHN

What do they do? Find City Hall, cry to the mayor?

                    (mocking)
"Ooo! The man wants too much money for a hotdog!"

                    CARMINE
Fuck no! They're gonna <u>pay</u> it!

                    JOHN
Foreign scum.

                    CARMINE
Then they leave New York pissed off because it was too fuckin' expensive.

                    JOHN
And they never come back!

                    CARMINE
Who gives a fuck! We got their money!

                    JOHN
Exactly! "Go on! Get outta here! Yuh Limey-Chink-Jap foreign scum!"

Carmine raises his coffee cup.

                    CARMINE
To foreign scum.

                    JOEY
Foreign scum.

                    JOHN
Foreign scum.

They toast and drink.

                    JOHN *(cont'd)*
Hey, Phil. Pour yourself a drink, put it on my tab.

Phil pours himself a drink.

                    PHIL
Sure thing. What're we drinkin' to?

                    JOHN
Foreign scum.

                    PHIL
Sounds good to me.

Angelina rises and begins to cross to the ladies room.

                    JOHN
Hey! Where you goin'?

                    ANGELINA
I'm going to the bathroom, John! Do I gotta ask permission?

JOHN
I'm just askin'!

ANGELINA
Well, where else would I be goin'!

JOHN
I don't know where the fuck you're goin'! I'm just askin'!

ANGELINA
I'm goin' to do the cha-cha with Trini Lopez, okay!

JOHN
I'm just askin'!

ANGELINA
Well, I'm gonna go to the bathroom. Is that all right with you?

JOHN
I was just worried about you, is all.

They both lose control and scream at each other at the same time.

ANGELINA
All day long you don't say two fuckin' words to me now you're worried about me?! You are so full of shit! I got no life with you around! No life! I can't even go pee without you sayin' somethin' about it! I'm gonna pee! Is that all right? Is it all right I go to the God damn bathroom? My dog has a better life than me! My dog! "Where you goin'? When you comin' back?" You drive me fuckin' crazy, John! I can't take it no more! Fuck you, John!

JOHN
Aw, Jesus! No one can even talk to you anymore! No one! I say the slightest thing you fly off the handle! Stop! Just stop! You demean yourself when you talk like that! Totally demean! Just makin' yourself lower if that's possible! Street trash! From the gutter! Just stop! Will you! The mouth on you! And on Christmas Eve! No respect for Christ or his mother or the Pope or nothin'! Crazy bitch! Shut up, will ya! Just shut the fuck up!

ANGELINA
You're worried about me going to the bathroom? John, you are so ambiguous it ain't funny.

Angelina shoots John a snooty look then exits to the ladies room.

JOHN
Crazy bitch.

CARMINE
Anyway...

JOEY
John, you know we'd do anything for you. Give up our lives if we had to.

CARMINE
Take a bullet.

JOEY
Both of us.

CARMINE
Any time.

JOEY
Day or night.

CARMINE
You call me up, three in the morning. You say "Hey, I need you to take a bullet for me." I'm there.

JOEY
Me, too.

John slowly begins to get sick to his stomach again. Phil begins to prepare a stomach powder for John but stops.

CARMINE
Take a bullet.

JOEY
In the heart.

CARMINE
The stomach.

JOEY
Right in the head, John. I would take a bullet in the head.

CARMINE
In the <u>face</u>.

JOEY
Me, too. Right in the face. Closed casket, I wouldn't give a shit.

CARMINE
I'd take a dozen bullets for you, John. Or a knife. A knife right in the gut!

JOHN
(interrupts)
Okay! I get it! I get it! Thank you!

CARMINE
We just want you to know how we feel about you.

JOHN
I know. You're both good boys.

JOEY
Carmine and me, we know you got guys to cover construction and food. I mean, that's your thing. That's all in place. But there's one thing

you don't have covered and Carmine and me, we'd like a shot at it. We wanna show you what we can do. Besides fillin' vending machines.

CARMINE

And runnin' cigarettes up from South Carolina.

JOHN

What're you thinkin'?

JOEY

Souvenirs.

JOHN

Souvenirs?

JOEY

We'd like to run that for you. With your permission.

CARMINE

And your blessing.

JOEY

I know a guy. He does the souvenirs for the Statue of Liberty, the Empire State Building. They knock out this souvenir crap in Hong Kong for pennies, sell it for two, three dollars. We could put the whole thing together for you, John. But only with your permission.

CARMINE

And your blessing.

JOEY

Tutto rispetto, John.

CARMINE

Tutto rispetto.

They take turns kissing John's pinky ring.

JOHN

One thing I always liked about you two; you know how to show proper respect.

CARMINE

You deserve it, John.

JOEY

You've been very generous with us.

CARMINE

And our families.

JOEY

My mother thinks you're a saint.

CARMINE

Mine, too.

JOEY

My mother has your picture hanging in her dining room. Right between the Pope and Frank Sinatra.

JOHN

Souvenirs.

JOEY

But only with your permission.

CARMINE

And your blessing.

JOHN

Twenty million people. If each one spends two bucks on a souvenir.

John takes out his pad and pencil and does the math.

JOHN *(cont'd)*

Carry the zero... zero, zero... That's forty million. Big step.

CARMINE

We're ready, John.

JOEY

We want to do good for the family.

Angelina peeks out from the ladies room. She sees John is talking with Joey and Carmine and ducks back in.

JOHN

I tell you what.
> *(thinks, then)*

You two put some sample stuff together. Whatever it is you want to sell. Put it together, show me.

CARMINE

All right!

JOEY

Yeah!

JOHN

I'm not sayin' you got it yet, but if I like what I see, the job is yours.

CARMINE

Oh, man!

JOEY

Yes!

JOHN

> *(calling)*

Angelina! Let's go!

ANGELINA *(O.S.)*

I'm not ready!

JOHN

Well, c'mon!

JOEY

I'll call this souvenir guy right away.

CARMINE

We'll show you some really good stuff.

JOHN

I'm going to Florida tomorrow for nine, ten days, so not this Friday but the Friday after, I want to meet with you guys, see what you come up with.

CARMINE

Not this Friday.

JOHN

But the Friday after.

CARMINE

We'll be ready.

JOHN

(calling)
Angelina!

ANGELINA (O.S.)

What!

JOHN

I gotta go!

ANGELINA *(O.S.)*

I need more time!

JOHN

We're on the inside with this thing. New York is ours. Queens is ours. The World's Fair is ours.

CARMINE

We won't call it the 1964 World's Fair.

JOEY

We'll call it John Esposito's World's Fair.

JOHN

I like that. That's nice. Remember, not this Friday.

JOEY

But the Friday after.

JOHN

After New Year's.

John crosses to the ladies room and opens the door a few inches.

JOHN *(cont'd)*

Are you ready or not!

ANGELINA *(O.S.)*

I'm not! God, stop rushing me!

JOHN

I gotta go!

ANGELINA *(O.S.)*

I'm so impressed!

JOHN

How much longer!

ANGELINA *(O.S.)*

It's gonna be a while.

JOHN

It's late, I gotta get home. Joey, run Angelina back to Howard Beach for me?

JOEY

Done. Put it out of your mind. She's already home. Safe and sound.

JOHN

Phil, if anyone calls and asks if I was with Angelina…

PHIL

Never saw her.

JOHN

Excellent.

PHIL

I didn't even see you.

JOHN

Even better.

JOEY

Did you see me and Carmine?

PHIL

I'm sorry, have we met?

Joey smiles. John hands Phil an envelope.

JOHN

Merry Christmas.

PHIL

Oh, thank you, John. Thank you very much. That's very kind of you. Thank you.

JOHN

What the fuck. It's Christmas for colored people, too.

John opens the ladies' room door a crack.

JOHN (cont'd)
I'm goin'.

ANGELINA (O.S.)
You're what?

JOHN
I gotta go now. Besides, you live the other way.

ANGELINA (O.S.)
What?

JOHN
You live in Howard Beach, I'm in Long Island!

ANGELINA (O.S.)
What's this, a geography lesson?

JOHN
Joey's takin' you home! I gotta go!

ANGELINA (O.S.)
Then go!

JOHN
I gotta!

ANGELINA (O.S.)
Then go!

JOHN
What?

ANGELINA (O.S.)
Then go!

JOHN
Okay.
 (beat)
Merry Christmas.

ANGELINA (O.S.)
Yeah, and a New Year that is both healthy and prosperous!

JOHN
Don't start with me!

They both lose control and scream at each other at the same time.

ANGELINA (O.S.)
Fuck you! This is the way we celebrate Christmas Eve together? You sayin' goodbye to me while I'm in the ladies room?! Eat shit and die, John! Sunovabitch! A gold wristwatch and a goodbye while I'm on the toilet! What a Christmas to remember! No class! No class at all! Merry Christmas, John! And let me wish you a new year that is both healthy and prosperous you two-face bastard!

JOHN

Don't start with me again! I'm in no mood for your shit! Understand! No mood! The mouth on you! Ignorance! You only show your ignorance! Low class! Low class! Please! You only lower yourself! Trash! Like your family! Low class, ignorant trash! Money grubbing, low class bitch! You're nothin'! Hear me! Nothin'! Sacrilegious bitch! You'll rot in hell for half the crap you say! Rot in hell!

JOHN *(cont'd)*

Crazy bitch.
(to Joey and Carmine)
I gotta go.

John closes the door then turns to Joey and Carmine and sighs.

JOEY

You can't help it.

CARMINE

You gotta go.

JOHN

I do.

JOEY

She'll be all right.

John prepares to leave.

JOEY *(cont'd)*

Goodbye, John.

CARMINE

Merry Christmas.

JOEY

Yeah, Merry Christmas.

CARMINE

Happy New Year.

JOEY

Happy New Year, John.

CARMINE

God bless you, John.

JOEY

Our best to your family.

CARMINE

Safe trip to Florida.

JOEY

Yeah, have a safe trip.

CARMINE

Night.

JOHN

Remember, it's a fair...

JOEY/CARMINE/JOHN

But it's for the whole world.

John exits. The instant the door closes Joey and Carmine hug and back slap.

JOEY

All right!

CARMINE

Yeah!

JOEY

We got it!

CARMINE

Big time!

As Joey and Carmine continue to talk Angelina peeks out from the ladies' room then goes back inside.

JOEY

Souvenirs!

CARMINE

They're gonna be ours!

JOEY

Every last one of 'em!

CARMINE

We're gonna be rich.

JOEY

You bet. This guy who makes souvenirs. I'll call him tomorrow. Get him started. I feel good about this.

CARMINE

Me, too. Maybe...

JOEY

Maybe what?

CARMINE

Maybe I've seen my last trip for cigarettes.

JOEY

Maybe I've seen my last jukebox.

CARMINE

I can't take another trip to South Carolina. I know three guys named Bubba.

JOEY

Our lives are gonna change plenty. And this all happened tonight.

CARMINE

On Christmas Eve.

JOEY

On Christmas Eve.

CARMINE

Can't no one ever tell me good shit don't happen on Christmas.
    (*suddenly*)
Ooo! That reminds me!

Carmine hands Joey an eight-track tape.

CARMINE (*cont'd*)

That's for you.

JOEY

You bought me something?

CARMINE

I didn't really "buy" it. The guy at Sam Goody's was such a prick I decided to lift a dozen eight-tracks.

JOEY

Love these eight-tracks!
    (*reads label*)
Vic Damone Sings Sinatra! Hey, c'mon!

CARMINE

You like?

JOEY

Love this! Hey, I'm gonna play this on my way home. Merry Christmas, Carmine.

CARMINE

Merry frikkin' Christmas to you, too. I love you like you was my brother, Joey.

JOEY

Same here, Carmine.

They hug.

CARMINE

I especially love you...

JOEY

Yeah?

CARMINE

    (*teasing*)
When you dance alone!

Carmine does a mock dance and the two laugh.

CARMINE *(cont'd)*

Woo! Woo! Merry Christmas, kid.

JOEY

You, too. Merry Christmas.

Carmine exits. Joey goes back to servicing the jukebox.

JOEY *(cont'd)*

You hear that, Phil?

PHIL

Huh?

JOEY

Me and Carmine. We might do all the souvenirs for the World's Fair.

PHIL

I didn't hear nothin'.

Phil exits to the back as Joey smiles and shakes his head. A beat then Angelina enters from the ladies' room.

ANGELINA

Did he go?

JOEY

John?

ANGELINA

Uh huh.

JOEY

Yeah, he left.

ANGELINA

Where's the other guy?

JOEY

Carmine, he just left, too.

ANGELINA

Man, I can really empty a joint, can't I?

JOEY

It's nothin' to do with you. They had to get home.

ANGELINA

Yeah.

JOEY

I'll run you back to Howard Beach as soon as I'm done.

ANGELINA

No rush.

She watches him finish up his work with the jukebox for a few beats.

ANGELINA *(cont'd)*

That what you do?

JOEY

Hmm?

ANGELINA

For John. That what you do?

JOEY

Long time. But I might be movin' up in the family. Makin' my move. You watch. But for now...

Joey jingles pocket change.

JOEY *(cont'd)*

"Joey Nickels." Jukeboxes, cigarette and vending machines.

ANGELINA

That's how you got your name?

JOEY

It's how all of us get our name. All of us who work for John, it's kinda tribal.

ANGELINA

What's that mean?

JOEY

Tribal. In some ways we're a lot like Indians. If you do a particular thing or there's something that's special about you, that thing becomes part of your name.

ANGELINA

Who told you that?

JOEY

Tony the Asshole.

Angelina breaks out laughing, then Joey.

ANGELINA

Tony the... Wadda pisser!

JOEY

Okay, there's no such guy. But you ever meet Frankie Four Aces?

ANGELINA

Sure.

JOEY

The story goes he was in a poker game, got four aces.

ANGELINA

Frankie Four Aces.

JOEY

Danny Cadillac.

ANGELINA

Always drives a Cadillac?

JOEY

Went to Florida to see his mother. The rental car joint was out of Caddies. Danny got on a plane and went back home.

ANGELINA

Wow.

JOEY

Won't even <u>ride</u> in another car. Carmine the Camel.

ANGELINA

The guy who just left.

JOEY

Makes two runs a week down to South Carolina for cigarettes. You ask him for a cigarette.

ANGELINA

It's going to be a Camel.

JOEY

Always.

ANGELINA

And you're Joey Nickels.

JOEY

My pockets, the trunk of my car, where I live, I got dozens of jars full of nickels.

ANGELINA

What you do becomes your name.

JOEY

Like Indians.

ANGELINA

Right. Like Indians.

She watches him for several more beats.

ANGELINA *(cont'd)*

Where'd you learn that?

JOEY

Learn what?

ANGELINA

The tribal thing, Indians.

JOEY

I read.

ANGELINA

Read what?

JOEY
Books.

ANGELINA
What kind?

JOEY
Ones that teach me stuff.

ANGELINA
I read, too. I bought a book. I'm reading it right now.

JOEY
What's it called?

ANGELINA
"Increase Your Word Power in Ninety Days" by some guy named Random House.

JOEY
How's that comin'?

ANGELINA
I dunno, this is only the third day. I'm still in the "A's."

JOEY
Ah.

ANGELINA
But I think it'll do me some good.

JOEY
Yeah. I heard you before. With John. What'd you call him again?

ANGELINA
Ambiguous.

JOEY
Ambiguous.

ANGELINA
Like that?

JOEY
I love it and I don't even know what it means.

ANGELINA
It means you're not clear, you're not for sure. You're one way and the other at the same time.

JOEY
Woa. Then that's a real put down.

ANGELINA
Good. I skipped ahead in the book and peeked at some other words. Next time I see John I'm going to call him fallacious.

JOEY
Fa what?

ANGELINA
Fallacious.

JOEY
Isn't that a sex thing? Something people do in bed?

ANGELINA
No. Fallacious means to be false or misleading.

JOEY
Oh, man. John's gonna be mad if he ever figures out what you're sayin'.

ANGELINA
He won't. He's too lazy and stupid to buy a dictionary. Even if he did he wouldn't know how to spell half of what I'm going to call him.
   (beat)
So what's a smart guy like you doing with John?

JOEY
I could ask you the same thing.

ANGELINA
Money.

JOEY
That's my answer, too.

ANGELINA
My mother, she's got a heart thing. It's expensive as hell. I don't want her in some city hospital so...

JOEY
I gotcha.

ANGELINA
So it works out, except for the part where I've got to stay home all the time and answer the phone on the first ring because that's the way John likes it. So I read. Book by book, I'm going to study myself into being smarter. You watch. I'll do it. I'll get smarter. Real smart.

JOEY
Sometimes I wish I was smarter. But then I tell myself at least I'm not one of the DeMarcos.

ANGELINA
Who's that?

JOEY
We lived next door to the DeMarcos when I was a kid. Now my family wasn't educated and stuff but the DeMarcos, they were the stupidest five people God ever made. I think they were sharin' a brain. Their idea of conversation was to grunt and point. Jesus Christ, they got through life on, I dunno, maybe fifty words. They used to fix cars in the driveway every weekend. The father would crawl under the car and you'd hear tell his kids "Gimme the thing! The thing!" And the kids would hand

him a hammer. And he'd go "No, no, the thing! The thing!" And the kids would hand him a screw driver. And he'd get pissed off and yell "Not that thing, the other thing! The thing!" And they'd ask him "What thing? The big thing or the little thing?" And he'd answer them! "Not the big thing or the little thing! The medium thing!" There was no hope for these people! The guy owns four thousand tools and he's got the same name for all of them, "The thing!" What he usually wanted was...

>   *(slowly)*

a crescent head wrench...

>   *(then)*

but he didn't call it that. He called it "The thing!"

The two become lost in each other's eyes.

JOEY *(cont'd)*

Simple things become difficult when you don't know how to say what it is you want.

ANGELINA

You know what you want?

JOEY

Always.

Angelina is the first to snap out of the gaze.

ANGELINA

I'll remember to tell that to John when I see him tomorrow.

JOEY

You won't see John tomorrow.

ANGELINA

Oh, right, it's Christmas. Whatever, the day after tomorrow.

JOEY

Not even then. He's headed to Florida for nine, ten days.

>   *(beat)*

He didn't tell you?

ANGELINA

No.

>   *(sarcastic)*

It must've skipped his mind. He's comin' back after New Year's?

JOEY

Not this Friday but the Friday after.

ANGELINA

Another New Year's Eve.

JOEY

And what? You got nothin' to do?

ANGELINA

Just like last year.

JOEY

You did nothin' last year?

ANGELINA

Oh, I did plenty. I did my nails and watched the ball drop in Times Square on television.

JOEY

You wanna do somethin'?

ANGELINA

What?

JOEY

I'm not doin' anything New Year's Eve. Wanna hook up, do somethin'?

ANGELINA

If John found out he'd kill you.

JOEY

Well, John ain't gonna find out unless you love him so much you gotta go tell him.

ANGELINA

What is it? You looking for some cheap and easy sex so you figure you'll buy John's goumada a hamburger then get laid?

JOEY

Hey, c'mon, listen this isn't about sex. This is about havin' a good time on New Year's Eve, that's all. And when I take a woman out I don't take her for no hamburger. I do it right. I put on a suit and tie, I clean the car, I pick her up and I don't blow the horn, I ring her bell, then I take her anywhere she says she wants to go. That's what you do when you take a woman out. You take her anywhere she wants to go. Anywhere.

ANGELINA

Anywhere?

JOEY

Anywhere you want. The Copa has Tony Bennett, we can go to the Waldorf, listen to Guy Lombardo, Times Square. You name it.

ANGELINA

Roseland.

JOEY

What?

ANGELINA

I want to go to Roseland. They got three orchestras. All night long. Non stop.

JOEY

Roseland.

223

ANGELINA

Yeah. Dancing.

JOEY

You really want to do that?

ANGELINA

Yeah!

JOEY

It's gonna be so crowded and you don't know. I could be a terrible dancer.

ANGELINA

But you're not. I heard John say you're a good dancer. Real good. He says you were all up in the Catskills one weekend and you won a dance contest with some woman you just pulled out of the crowd.

JOEY

Oh, that. That was...

ANGELINA

He says you and this woman did such a good job her husband got all kinds of jealous. Carmine had to beat him up.

JOEY

Oh, that. Yeah, well, Carmine's always beating people up.

ANGELINA

What's the deal? You don't want to go dancing with me?

JOEY

No, no. It's just that...

ANGELINA

What?

JOEY

I know a lotta people at Roseland. And I take my dancin' very serious. My mother and father were ballroom dancers. I mean they competed and stuff. So did I. I used to teach ballroom in the Poconos. Our house is wall to wall trophies.

ANGELINA

And what? You think I'm gonna cramp your style? Hurt your rep?

JOEY

No. No. It's just that a lotta women have trouble keepin' up.

ANGELINA

Listen, I was born to dance. My mother ran a dance studio in our basement. Before she met my father she was a God damn Rockette.

JOEY

So?

ANGELINA
So there ain't nothin' you can do on a dance floor I can't keep up with.

JOEY
Angelina, if I take you to Roseland you'll wind up watching me dance with some other woman who knows how.

ANGELINA
That other woman...

JOEY
Yeah?

ANGELINA
Is me.

JOEY
Think so?

ANGELINA
Know so.

JOEY
Let's see.

ANGELINA
Your funeral. Got a nickel?

JOEY
It's my last name.

Joey hands Angelina a nickel. She puts it in the jukebox and surveys the selection.

ANGELINA
Some rock and roll?

JOEY
That's for cowards and amateurs.

ANGELINA
Something that takes some style?

JOEY
If you got any.

Angelina smiles then pushes a button on the jukebox. She turns to face Joey. She tilts her head back, arches her back and takes the pose of a professional ballroom dancer. Joey, not about to be outdone, does the same. A romantic period song like *"Crying"* begins to play.

The song, slow, sultry and full of love unfulfilled seems to fit the moment perfectly. Angelina makes the first move and Joey is right with her. They dance separately, mirror images of each other, not yet touching and the distance between them is exquisite.

During the song the lights will dim until Joey and Angelina are bathed in a warm spotlight. A mirrored ball sends specks of starlight floating across the walls.

By now Joey has Angelina in his arms and they sweep across the floor effortlessly, as though they have done this dance a thousand times. Their dance is pure splendor and romance as Joey dips and twirls Angelina with ease.

The dance is nothing less than a timeless expression of grace and intimacy. She spins out of his arms then back into a tight embrace, they look into each other's eyes, and hold this pose as...

The lights fade to black.
END ACT ONE

ACT TWO

SCENE 1

Before the lights come up we hear *"You Gotta Shop Around"* by Smokey Robinson playing on the jukebox.

It is nine days later. The lights come up to reveal Joey and Carmine at a table with LENNY GREEN. Lenny is a pleasant, timid and overweight middle-aged man. Potential souvenirs for he upcoming World's Fair are scattered on the table along with paperwork and order pads.

Phil hunches over the counter reading a newspaper as always.

The song fades at some point during the following.

                      LENNY
Okay. Next on our list. Souvenir spoons.

Joey and Carmine examine a sample spoon.

                      JOEY
Lookit this. The handle has writing on it that says "1964 World's Fair." Hey, Phil you see this?

                      PHIL
I didn't see nothin'.

Joey and Carmine exchange a smile.

                      JOEY
Nice lookin' spoon.

                      CARMINE
And it's silver.

                      LENNY
Polished steel actually.

                      JOEY
We'll say it's silver.

                      CARMINE
Yeah. Fourteen karat silver.

                      LENNY
Ooo, we can't do that.

                      CARMINE
Why not?

                      LENNY
Because it's not silver. Not even silver plated.

CARMINE
So?

LENNY
So it's against the law.

CARMINE
What law is that? The You-Can't-Call-it-Silver-Law?

LENNY
But the government says you can't do that.

CARMINE
The government says a lotta stuff they really don't mean.

JOEY
We're going to say this is solid silver.

LENNY
And what are you going to do when people find out it's <u>not</u> solid silver?

CARMINE
You mean what are we gonna do when people get back to Swamp Dump, Florida? And the spoon turns green two years later? And they jump in their car and drive back to Queens? Back to the World's Fair? To complain?! But all they can find is two Puerto Ricans playin' handball? Because the World's Fair is fuckin' <u>gone</u>? Is that what we're supposed to worry about?

JOEY
We want little tags that say "solid silver."

CARMINE
Write that down. "Solid silver." Write it down!

Lenny writes it down as Carmine takes Joey aside.

CARMINE *(cont'd)*
Joey, c'mere. Know what I like about these little spoons?

JOEY
What?

CARMINE
They're little. I mean if a couple thousand of them got "lost" no one would know.

JOEY
Jesus, Carmine!

CARMINE
What!

JOEY
We don't even have this job yet and you're already figuring out ways to skim.

CARMINE

Hey, it never hurts to plan ahead. By the way, I put forty cases of cigarettes in your garage.

JOEY

Again!

CARMINE

Your mother wanted three cases for her trouble but I got her to take two.

JOEY

Hey, Carmine!

CARMINE

They'll be gone tomorrow. Swear to God!

JOEY

Next time I want you to ask me first. "Joey, can I put forty cases of cigs in your garage?" I want you to do that.

CARMINE

Why?

JOEY

So I can say "no."
(*suddenly*)
Shh! Careful, it's John!

CARMINE

I see 'im. I see 'im.

John enters followed by Angelina. Again he doesn't bother to hold the door for her. Joey and Angelina exchange furtive glances then she crosses to a table where she sits and quietly studies her book.

CARMINE (*cont'd*)

John!

JOEY

Hey, John!

CARMINE

Back from Florida!

JOEY

How was it?

JOHN

Hot, humid, full of Jews and alligators.

CARMINE

Well, you look good, John.

JOEY

Well rested.

CARMINE
Got some nice color.

JOEY
Very nice.

CARMINE
Nice tan.

JOEY
When'd you get back?

JOHN
Yesterday. As soon as I heard the terrible news about Frankie Four Aces.

CARMINE
What a shame.

JOEY
A tragedy.

CARMINE
Right in front of his favorite seafood joint.

JOEY
And they whacked him goin' in. Not on his way out. That means he didn't even get to have dinner.

CARMINE
That's not right.

JOEY
Shot him eight times. Like a dog.

John looks like he might become sick during the following. Phil prepares a stomach powder for John.

CARMINE
And he took one in the eye which means a closed casket.

JOEY
Who shoots someone in the eye?

CARMINE
My mother says you don't get to see the face of God if they shoot you in the eye.

JOEY
Well, maybe if they shoot you in both eyes.

CARMINE
Right. Frankie can still see God with his good eye.

JOEY
Wait, what are we talkin' here? God can fix the bad eye.

CARMINE
Well, if He can fix one eye He can fix 'em both.

JOEY

If you were shot in both eyes.

CARMINE

My mother is so fuckin' stupid! "Can't see the face of God?"

JOEY

God'll fix it!

CARMINE

He can fix anything!

JOEY

Even if you got a million bullets in you!

JOHN

Stop!

CARMINE

Oh. Sorry, John.

JOHN

It's okay. I just... I'm... I'm okay...

CARMINE

My fault.

ANGELINA

You want a bucket or something, John?

JOHN

Naw, naw. I'm all right.
(then)
Maybe.
(then)
False alarm. I'm okay.

ANGELINA

You sure?

JOHN

Yeah.

ANGELINA

What do you want me to do now, John?

JOHN

Just go sit. Do whatever the fuck it is you do.

Angelina crosses to a table and sits.

JOHN *(cont'd)*

The piece of shit who did this to Frankie. The person who has slapped the face of our family. We will hunt him down like a dog. We'll find this cock sucker and make him <u>beg</u> for death.

JOEY

Beg for death.

CARMINE

Beg for death.

JOHN

Beg for death.

CARMINE

Beg for death.

Carmine, Joey and John all realize Lenny has been staring at them with a look of absolute amazement. All eyes slowly turn to Lenny.

JOHN

Who's the fat guy?

CARMINE

Oh, him.

JOEY

This is Lenny. He's the souvenir guy I was tellin' you about.

CARMINE

We've been taking care of that. Just like you said.

JOEY

I mean, we haven't ordered anything. We just put together some samples.

CARMINE

Just like you said.

JOHN

Samples, huh? For the New York World's Fair?

JOEY

It's a fair...

CARMINE

But it's for the whole world.

JOHN

Okay, let's see what you got.

CARMINE

Really?

JOHN

Yeah.

JOEY

Right now?

JOHN

No, a million years from now! Of course right now. C'mon, I'm standin' right here, I wanna see. Angelina!

ANGELINA

What!

JOHN

C'mere!

ANGELINA

What for?

JOHN

I want you to see this stuff.

ANGELINA

What stuff?

JOHN

This stuff over here! C'mon! I need a woman's opinion. It'll only take a second.

ANGELINA

I just sat down.

JOHN

Well now I'm asking you to get up.

They both lose control and scream at each other at the same time.

ANGELINA

Jesus Christ, make up your mind. Sit down, stand up, go here, go there! Like I'm some kinda dog! I'm not a dog, John! I'm a human being with feelings an' stuff! Understand! Not a dog! Human being! If you wanted me over there you should've said "Hey, stay here for a minute. I want you to see somethin'." But no! You tell me to come over here, two seconds later you want me to go over there! This shit is drivin' me nuts, John! Drivin' me nuts! Eat shit and die!

JOHN

Aw, for Christ's sake I'm askin' you nice! Do me one little favor! One little thing! Is this too much to ask? Get up and walk ten feet over here! I didn't know they had anything over there until you came over here. Do you have to? Do you have to! Please! Stop! Would you please! Is it too much to ask? There's no talking to you! Get up! Please? C'mon, I'm askin' you nice. Do this one thing for me, 'kay? C'mon, act like a human being just this once! Please? C'mon...

As Angelina crosses to John.

ANGELINA

Asshole.

JOHN

(sotto to Joey and Carmine)
Women see stuff different from men. They're all fucked up.

(to Angelina)

Take a look with me. This is souvenir stuff for the World's Fair.

ANGELINA

World's Fair?

JOHN

Yeah. It's a fair but it's for the whole world.
> *(to Lenny)*

Go 'head.

LENNY

Hmm?

CARMINE

Show him.

No response.

CARMINE *(cont'd)*

Show John what you got!

LENNY

> *(snapping out of it)*

Oh, I'm sorry.
> *(then)*

I uh... let's see... I've been showing samples here... I was about to show the World's Fair T-shirt.

Lenny holds up a World's Fair T-shirt.

CARMINE

Very colorful.

LENNY

And these days, the new trend in T-shirts is "one size fits all."

CARMINE

One sit fits all, huh?

JOHN

They oughta call it "one size fits all except you." Listen, Chunky. If I decide to do business with you, don't try and gimme this "one size fits all" bullshit. I want fat people to buy T-shirts, too.

JOEY

We'll sell 'em for what?

CARMINE

Five bucks.

JOHN

Yeah, five bucks. I like that. Round numbers. Five bucks.

LENNY

No one ever charges more than two dollars.

JOEY

We're chargin' five.

LENNY

Well go ahead but you'll get murdered by your competition.

John, Joey and Carmine break out laughing.

LENNY (cont'd)

What?
    (beat)
What!

JOHN

Could you say that again?

LENNY

Say what?

CARMINE

The last part.

LENNY

You'll get murdered by your competition?

They break out laughing again.

CARMINE

"Murdered."

JOEY

I know! I know!

JOHN

You gotta love that!

CARMINE

You gotta!

JOHN

Competition!

CARMINE

That is so cute!

JOHN

Lenny, is it?

LENNY

Yes.

JOHN

My friends and I, my associates, when we do business, we do it so well, we do it with so much heart and and and... enthusiasm that... we don't <u>have</u> any competition.

Lenny stares at John, Joey and Carmine as things finally begin to make sense to him.

235

LENNY
Oh, my God.

JOHN
What?

LENNY
I think I understand.

CARMINE
You do?

LENNY
Yes, I get what you're saying.

JOEY
Good. Show John what else you got.

LENNY
Very well.

Lenny holds up various items and rattles them off quickly.

LENNY *(cont'd)*
We have the New York World's Fair metal ashtray, ceramic ashtray, imitation gold bracelet.

JOEY
Pure gold.

LENNY
(quick to cover)
How stupid of me. Of course it's pure gold.
(then)
The New York World's Fair license plate frame, playing cards, key ring, nite lite, coffee mug, the comb, the brush, the comb and brush set, nut dish, pickle dish, candy dish, toothbrush, pennant, thermometer, the poster, the Souvenir World's Fair Coca Cola cup...

ANGELINA
Don't you need permission from Coca Cola?

CARMINE
We asked them and they were delighted about the whole thing.

LENNY
World's Fair sun visor, baseball hat, beer stein, coasters, shot glasses, swizzle sticks, flash light, pen, pencil, pencil box, salt and pepper shakers, snow globe, paper weight, tie clip, cuff links, note pad, hair clip, lapel pin, rain bonnet, umbrella and the Pieta nite light.

John stares stone faced at all the merchandise. No one can tell if he's pleased or not. After several long, silent beats.

JOHN
Is that everything?

CARMINE
Yeah.

JOEY
That's everything.

JOHN
Angelina.

ANGELINA
What?

JOHN
What do you think?

ANGELINA
You're asking me?

JOHN
Yeah, I'm asking you.

ANGELINA
My honest opinion?

JOHN
No, I want you to lie and make up a bunch of shit! Of course, your honest opinion!

ANGELINA
You want to know what I think?

JOHN
Yeah and don't hold back.

ANGELINA
I think if you don't order a million of each and every one of these things you're out of your God damn mind, John. This stuff is unbelievable.

JOHN
You like it?

ANGELINA
I <u>love</u> it! It's gorgeous! All of it! If I was going to the World's Fair I'd want one of everything. All this stuff! Lookit this stuff! Just lookit! It's beautiful!

Angelina shakes a snow globe.

ANGELINA *(cont'd)*
Look, it's snowing in Queens. These guys are smart, John. Not like the other gorillas who work for you. These two got brains.

CARMINE
Thank you.

JOEY

You're very kind.

CARMINE

Thank you very much.

ANGELINA

May I make one tiny suggestion?

LENNY

Of course.

ANGELINA

Pot holders. My mother collects them. Everywhere I go, I get her a souvenir pot holder.

JOEY

Pot holder.

ANGELINA

She don't use the pot holders. She hangs them over the stove in a special place. When she's makin' dinner she can look at her pot holders and dream about all the places she's never been.

CARMINE

Great idea.
   (to Lenny)
Write it down.

LENNY

Huh?

CARMINE

Pot holders! Write it down!

Lenny writes it down.

JOHN

Angelina's right. This stuff is beautiful. I love this shit. It oughta sell like hotcakes. Angelina, thanks.

ANGELINA

You're welcome. I'm always glad to act in a supplementary manner.

Angelina throws Joey a secret smile then crosses back to her table where she sits and reads.

JOHN

This is terrific what you guys did. I'm pleased. Very, very pleased. I never expected to see so much.

CARMINE

We wanted to do a good job, John.

JOEY

Show you we're serious about all this.

JOHN

Well, you did. You did. Joey, call Tommy Two Tone. Tell him we're going ahead with this. Hold on... hold on...

(to Lenny)

How long does it take for this crap to get here from Hong Kong?

LENNY

Two months.

JOHN

(to Joey)

Tell him in two months we'll need warehouse space.

JOEY

You got it!

Joey crosses to the pay phone, closes the door and makes the call.

JOHN

Very nice, Carmine. You did good.

LENNY

Ooo, there's one more thing you haven't seen. And this will sell big! Everyone's going to want one of these!

Lenny takes out a Frisbee with World's Fair artwork on it.

JOHN

What the fuck is that?

LENNY

It's new. It's called a Frisbee.

CARMINE

What the fuck is a Frisbee?

LENNY

It's a toy. Kids love them! Adults love them, too.

Carmine takes the Frisbee and bangs it on the table.

CARMINE

(sarcastic)

Ooo, yeah! Great! Wadda great toy! I want one for Christmas!

Lenny takes the Frisbee back.

LENNY

No, you throw it.

JOHN

Yeah, right. You throw it <u>away</u>.

LENNY

No, you throw it <u>to</u> someone. They catch it and they throw it back. Once you see it fly, it's amazing.

CARMINE
(mocking)
Ooo, it flies!

JOHN
(mocking)
I'm scared!

LENNY
At least take a minute to see how it goes. But not in here. There's not enough room.

JOHN
The parking lot?

LENNY
Yes, that'll be perfect.

Lenny crosses to the door followed by Carmine and John.

LENNY *(cont'd)*
I'm not an expert thrower or anything. But if you throw it right it can really zing.

JOHN
Ooo, it zings!

CARMINE
I don't know if I should zing. I'm Catholic! I'm savin' it for when I get married!

JOHN
Angelina, wanna see the Frisbee?

ANGELINA
Like I wanna get pregnant.

John, Carmine and Lenny exit. Angelina crosses to the jukebox, puts in a nickel but doesn't press a button. After a few beats Joey hangs up the phone and exits the phone booth.

JOEY
Where'd they go?

ANGELINA
Outside for a minute.

JOEY
Oh, well... hiya.

ANGELINA
Hi.

JOEY
How you been?

ANGELINA
Okay. How you been? Busy?

JOEY
Always. Jukeboxes to fill... Cigarette machines... Nickels to roll.

ANGELINA
Joey Nickels.

Joey smiles.

JOEY
That's right.

ANGELINA
Like the Indians.

JOEY
Like the Indians. Thanks for doin' that. With the souvenirs. Saying what you did.

ANGELINA
I meant it. You worked hard, you should sell a lot of those, move up in the family.

JOEY
How you doin' with your book, increasing your word power.

ANGELINA
I'm up to the "r's."

JOEY
Good for you. Keep at it.

ANGELINA
I will. I'm totally committed to it. I approach it with an absolute resolve.

JOEY
(impressed)
Yeah, you're up to the "r's."

ANGELINA
You hear about Jimmy Two Tone? He's getting married this spring to Tammy.

JOEY
Tammy DeLatura.

ANGELINA
Of course, after the wedding her name will be Tammy Two Tone.

They share a smile.

JOEY
It don't work like that.

ANGELINA
I guess not. Going to the wedding?

JOEY

Jimmy asked me to be an usher.

ANGELINA

I'm going to be a bridesmaid. Looks like we'll both be there.

Angelina pushes two buttons on the jukebox and "*Oh What A Night*" by the Dells begins to play. She begins to dance. It's all very dreamy and seductive.

ANGELINA

There's a band at the reception. Maybe we could dance.

JOEY

Not a good idea. People might get suspicious.

ANGELINA

True. Then again, if we're both in the bridal party and we don't dance... people might get even more suspicious. Especially John. "What's goin' on with Joey and Angelina? They're dancin' with everyone but not with each other."

JOEY

Yeah, well if we dance we've got to keep it simple.

ANGELINA

Sure. None of this.

She does a sexy dance move.

JOEY

Yeah, I'd hold off on that.

ANGELINA

Or this.

She does another sexy dance move.

JOEY

Also that one.

ANGELINA

We'll keep it simple... dance like all the old ladies and children.
(beat)
Some of them moves we did at Roseland, Joey... New Year's Eve.

JOEY

We got looks from the crowd.

ANGELINA

Were there other people at Roseland that night?

JOEY

A couple thousand.

ANGELINA

Didn't see them.

>   *(beat)*

When I got back home that night channel five was running these old movies... these black and white British films about, I don't know, British people. There were these five British guys and they're standing by this fireplace with glasses of champagne and one of them holds up his glass and says "To the Queen!" Then they drank their champagne and threw their empty glasses into the fireplace. And one guy, he's the only one who's American, he goes "Why'd you do that?" And the British guy goes "So the glass can never be used again for a lesser purpose."

JOEY

Woa!

ANGELINA

I know. The British are so weird.

>   *(beat)*

Then I thought of my shoes, my dancing shoes, the ones I wore that night. My favorite dancing shoes, Joey. The ones that cost eighty-five dollars. Shoes I bought with my money! Not John's! I jumped out of bed, marched out to the backyard, put them in the barbecue and set them on fire. I stood there at four in the morning watching my dancing shoes burn and told myself "They will never be used for a lesser purpose."

They exchange tender smiles, finally.

JOEY

You remember how hot it got at Roseland? All them people on the dance floor? You got so hot you took off your stockings, shoved them in my pocket.

ANGELINA

I forgot all about that!

JOEY

I didn't. I found your stockings the next day. I put them under my mattress. At night, I reach down and I breathe them into my face. I smell them and you, your hair, your skin, you're all over me. It's you like you're right there in bed with me but you're not. I'm just holding stockings. Then I weep like a baby.

ANGELINA

You keep my stockings under your mattress?

JOEY

My mother found them. Now she thinks I like dressing up like a woman.

ANGELINA

Didn't you tell her where they come from?

                             JOEY
How can I? What can I say to her? "Ma, I've fallen in love with a woman who can never be mine so..."

                           ANGELINA
I'll always be yours.

They kiss. As they kiss Phil enters from the back. He sees them kissing, turns right around and exits.

                        ANGELINA *(cont'd)*
I worry all the time that John might kill me. Then I think he might kill you and I worry even more. I can't do this, Joey. There's no future for people like us. Not inside this family. And there's no way out. Not when there's guys like John around. We could get away with it for six months or a year but sooner or later, all we'd have to do is trip up once, just once, and it would be all over for us.

Suddenly we hear three gunshots right outside. Angelina and Joey duck as we hear Lenny scream.

                          LENNY *(O.S.)*
Aaahhhh!!!

                             JOEY
What the...!

                           ANGELINA
Don't talk to me, Joey. It's over. I don't want to know you.

Angelina quickly exits to the ladies' room as John, Carmine and Lenny enter. Lenny is in a state of shock as Carmine holds up the Frisbee and examines the two bullet holes he put in it.

                            LENNY
You people are insane!

                            JOHN
Aw, we were just havin' fun.

                           CARMINE
Lookit that, John. Two hits out of three. Nice shootin'?

                            JOHN
Very nice.

                            LENNY
That was my only sample! You didn't have to shoot it!

                            JOHN
Listen, fat guy... can I give you my personal opinion about this Frisbee thing? It's crap. It's a plastic piece of plastic crap that's never gonna catch on in a million fuckin' years.

LENNY
We weren't throwing it right. When you throw it you're supposed to <u>flick</u> your wrist. Kinda <u>flick</u> sorta.

CARMINE
Look at us. I'm serious. Look at us.

Lenny does.

CARMINE *(cont'd)*
Do any of us look like we're guys who "flick?"

JOHN
Leave your samples here. I'll call you tomorrow, tell you how much we want. And when you tell me how much it's costing me, I want to be <u>shocked</u> at how low your prices are. I mean fuckin' <u>shocked</u>!

CARMINE
John likes being shocked.

JOEY
Makes his day.

JOHN
I want to drop the phone! I wanna be absolutely, totally <u>shocked</u>!

LENNY
Shocked.

JOHN
That's right. Shocked in a good way.

LENNY
Uh huh.

JOHN
'Cause if your prices are too high I might be shocked in a <u>bad</u> way.

CARMINE
You don't want that.

JOEY
Makes John cranky.

JOHN
And when I get cranky...

CARMINE
You don't want to know.

LENNY
Shocked.

JOEY
In a good way.

JOHN
We'll talk tomorrow.

Lenny forces a smile then exits.

Meanwhile Angelina enters from the ladies' room. She stops at Joey's coat which is hanging on a coat hook. She furtively stuffs something in the pocket.

JOHN *(cont'd)*

Angelina!

They both lose control and scream at each other at the same time..

ANGELINA

What! I'm right here! Jesus Christ, you don't have to yell at me like that! Like I'm some kinda piece of meat or somethin'! You're like an animal, John! An animal! Yell this! Yell that! No decorum or nothin'!

JOHN

How the fuck was I supposed to know you's there! Don't start! Don't start with me! Not now! You and your fuckin' attitude! I'm an animal?! Stop! Stop! Aw, you're breakin' my heart! Stop!

JOHN *(cont'd)*

We gotta go, is all.

ANGELINA

We just got here.

JOHN

Well, now we're leaving.

ANGELINA

Where we goin'?

JOHN

Sheepshead Bay, c'mon.

ANGELINA

Where, that place again?

JOHN

Never mind what place. We're just goin'.

ANGELINA

You gonna make me sit outside again?

JOHN

Whatever! C'mon!

ANGELINA

Great, I get to sit in the car with the motor runnin' for two hours again. There's a fun night. You know what, John? You think you're audacious but you're not. You're fatuous is what you are. Every last bit of you is fatuous.

John flashes with anger and grabs Angelina by her wrist. Angelina writhes with pain as John seeks to put her in her place.

JOHN

What do you think? You think you're better than me all of a sudden?

ANGELINA

My arm!

JOHN

You think this two dollar book makes you better than me now?

ANGELINA

You're hurting me!

JOHN

You learn ten new words and now you're what? Smart or somethin'? Is that it? We can all kiss your ass now 'cause you learned ten new words?

ANGELINA

My arm! It hurts!

JOHN

I'll break it if I want! You hear me? You hear me!

ANGELINA

I hear you!

JOHN

You listen to me. You were trash when I found you, now you're trash in a mink coat! Don't you _ever_ talk to me like that again! You understand? Not _ever_! You understand!

ANGELINA

Yes!

JOHN

I don't want to remind you of who you are again.

John lets go of Angelina. She cries from humiliation as she runs out of the diner. John watches her go, then exits after her.

Carmine sees the look on Joey's face.

CARMINE

Joey.

No reply.

CARMINE *(cont'd)*

Joey.

JOEY

What?

CARMINE

Wipe that look off your face before someone sees it.

JOEY

What look?

CARMINE

The one that says you wanna kill John.

Joey snaps out of it.

CARMINE (cont'd)

You in love with that girl?
(beat)
Are you in love with her?

No reply. Instead Joey crosses to his coat and puts it on.

CARMINE (cont'd)

Jesus, Mary and Joseph! You're in love with her! When you took her out last week did you bang her? Uh oh! I think you did. Either you banged her or she banged you or the two of you, you banged each other.

JOEY

Sometimes people fall in love, Carmine, without bangin'.

CARMINE
(news to him)
Like who?

Joey reaches in his pocket and feels something he didn't expect to find. He takes out Angelina's panties.

CARMINE (cont'd)

Oh, my God it's her underwear! She left you her underwear! Oh, that's sick! So sick! If John finds out he'll kill us both! Her underwear! Why the hell would you want her underwear! That's so twisted! That's...

JOEY

Shut the fuck up!

Joey puts the panties away.

CARMINE

You gotta forget about her, Joey! You gotta put her out of your mind. We're plugged into this World's Fair thing now. Big time. We're in. We got it. No more nickels. No more trips to Hillbilly Land. We're gonna be rich. We're gonna make a fortune. We're on our way, Joey. We're gonna live like kings!

JOEY

Kings? You think we're gonna be kings? What king would watch a man strong arm the woman he loves? That's what I did. I stood here and I watched that. She was in pain. She was in tears. I wanted to rip John's throat out with my bare hands but instead I stood here and I did nothing. I did <u>nothing</u>! Now you wanna call us kings? How could you possibly say that? Saying you're a king don't make you one. You can spend dough like a king, dress like one, eat like one, talk big like a king, drive a big car like a king but none of that don't make you one. You gotta <u>be</u> a king! Have the <u>heart</u> of a king! Have the courage of a king! The the the the guts and the bravery of a king! Stand face to face with what you know is wrong and risk your life to end it. You ever done that? I haven't. We ain't kings. We ain't nothin'. Haven't you noticed? Can't you tell?

Joey exits as Carmine looks.

(The LIGHTS fade to BLACK.)

ACT TWO

SCENE 2

It is several months later and the World's Fair has launched. Phil has hung a banner that reads "Welcome World's Fair Visitors." World's Fair souvenirs are for sale at the counter, boxes containing World's Fair souvenirs are piled high where ever space permits and, if we can see it, a sign outside offers World's Fair parking for ten dollars.

As we begin Joey, dressed in a tuxedo, sits at a table counting huge stacks of money. He's almost finished and keeps a tally on a slip of paper as he places the stacks of cash into a Macy's shopping bag.

Phil is cleaning cutlery and a large assortment of knives, forks, serving spoons and carving knives are scattered about the counter.

"Poetry in Motion" by Bobby Vee plays on the jukebox. Phil also counts money at the counter.

PHIL
You gonna dance?

JOEY
Hmm?

PHIL
I asked if you're gonna dance. You love this song. You used to dance to it every time it played.

JOEY
Don't have time.

PHIL
That's what happens when you start making money, kid. You stop doing the things you did for fun.

JOEY
Can't be helped. You got your parkin' lot money?

PHIL
All set to go.

JOEY
How's that comin'?

PHIL
Never thought I'd live to see it. People paying ten dollars to park their car in Queens. In the <u>bad</u> part of Queens. You know. The part where colored folks live.

JOEY
Aw, hey... c'mon...

250

PHIL
I'm kiddin'.

JOEY
How are the souvenirs doin'?

PHIL
Can't keep enough of them in stock. I run out of everything all the time. Word is you and Carmine are making it hand over fist.

JOEY
We're doin' okay.

PHIL
Just okay? Carmine bought himself a Cadillac, the official dream vehicle of Negros.

JOEY
It's a beauty, isn't it?

PHIL
How about you? When you buying a new car?

JOEY
I dunno. I drive by the Caddy showroom on Queens Boulevard, I slow down, I look...

PHIL
Listen to me. You're doing it wrong. You drive by, you slow down, you <u>stop</u>, you get out of that piece of crap you drive, go inside and buy yourself a Cad-illi-ack!

    (mimes driving)

Mmm mmm <u>mmm</u>!

JOEY

    (laughs)

Okay.

PHIL
Tell the man "I want the leather and the eight track! Toss in a couple of blondes while you're at it! I want <u>all</u> the options!"

JOEY
When I go to buy, you come with me.

PHIL
I will. You could have gone to the wedding tonight in your new Caddy. Could have pulled up to the church in <u>style</u>.

JOEY
That's right. Jimmy Two Tone gets married in less than an hour. You goin'?

PHIL
Am I what? Am I what! Is a colored man going to an Italian wedding? Are you kidding? You can't be serious.

JOEY

Well, I...

PHIL

(sarcastic)

Maybe I could dance with the bride while I'm there. Hold her close. Maybe run my hands up and down her ass. Give her a soul kiss. That'd be nice. People would love that! Then people can do that riddle I like so much: "What's black and white with six bullet holes in it." No, I'm not going to be the only colored man at a Sicilian wedding.

JOEY

Sorry. I wasn't thinkin'.

PHIL

It's all right. You're just young. You live in the world that's going to be. Not the one that is. Am I goin' to Jimmy's wedding. You're somethin' else.

Lenny Green enters from outside carrying a fairly large, cardboard box labeled "World's Fair T-shirts." He struggles over to a table where puts down the box and takes a breather.

LENNY

Damn, this thing gets heavier every time!

JOEY

You're makin' deliveries?

LENNY

It's the only way I can see any money out of this! I found out the trucking service gets twenty-two dollars to run a load out here. I told myself "Hell, I've got a truck!"

PHIL

That T-shirts?

LENNY

Yeah.

PHIL

What else you bring?

LENNY

Beer steins and pennants.

PHIL

Snow globes?

LENNY

Tomorrow.

PHIL

You said they was comin' today.

LENNY
(losing it)
Okay, so I fucked up! All right? So shoot me!
(panics instantly)
No, don't! It's just an expression! No shooting! I was just... I was... I tell you what. I'll bring the snow globes first thing tomorrow morning. Swear to God.

PHIL
Good enough.

Carmine enters from outside wearing a God-awful tuxedo.

JOEY
Woa!

PHIL
Look out now!

LENNY
Wow!

JOEY
Mama!

Carmine strikes some poses.

CARMINE
Huh? Huh?

PHIL
Lookin' good, Carmine!

CARMINE
You like?

LENNY
Very classy.

CARMINE
Huh?! Huh?!

PHIL
Some threads!

LENNY
Perfect fit.

CARMINE
Man, drivin' here in my new Caddy, wearin' this... I'm thinkin' to myself "I wish I had a camera! Someone, please take my picture!"

Carmine strikes another pose.

PHIL
You look like one of The Four Tops.

253

CARMINE
Great. Am I gonna get laid tonight or what?

JOEY
You look so good I might fuck you myself!

CARMINE
Be gentle! I'm a virgin!

Joey and Carmine laugh and exchange playful punches.

PHIL
(to Lenny)
C'mon, I'll show you where that goes. You look great, Carmine.

CARMINE
Thanks, Phil.

Phil exits into the back as Lenny follows carrying the box. Joey finishes putting stacks of cash into the shopping bag.

CARMINE *(cont'd)*
How's the money lookin'?

JOEY
It's like a dam burst and I can't stop it from pourin' in.

Joey shows Carmine the slip of paper with the money count on it.

CARMINE
Holy shit! This for the week?

JOEY
That's for the last two days.

CARMINE
Mama! I keep tellin' you, Joey. We could skim ten percent, John would never miss it.

JOEY
And I keep tellin' you I like to <u>look</u> at the East River, not live at the bottom of it.

CARMINE
Still, it would be nice to have the extra dough.

JOEY
We're making ten times what we used to make, Carmine!

CARMINE
Still, I got my eye on a white Caddy.

JOEY
You just bought a Caddy.

CARMINE
The one I want is a convertible. I'm gonna use it to drive to and from

my boat.

JOEY

You don't have a boat.

CARMINE

(twinkles)

Not yet.

(then)

Listen, a couple dozen boxes of souvenirs "fell off the truck."

JOEY

Again?!

CARMINE

Yeah, and I ran outta room where I stash my stuff so I put this load in your garage.

JOEY

Aw, Carmine!

CARMINE

I didn't bother your mother. I know she's sick. I lifted up the door, put the stuff in and took off.

JOEY

Carmine!

CARMINE

It's just for a while. It'll be there a day, maybe two. My guy from Jersey comes in, it'll be gone.

JOEY

Do me a favor, make this the last time. I mean it. If you wanna pick John's pocket, risk your life, fine. But don't involve me.

CARMINE

It's the last time. I promise. Now, c'mon. Lighten up. You look good. You might actually get laid at this wedding.

JOEY

Aw...

CARMINE

Hey, if a guy can't get laid at an Italian wedding he oughta hang up his dick and quit. You know how women get at weddings. All sentimental and horny. You talk to some chick, she says "The bride is so beautiful!" You say "I'd get married, too if I could find the right girl." Next thing you know you're bangin' her brains out in the men's room!

JOEY

That is so romantic!

CARMINE

You know who's gonna be there? The Russo sisters. All three of them. You gonna bang one of the Russo sisters?

JOEY

Nah...

CARMINE

You're not gonna make me bang all three, are ya?

JOEY

I think so.

CARMINE

That's a lot of heavy lifting. You got your eye on someone else?

JOEY

No.

CARMINE

Well, you must have some sort of plan worked out for the wedding.

JOEY

I'm gonna sit and watch Jimmy and Tammy get married, go to the reception, have dinner, dance a little, drink a little, go home.

CARMINE

What the fuck kinda plan is that!

JOEY

It's my plan. It's what I'm gonna do.

CARMINE

What about havin' fun? What about women? What about a little bah-bing?

JOEY

I'm not gonna bah or bing.

CARMINE

Sure you are.

JOEY

No, I'm not. I'm in love with someone, Carmine. With my whole heart and soul.

CARMINE

So?

JOEY

So nailin' some woman I don't even care about would be an infamnia... a disgrace. I could never do that to the woman I love. Never. I don't ask you to understand it, just respect it. It's how I feel about Angelina. I sent her flowers today. Two dozen white roses with a note that says I wished it was her and me gettin' married on this day. I wiped my tears with the card.

CARMINE

I never loved anyone like that.

(beat)

What's that feel like?

JOEY

Right now, not so good.

Angelina enters on the run. She wears a bridesmaid's dress. She talks a mile a minute as she passes Joey on her way to the ladies' room, furtively looking outside throughout.

ANGELINA

Joey, listen, I only have a few seconds. I ran ahead. I told John I have to pee. When he came by my place to pick me up I went to get my purse in the bedroom for a few seconds. Then I remembered I never took your card off the flowers! When I come out John was standing right by the flowers but I don't know if he read the card or not! Christ! I am so sorry, Joey!

Angelina exits to the ladies' room. Carmine peers outside.

CARMINE

John's comin'. What are you going to do?

JOEY

Nothin'. Maybe he didn't read the card.

CARMINE

What if he did?

JOEY

If he did, I don't think I'm goin' to Jimmy's wedding.

CARMINE

Man! Everything was goin' so good, now this!

JOEY

Shhh! It's John. It's John.

John enters dressed for the wedding.

CARMINE

Hey, look it's John!

JOEY

Hey, John.

CARMINE

Wadda yuh know, it's John! Heh heh! John of all people!

JOHN

What, you surprised to see me? Angelina just run in. I gotta drop her off before I pick up my wife! What! You think I'd pick up my wife with Angelina in the car? What kinda guy do you think I am! Huh?

CARMINE

No, I didn't mean it that way. I just mean it's great to see you, John. You look nice, John.

JOEY
Very nice.

CARMINE
Elegant. Real elegant, John. *Il meglio*. You're gonna be the best lookin' guy at this wedding.

JOHN
You think?

CARMINE
Fuckin' A.

Phil enters from the back.

PHIL
Hey, John. You hungry? Something to eat?

JOHN
Naw... I'm on my way to a wedding. They got food there.

PHIL
Gotcha.

Phil crosses to John and hands him a letter sized envelope stuffed with cash.

PHIL *(cont'd)*
Parking money.

JOHN
Fatter than last week.

PHIL
Looks like it.

JOHN
You take your cut?

PHIL
No, that's up to you. If you want to do that... That's not for me to do.

JOHN
(to Carmine and Joey)
The man knows how to show respect.
(to Phil)
I'll count this, get back to you later.

PHIL
Whatever you say, John. It's fine with me. Sure you don't want anything?

JOHN
I'm sure. They got food at the wedding.

Phil nods and exits to the back.

JOEY
Money's all counted, John. Put away.

JOHN
How'd we do?

JOEY
Fantastic and it's only for two days. Weekdays, not even a weekend.

Joey shows the tally slip to John.

JOHN
Holy shit.

CARMINE
Huh? Huh?

JOHN
This is two days?

JOEY
Yesterday and the day before.

JOHN
Un-fuckin'-believable. Never in my wildest dreams did I think we could make this much money sellin' T-shirts an' snow globes.

JOEY
All of it in cash.

CARMINE
And it's totally legal except for the bribes, extortion, arson and blackmail.

JOHN
Un-fuckin'-believable what we're pullin' in.

John throws his car keys to Joey.

JOHN *(cont'd)*
Joey, be a good boy. Put the cash in my trunk.

JOEY
You got it.

JOHN
Put it under the mat. You'll have to take out the spare.

JOEY
Done.

JOHN
My car is down at the end of the lot. I didn't want no one puttin' a ding in the door. Fuckin' people in Queens don't give a shit about dings.

JOEY
I see it.

JOHN
You don't mind, Joey?

JOEY
Naw. Not at all, John. Right back.

Joey exits outside. John crosses to Carmine and they sit at a table.

JOHN
(sneers)
He don't mind at all.

CARMINE
Hmm?

JOHN
Joey… he says he don't mind.

CARMINE
What, runnin' out to your car? Neither would I. If you asked me I woulda. Be glad to.

JOHN
My wife tells me Rosey's got the flu.

CARMINE
Joey's ma… Yeah, he told me.

JOHN
I dropped by to see how she was. Drop off some cannoli. Pay a visit.

CARMINE
That's so like you, John. Caring about people.

JOHN
I parked in her driveway. On the way out Joey's mother says "Why don't you take the shortcut through the garage."

CARMINE
Uh huh.

JOHN
So I went out through the garage.

CARMINE
Yeah.

JOHN
Guess what I seen in Joey's garage.

CARMINE
I dunno.

JOHN
Go on, take a guess.

CARMINE
No idea.

JOHN
Take a guess!

CARMINE

Old tires?

JOHN

A hundred boxes of World's Fair shit. Stacked from the floor to ceiling. A hundred boxes.

CARMINE

Really?

JOHN

Maybe more. And all of it was stuff that's moving fast. Ash trays, pencils, pens, snow globes... Stuff we run out of all the time. Looks like Joey don't run out.

CARMINE

You sure?

JOHN

I know what I seen.

CARMINE

Maybe...

JOHN

Maybe what?

CARMINE

Maybe Joey's keepin' it there until it's time to sell it. You know, storin' it.

JOHN

We've got two storage spaces right near the fair. Neither one is full. My guess is this is swag Joey has stolen from me to sell on his own. I will only ask you one time, Carmine. Do you know anything about this?

CARMINE

Me? About the boxes? I uh... His garage, huh? You want to know if I...

Angelina enters from the ladies' room. John and Carmine totally ignore her and she senses the tension.

ANGELINA

Oh, hi. I'll uh... I'll be over here.

Angelina crosses to another table where she sits. John and Carmine continue their uneasy silence. Finally...

JOHN

I said I would only ask you once.
    (beat)
I'm waiting. Did you know?

CARMINE

No.

JOHN

Joey wanted this life. I never went to him. I never went to Joey and asked him to become part of this family. He came to me. He came to me and asked if he could be part of this. And I said I would give him this life. I would take him into my family and he would have all that comes with it. What did I ask of him in return? His brain, his hands, his mind, his soul? Did I even so much as ask him for his affection? Did I ask him for that? Not even. Not even. I asked Joey and guys just like him for one thing. Their respect. With that, everything else falls into place. I don't care if Joey sold a stick of gum behind my back. He has lost his respect for me. That means he has lost his place with us. He does not belong in my family. Not anymore.

CARMINE

John...

JOHN

He does not belong.

CARMINE

John, maybe if you...

JOHN

I seen Vincent.

CARMINE

Vincent?

JOHN

We talked. Vincent knows everything. Now I'm going to tell you something about Joey and this comes direct from Vincent. The capo di tutti capi.

(then)

Take my hand.

No response.

JOHN *(cont'd)*

Take my hand.

Carmine takes John's hand. John's grip is powerful and Carmine winces with pain.

JOHN *(cont'd)*

Joey does not live to see tomorrow.

CARMINE

John...

JOHN

Say it.

CARMINE

John...

JOHN

Say it.

CARMINE

He's my best friend.

JOHN

Say it.

CARMINE

... like my brother...

JOHN

Say it!

CARMINE

... not tomorrow...

John lets go of Carmine's hand.

CARMINE *(cont'd)*

John...

JOHN

Hmm?

CARMINE

Ever hear of the Yakuza?

JOHN

Who?

CARMINE

They're Japanese. They got this ceremony where they...

JOHN

(interrupts)
Stop your bullshit! Do you wanna do this or do I go to someone else?

Carmine, petrified with guilt and fear thinks for several long beats, finally...

CARMINE

Joey and me... we made a promise to each other. If one of us ever had to go... it would come from the other.

JOHN

Then you get to keep your promise and you keep it tonight.

CARMINE

My tux, John...

JOHN

What about it!

CARMINE

I didn't bring a piece. It would ruin the shape of the tux.

John takes out a gun and places it on the table.

JOHN

When you're done, you take over for Joey and keep his end.
>(beat)

You should smile. Tomorrow you start makin' even more.

Carmine stares at the gun then slowly picks it up. A beat, then Joey enters from outside.

JOEY

Done. I had to move the wedding present to one side, John.

No reply.

JOEY (cont'd)

Big present. What is it? A punch bowl maybe?

No reply.

JOEY (cont'd)

Well, the cash is under the mat next to the jack. Like you wouldn't see a bag that size!

Joey crosses to the table to return John's keys. He sees the gun.

JOEY (cont'd)

What's up?

JOHN

I know what's goin' on, Joey. I know all about it.

JOEY

Know about what?

JOHN

What do you think?

Joey looks to Angelina. The two exchange looks of panic.

JOEY

When did you find out?

JOHN

Today. I found out today.

JOEY

Figures.

JOHN

They haven't invented the words that can tell you the shock and hurt I feel from all this.

JOEY

Well, I felt bad too, John. And I'm glad it's finally over. Hiding it was the most painful part. I've always loved and respected you. I never liked goin' behind your back. I just want you to know one thing, John.

Angelina had nothin' to do with this.

JOHN

I never thought she did.

JOEY

Well, good 'cause she didn't. It was me. All me. I told her if she didn't go along with me, I would tell you that she <u>did</u> anyway. And she fought me, John. Oh, she fought me. Over an' over, she said no, it's not right, it wouldn't be right to do that to you. It wouldn't be fair. You've been so kind and generous to us both why betray you like that? But I kept at her with all kinds of threats until she finally caved in. It was me. It was all me. She's innocent. Totally innocent.

ANGELINA

No, I'm not innocent. Not innocent at all. I'm in love with Joey. Have been for a long time. Since I first seen him practically. Force me to go out with him? Force me to be with him? The only force he ever used was his smile. I love you, Joey.

JOEY

I love you, too.

They smile at each other.

JOHN

You two are having a thing?

JOEY

Yeah.

ANGELINA

That's what this is about.

JOHN

No.

JOEY

No?

JOHN

I found crates of World's Fair shit in your garage.

JOEY

Oh. So you...

JOHN

Not until now. Guess it's my lucky day.
    (beat)
Carmine...

CARMINE

Here?

JOHN

Wherever you want. I just want it done. Both of them.

Carmine gestures at the men's room.

CARMINE

C'mon... If I don't do it now...

JOEY

I know. You'll lose your nerve. At least we're keepin' our promise.

CARMINE

Yeah.

JOEY

I have to go, and it's going to come from you.

Carmine nods then gestures with the gun. Joey and Angelina look at each other, hold hands, then exit into the men's room as Carmine follows. The instant Carmine exits into the men's room we hear six gun shots. The shots are loud, almost deafening as we see flashes of light. Phil and Lenny enter from the back having heard the gun shots. After several long, silent beats, Carmine enters from the men's room, smoking gun in hand.

JOHN

Dead?

Carmine nods.

JOHN *(cont'd)*

The girl?

CARMINE

Hmm?

JOHN

Her, too?

Carmine nods.

JOHN *(cont'd)*

You sure they're dead?

CARMINE

Go in an' look if you want. But be careful. The floor's slippery. Blood. It's everywhere.

John begins to feel sick to his stomach. Phil prepares a stomach powder for John.

JOHN

Right.

CARMINE

(pointing)
And don't trip on that thing over there...

JOHN

What thing?

CARMINE

It's a piece of Joey's skull and some of his brain. The bullet went up through his chin but come out the back of his head.

John feels more sick.

CARMINE *(cont'd)*

Go on, take a look. A gun this size does a lotta damage. There's a hole in her... you can see daylight through it!

JOHN

Phil... go look for me...

PHIL

Excuse me, John?

JOHN

Go look. Tell me what you see.

As Phil crosses to the men's room.

PHIL

First no snow globes now this!

Phil exits into the men's room for a few beats, then comes back out. All eyes are on Phil. Phil looks at Carmine, John and Lenny for several long beats.

PHIL *(cont'd)*

Dead.
(beat)
Man, it'll take forever to clean up that mess.

John feels more sick.

JOHN

Hnn!

PHIL

And her, well... She used to have a pretty face.

JOHN

Enough! I don't wanna hear no more!

PHIL

Sorry, John.

CARMINE

It had to be done, John.

JOHN

I know. Had to be. There's no way I could let an insult like that go unpunished.

CARMINE

I'll wait until late tonight, take them out to this place I know in Jersey.

JOHN

Fine.

CARMINE

I'll never get my trunk clean. No matter how much newspaper you put down it always soaks through. Brand new Caddy, too.

JOHN

I'll buy you another one.

CARMINE

No.

JOHN

I want to.

CARMINE

No, I couldn't.

JOHN

I insist.

CARMINE

Really?

JOHN

Whatever you want.

CARMINE

Did have my eye on a convertible.

JOHN

It's yours.

CARMINE

Well, thank you, John.

JOHN

What about him?

LENNY

What about me?

JOHN

You see any of this?

LENNY

Are you kidding? I wasn't even here! I was never here at all today. I haven't been out to Queens for days. In fact, I'm not even in New York City. I was with my wife and sister-in-law all weekend. We left early this morning for Atlantic City. We're still there. We're having a wonderful time, by the way.

CARMINE

He'll be okay. Walk John out to his car?

LENNY

Sure.

Lenny escorts a weakened John to the door.

CARMINE
You going to the wedding, John?

JOHN
Maybe later.

CARMINE
You rest up. Feel better.

JOHN
Thanks.

CARMINE
Tell Jimmy I'm sorry I missed his wedding.

JOHN
I'll make up an excuse.

CARMINE
Thank you.

John and Lenny exit. Carmine calls after John.

CARMINE *(cont'd)*
I'll call you tomorrow after I bury the bodies.

JOHN *(O.S.)*
Ooooh!!!

A beat, then Joey and Angelina enter.

ANGELINA
He gone?

CARMINE
John? Yeah.

ANGELINA
We heard what you did.

JOEY
Why'd you do that, Phil?

CARMINE
Yeah, how come?

PHIL
I've seen all the wiseguys in this family. For years. Each and every one of them stopped here on their way up or on their way out. Big guys, small guys, loud, quiet, half crazy, all crazy... Guys with gold teeth, gold jewelry, wads of cash so big one hand couldn't hold it all. Guys who carried guns, knifes, shotguns, ice picks, baseball bats. Eyes like sharks. Cold blooded killers who could drink coffee, laugh and relax after just having choked someone to death. Brave men. All of them brave. But not so brave they would ever, not for one second, risk their life for a friend.

I've never seen that. Not until now. Not until tonight.
>(beat)

You also ran cash and Christmas presents down to my sister and my nephews. Ain't a lot of white men who would do that. Take the time to stop and knock on my sister's door.

CARMINE

I never really knocked. I just slowed down, threw the presents out the window.

Phil smiles.

PHIL

I'm going to take a nap. There gonna be any more murders tonight?

CARMINE

No, not tonight. I'm done with my killin' spree.

PHIL

Thank God.

Phil exits to the back.

JOEY

Jeez, Carmine I thought for a second there you might...

CARMINE

I might what?

JOEY

You know.

CARMINE

No, I had enough of that.
>(beat)

All I wanted to do was keep my promise to my best friend.

JOEY

If one of us ever has to leave...

CARMINE

It would come from the other.

JOEY

Now I've got to leave.

CARMINE

No one's gonna look for you, Joey. They think you're dead. But you'd better get dead and stay dead.

They smile.

CARMINE *(cont'd)*

Where you gonna go?

                              ANGELINA
Some place that has dancing.

                                JOEY
Yes, a place that has dancing.

                              CARMINE
You wouldn't have a slutty sister by any chance, would you?

                              ANGELINA
Sorry.

Without any warning John begins to enter the diner. Carmine, Joey and Angelina have less than a second before John sees what's going on. In a flash Angelina drapes herself lifeless over a stool. Joey drops into Carmine's arms lifeless as well. Carmine picks up the largest carving knife he can find from the counter. John enters.

                                JOHN
Carmine, before I forget...

                              CARMINE
John! You're just in time! We're gonna cut up the bodies!

John instantly feels sick.

                                JOHN
Never mind!

He runs out of the diner holding his mouth.

                        JOHN *(O.S.) (cont'd)*
Aaarrrfff!

Carmine, Joey and Angelina sigh with relief.

                              CARMINE
Close.

                                JOEY
Too close.

Carmine hands Joey the keys to his car.

                              CARMINE
Here. Better not drive your piece of crap.

                                JOEY
You're kidding.

                              CARMINE
Take it. John's buying me a new Caddy anyway. C'mon, go. If someone sees you two, Phil and me get a family plot in Jersey. Go on. Beat it.

Joey hugs Carmine goodbye.

JOEY
I knew you wouldn't.

CARMINE
Maybe my aim is just bad.

JOEY
Gonna miss you.

ANGELINA
I was wrong about you, Carmine. You're a prince. A kingly man.

CARMINE
You'd better scram. Take care of my best friend. Go scram. There's a full tank of gas.

Joey and Angelina begin to exit then pause at the door.

JOEY
Carmine, what's the stupidest name you ever heard?

CARMINE
Hands down it's gotta be Bubba.

JOEY
If you ever get a postcard from Bubba... Maybe you'll wanna come visit?

CARMINE
I just might.

Joey and Angelina laugh and exit as Carmine watches them go.

CARMINE *(cont'd)*
Bubba...

Carmine crosses to the jukebox, puts in a coin and plays *"Calendar Girl."* He dances. He dances badly - but he dances.

(The LIGHTS fade to BLACK.)

THE END

THE KING OF CITY ISLAND

CAST

CAZZIE, late thirties or older, a Bronx blue collar, charismatic tough guy. Larger than life, a man who can never get enough.

DONNA, thirties or older, Cassie's faithful, long-loving, long-suffering girlfriend. Attractive, capable, smart but growing weary of Cazzie's empty promises.

AMBROSE, Cazzie's younger brother. A bright, tender, tranquil, religious man who believes there is good in all people.

MURIEL, thirties or older. A beautiful woman of the large and lovely variety struggling with low self-esteem. Loud, animated, outspoken.

DANZINGER, thirties or older, a large, crude, filthy weasel of a man.

LUNTZ, thirties or older, a small, crude, filthy weasel of a man.

ACT ONE

SCENE 1

The setting is the backyard of a house in City Island, New York. Like many of the homes found there, this is a simple house set against the spectacular backdrop of Long Island Sound. The backyard is cluttered with a fair amount of waterside junk, a badly weathered dingy, a rusted outboard engine, oars, etc. One can enter this backyard from either the back of the house, an alleyway that leads to the street or from an unseen dock.

It is late afternoon in the spring and, as we begin, DONNA DEMARCO is setting a small outdoor table for dinner. When she is certain the table looks flawless, she takes a newspaper, opens to a page, folds the paper back then places it on the table.

MURIEL GRECCO peeks over the backyard fence. She's a large woman Donna's age. We can only see her head.

MURIEL
Holy crap did I ever clean up! It was rainin' dough. I had to come home just to count it all. Looks like six hundred bucks so far.

DONNA
You made six hundred dollars this week?

MURIEL
No, I made six hundred dollars in the last three hours!

DONNA
What?

Muriel steps into view. She's wears a nun's habit and is smoking a cigarette.

MURIEL
And I'm not done. As soon as my feet stop swellin' I'm going right out again. There's a lot of bars I haven't hit yet.

DONNA
Good God, Muriel what on earth are you doing?

MURIEL
It's Friday, payday for most guys. Where do they go? Home to their wife and kids? No. They go to bars. Dark, cheap, stinky, smelly bars where they drink, watch the ball game and tell each other lies.

DONNA
I don't get it. What's the nun costume got to do with all that?

MURIEL
Guilt! These guys look like they're having a good time, but down deep they're full of guilt. They know they should be home, but they're not. It's killin' them. I walk in, all sweet and angelic, white pasty face, and

got this tambourine in my hand. "For the cripple children. For the crippled children." Oh, they can't toss their money in fast enough. One guys tosses in a buck and all the others do the same. Buck after buck, fives, tens and even a few twenties. They all wanna look like "big men" to their buddies. But they're not. They're just stinky, drunken losers too scared to go home.

DONNA

So you're collecting money for crippled children?

MURIEL

Hell no! I'm collecting money for me!

DONNA

Muriel!

MURIEL

Hey! Hey! Cripple kids got a hundred different charities collecting money for them. All I got is me! I got rent to pay, a phone bill that's overdue, clothes to buy. Large and lovely fashions aren't cheap, you know.

DONNA

Muriel...

MURIEL

Don't gimme that look. I'm a single woman with no job skills trying to survive in a male-dominated workforce. And I don't get to keep all the six hundred. Cazzie gets ten percent.

DONNA

Cazzie put you up to this?

MURIEL

Hey, I'm glad he did! I also owe him rental on the nun's outfit and the tambourine.

DONNA

Good God.

MURIEL

I covered Williamsbridge, Bronxdale and Co-op City. I still need to hit Pelham Parkway and Eastchester.

DONNA

With your tambourine and nun's habit?

MURIEL

Yeah.

DONNA

Saying it's for crippled children?

MURIEL

Does that bother you?

DONNA

Well, since you asked, yes, it does.

MURIEL
Okay, I respect that. I promise I won't say cripple children no more.

DONNA
Thank you.

MURIEL
From now on it's blind orphans.
(suddenly)
Ooo... eating outside tonight?

DONNA
It's such a beautiful evening I thought we would.

MURIEL
Whatcha makin', huh? A little salad? A little wine?

DONNA
And some chicken.

MURIEL
Ooo!

DONNA
It's no big deal.

MURIEL
Maybe not to you but it means a lot to a man. A man sees his dinner didn't come from a microwave...

DONNA
Yeah?

MURIEL
It does things to him. It makes him grateful. Get my drift?

DONNA
I get your drift.

MURIEL
I'm not kiddin'. When I had a boyfriend, many years ago, before my glands shut down and made me bloat, I made Dominic a homemade veal cutlet thing. It was easy. Something I threw together in a coupla minutes. But Dominic was impressed. And grateful. Mama mia was he grateful! When he finished he <u>threw</u> me on the table where he "took" me! And believe you me, I got "tooken."

DONNA
Well, that's-

MURIE
Kissin' and grabbin' and gropin', shovin' dishes and food out of the way.

DONNA
I guess he just-

MURIEL

I'm tellin' yuh, I was finding sesame seeds in the damndest places for weeks.

DONNA

Muriel.

MURIEL

Even a crouton.

DONNA

Muriel!

MURIEL

Like I'd be taking a shower and all of a sudden...

DONNA

Muriel! I believe you!

MURIEL

Just be careful at the end of dinner, hon. Cazzie's like all men. He's a beast. A hot, sweaty, smelly, hungry, horny, jungle beast.

CASHMERE MARINO (Cazzie), enters looking exasperated.

MURIEL *(cont'd)*

You! You're an animal.

CAZZIE

You're an idiot.

MURIEL

A jungle animal.

CAZZIE

A certifiable nut. And what are you doing here? Why aren't you hittin' the bars?

MURIEL

It's a slow night. I only made two hundred dollars so far.

CAZZIE

Then get out there and earn more with the cripple children thing.

MURIEL

At Donna's request I'm dropping the cripple kid thing and replacing it with blind orphans.

CAZZIE

I don't care if it's midgets with prickly heat! Go shake your tambourine!

MURIEL

Okay, okay! I'm going!

Muriel goes to exit but stops.

MURIEL *(cont'd)*

Dominus vobiscum!

CAZZIE

Get outta here! And don't damage the uniform!

Muriel exits.

CAZZIE (cont'd)

Jeez! You try and help some people! Help her pay some bills, launch her in a new career, and what does she do? She stands around gabbin' with you!

DONNA

Well, put all that behind you. It's Friday night and you're home. How was your day, Cazzie?

CAZZIE

For shit. The worst. This guy Angelini, he's gonna drive me nuts. He knows the clearance on the drawbridge is thirty-five feet. He knows that. Everyone knows it. There's a gigantic sign, "Clearance, Thirty-Five Feet." What's he do? He buys a sailboat with a mast thirty-<u>six</u> feet high. From waterline to the top of the mast, thirty-six feet. He did it just to drive me nuts. Just to make me crazy! He went through the bridge four times today! Four times! Turn on the warning lights, sound the bell, the siren, lift the bridge, wait for him to pass, lower the bridge… Four times! Ruined my whole friggin' day! I swear, I'd pop Angelini right in the jaw if his whole family wasn't in the Mafia.

DONNA

His whole family is not in the Mafia.

CAZZIE

Of course it is.

DONNA

No, just his mother. And she's very nice. I do her hair all the time.

CAZZIE

Well, tell her that her son is a royal pain in the ass.

(a beat, then)

We eating outside tonight?

DONNA

The weather's so nice I thought it would be romantic.

CAZZIE

The Mets play at eight o'clock. I want to watch the game.

DONNA

I could bring out the portable TV. You can watch it on that.

CAZZIE

Eh… that's black and white. It's so much nicer to watch the Mets lose in color.

(notices newspaper)

What's this?

DONNA
Today's newspaper.

CAZZIE
Why's it open to this page?

DONNA
I thought you might like to read the ad.

CAZZIE
(reading)
Male Impotence Cured.

DONNA
Not that ad. The other one.

CAZZIE
The Mirage Hotel? In Atlantic City?

DONNA
Uh hmm.

CAZZIE
(reading)
Fourth of July Wedding Special?

DONNA
Uh huh.
(almost memorized)
A wedding service in their twenty-four hour chapel, a champagne dinner in their Dreams of Tomorrow restaurant and a night in the honeymoon suite. A hundred and forty-nine dollars, for everything. Everything. It sounds like a great deal, Cazzie.

CAZZIE
Sure, it <u>sounds</u> like a great deal. Until you get there. Then they've got you. They know you drove a million miles so they start throwing on the extras.

DONNA
Extras?

CAZZIE
Sure, they'll marry you but it'll be their rock bottom, no frills service. You want a veil, a little bouquet of flowers, music... that all costs extra. You want a video of the ceremony? That's extra, too. You want them to fling rice at you when they're done? Extra.

DONNA
I don't think they can advertise one thing then charge another. That's against the law.

CAZZIE
This is Atlantic City, Donna. They can get away with anything. The dinner is probably hamburger. You want steak? Extra. The honeymoon suite

is a closet. You want nicer? Extra. Before you know it, their wedding special hasn't cost a hundred and forty-nine dollars. It cost two hundred.

DONNA
I'll pay the difference. I'll pay for the whole thing.

Cazzie simply stares silently at Donna for a few beats, then.

CAZZIE
Boy, you really like to hack off my balls, don't you?
    (mocking her)
"I'll pay the difference. I'll pay for the whole thing." You really like to chip away at the groin area until there's nothing there.

DONNA
Then you pay.

CAZZIE
I would except there's a principle involved. This is nothing more than a rip off designed for suckers.

DONNA
It's just that you said we'd be getting married and soon.

CAZZIE
And we are. But I don't want a cheesy wedding in some all-night chapel with a Korean Elvis. I want a nice wedding in a church.

DONNA
When?

CAZZIE
When? How about when the New York City Drawbridge Operators get a new contract with the city so I'll know how much money I'll be making. It would be stupid if I jumped into a marriage without knowing if I can support us properly. Don't you think? Huh? I'm trying to make sure our future is solid, rock solid.

DONNA
So, when your union signs a new contract.

CAZZIE
We tie the knot.

DONNA
Promise?

CAZZIE
Promise.

DONNA
Cazzie, I love you so much. I'll make you a good wife. Children. I'll give you beautiful children who adore you. You want all that, don't you?

CAZZIE
Yes. But right now what I want even more...

                        DONNA

Yes?

                        CAZZIE

Is a beer.

                        DONNA

Sure. 'right back...

Donna goes to exit, then stops.

                        DONNA *(cont'd)*

When the bridge operators and the city sign a new contract?

                        CAZZIE

That very <u>day</u>.

                        DONNA

Promise?

                        CAZZIE

Promise.

                        DONNA

Love you.

                        CAZZIE

Beer?

                        DONNA

Right away.

Donna exits into the house. Cazzie strolls over to the nicely set table and helps himself to a bit of food. After a few beats

AMBROSE MARINO, Cazzie's brother, enters. Ambrose wears brightly colored shorts, a screamingly loud Hawaiian shirt, sandals and a hat designed for shade, not style. He carries a backpack. Cazzie doesn't recognize his brother at first.

                        CAZZIE

If you're looking for Orchard Beach, it's a half mile that way.

Cazzie helps himself to more food.

                        CAZZIE *(cont'd)*

I said the beach is that way. Just follow the smell of suntan lotion and beer cans.

Cazzie helps himself to more food.

                        CAZZIE *(cont'd)*

You homeless or something? We've got a really nice place for homeless guys on City Island. You see that jetty out there. It goes out into Long Island Sound. If you're homeless, just walk out on the jetty, then jump the fuck off. Loser.

                    AMBROSE

Hello, Cazzie.

Cazzie realizes who it is.

                    CAZZIE

Ambrose? My God! Ambrose!

The two brothers cross to each other. Cazzie offers a manly handshake but Ambrose turns it into a giant hug.

                    AMBROSE

God, is it good to see you!

                    CAZZIE

Ha! Look at you!

                    AMBROSE

Look at you.

                    CAZZIE

You're a man, for Christ's sake. A full grown man!

                    AMBROSE
            (indicates stomach)

Maybe a little too full grown, eh?

                    CAZZIE

Whadda ya talkin'? You wanna see a gut? Here... here's a gut. A lotta beer and burgers went into that.

Cazzie sticks out his stomach.

                    CAZZIE *(cont'd)*

Huh? See that? Huh?

                    AMBROSE

Mine's bigger.

Ambrose sticks his out. They pat their stomachs and laugh.

                    CAZZIE

Naw naw... I've got the gut of a New York City Municipal Employee. I win. God, Ambrose, how long has it been? Twelve, fifteen years?

                    AMBROSE

Eighteen.

                    CAZZIE
            (shocked)

Get the fuck away!

                    AMBROSE

Eighteen years just last month.

                    CAZZIE

Get the fuck away!

                              AMBROSE
The day I was ordained as a priest.
                              CAZZIE
Get the...

Ambrose holds up a finger and manages to stop Cazzie just in time.

                          CAZZIE *(cont'd)*
Sorry. You're probably not used to hearing language like that. So
what are you, on a vacation? A... what do they call it... a sabbatical?
Something like that?
                              AMBROSE
Something like that.
                              CAZZIE
Hey, you gotta see Donna. She'll shit when she sees you.
        (yelling loudly)
Donna!
        (beat)
Donn-ah!!!
                           DONNA *(O.S.)*
I'm busy!
                              CAZZIE
        (yelling)
Get out here!
                           DONNA *(O.S.)*
I'm takin' a chicken out of the oven!
                              CAZZIE
Get out here!
                           DONNA *(O.S.)*
I'm... busy!
                              CAZZIE
Ambrose is back.

A beat, then Donna appears at the back door drying her hands on a kitchen towel.

                              DONNA
If this is some kind of trick I'm gonna...

Donna sees Ambrose.

                          DONNA *(cont'd)*
Ambrose? Oh, my God! Ambrose!

Donna runs to Ambrose and he sweeps Donna off her feet as they hug.

AMBROSE
Donna!

DONNA
Oh, my God! I don't believe it! I don't believe it! Let me look at you. You haven't changed. Not one bit.

AMBROSE
And you, Donna... you're more beautiful than ever.

DONNA
Aw...

AMBROSE
Look at you. When I left you were a girl. Now... now you're a woman. A beautiful, fertile, woman.

DONNA
(embarrassed)
Ambrose...

AMBROSE
Look how full and round and fruitful you are. You've had children?

DONNA
No.

AMBROSE
There's still time. Because you're a ripe, beautiful woman bursting with—

CAZZIE
(interrupts)
Yeah, right sure, she's burstin'. Take it slow, guy. Don't think I've forgotten how you used to steal my girlfriends.

DONNA
Oh, for Christ's sake, Cazzie. He's a priest.

CAZZIE
That makes me worry even <u>more</u>. Ambrose, you want a beer? Donna, get Amby a beer.

AMBROSE
No thank you. I don't drink.

CAZZIE
You don't?

AMBROSE
Not for many years.

DONNA
You don't drink at all?

AMBROSE
Nothing.

CAZZIE

Not even beer?

AMBROSE

Not even beer.

DONNA

Are you hungry? You must be starving. We're eating al fresco tonight. Al fresco... that's Italian for outdoors.

CAZZIE

He knows what al fresco is! He's a college graduate, for God's sake!

DONNA

I'm sorry.

AMBROSE

Thank you, Donna. Yes, I'd love to join you.

DONNA

We're having chicken.

AMBROSE

I'm sorry. I don't eat meat.

CAZZIE

It's not meat. It's chicken.

AMBROSE

Chicken is meat and I don't eat it.

CAZZIE

Chicken barely qualifies as meat. It's more like fish with feathers. You look up chicken on some food charts and they've got it right between broccoli and Ding Dongs.

DONNA

Ambrose, I've got vegetables and tons of salad and a big loaf of Italian bread. You can eat that, can't you?

AMBROSE

Yes. Thank you, yes.

DONNA

Great, great... back in two seconds.

Donna smiles and happily exits into the house.

CAZZIE

I'll bet you don't smoke, too.

AMBROSE

Of course not.

CAZZIE

I don't get it. The church tells you you can't have sex so you go ahead and make it worse by giving up everything else.

AMBROSE
It's something I've chosen to do on my own, Cazzie. I don't expect you to understand it right away.

CAZZIE
Don't expect me to understand it in a million years.

AMBROSE
A few years ago I spent six months with an order of Trapist monks in Gethsemane.

CAZZIE
Where's that? Egypt?

AMBROSE
Kentucky.

CAZZIE
Close enough.

AMBROSE
None of the brothers smoked or drank. Very few ate meat. And all of them had taken a vow of silence. Their leader, Father Bernard, had not spoken a word, by choice, in fifty-three years.

CAZZIE
Aha.

AMBROSE
And even though he was almost ninety, each night, when the sun was setting in the green hills to the west, he would climb to the top of a bell tower, his own private sanctuary, and pray.

CAZZIE
Aha. Well, if you tiptoed up the stairs to that bell tower.

AMBROSE
Yes?

CAZZIE
And snuck up on Father Bernard... real quiet...

AMBROSE
Uh huh...

CAZZIE
You would hear him saying...
 (screaming)
"I'M SO FUCKIN' HORNY!"
 (laughs)
"Man, I gotta get laid or somethin'! Gimme a vodka! Where's my cigarettes!"

Cazzie has a good laugh over his joke. Ambrose is not amused.

CAZZIE *(cont'd)*
C'mon, lighten up. The Catholic church can use a few laughs, huh?

Donna enters from the house carrying bowls and trays of food. They sit for dinner.

CAZZIE *(cont'd)*
So, this is what you've been doing all these years? Hanging out with monks who don't say nothin'?

Cazzie is completely into his food. Donna is riveted by everything Ambrose says.

DONNA
Ooo, Ambrose... you've been with monks?

AMBROSE
Last year, for a short while.

DONNA
What else have you been doing?

AMBROSE
Well, a few years ago I had the summer off so I hitchhiked across America. It took me over three months.

CAZZIE
Fuckin' traffic, it's insane!

AMBROSE
No, I stopped along the way.

CAZZIE
What for?

AMBROSE
To meet people.

CAZZIE
Why would you want to do that?

AMBROSE
To learn. I would stop to live and work with the people I met.

CAZZIE
(no clue)
Aha.

DONNA
That's beautiful. We've kept all your postcards. They're on the wall in the bathroom in the basement.

CAZZIE
It's like watching a travelog every time I take a dump.

AMBROSE
I was assigned to a parish in Reno. Worked in a Catholic college in San Francisco. A halfway house in San Diego. For five years I was an aide to a Bishop in Tokyo.

DONNA
Cazzie, are you listening to all the places Amby's been?

CAZZIE
Yeah, places that end in "o."

AMBROSE
After my time with the Trapists, I was transferred to a missionary position in China.

DONNA
Red China?

CAZZIE
(sarcastic)
No, Blue China. The one small section of China where they forgot to have communism.

DONNA
Stop. Ambrose, I've missed you so much.

AMBROSE
I've missed you, too.

DONNA
A few postcards each year is not enough.

AMBROSE
I know. I've been gone a long time, missed a lot.

DONNA
Yes, you have.

AMBROSE
I missed your wedding.

Donna looks embarrassed. Cazzie stops eating.

AMBROSE (cont'd)
I wasn't here to share the happiest day in your lives. I'm sorry. After dinner, do you know what I'd love to do? I'd like to sit down, relax and look at the photo album of your wedding day. Donna, you must have been the most beautiful of brides.

Donna looks very upset. She looks to Cazzie, then Ambrose, then.

DONNA
(mumbling)
I'll... I'll get some more bread.

Donna exits into the house on the verge of tears.

AMBROSE
What did I say?

CAZZIE

You said the "m" word.

AMBROSE

Huh?

CAZZIE

Marriage.

AMBROSE

What about it?

CAZZIE

Donna and me, we're not married.

AMBROSE

But she... she set out this dinner, you're living together, you've known her for twenty years.

CAZZIE

We're not rushing into anything. We don't need a piece of paper to know we're together.

AMBROSE

Oh, my. Oh, my! It's just that, from what I saw, I assumed...

CAZZIE

It's not a problem. She'll have a good cry, I'll go in and talk to her, make everything all right. I'm gonna miss the beginning of the Met's game but I'll do it. It's just one more thing I gotta take care of.

AMBROSE

What do you mean?

CAZZIE

It means if something gets fucked up, I gotta take care of it. I never come home and people say "Welcome home, Cazzie. Look around, everything is okay." No, I always come home to problems. Shit I gotta take care of. I got three cases pending in court, my stupid-ass lawyer can't put two words together, assholes down the street owe me money for months, the drawbridge operators have no contract with the city, my crazy, fat neighbor is always on my back. Now Donna's hysterical cryin' upstairs. All this shit goes wrong and I gotta fix it. Do me a favor while you're here, will ya? When it comes to other people, could you at least make some small effort to be fuckin' sensitive?

The lights crash to black.

SCENE 2

It's early morning a few days later. The backyard is empty as we hear the SOUND of an approaching boat. Cazzie enters from the house eating a donut.

CAZZIE
All right!

Cazzie rushes to the water's edge as the boat draws nearer. The boat's ancient outboard motor gurgles and sputters loudly and a large cloud of engine fumes waft by.

CAZZIE *(cont'd)*
Bring it around to the port side!
(pause)
The port side!
(pause)
Port side. Port! Port! Port!
(pause)
The other port side!
(pause)
The left side!
(pause)
Left! Left! Bring it around to the left side!
(pause)
Your other left, you stupid, fuckin' idiot! Yes, that's it. On the left.

The boat is finally docked. The engine sputters and knocks as it stops.

DANZINGER enters.

DANZINGER
Jeez, I'm sorry about that, Cazzie. Port, starboard, right, left. I don't know why I can't get that right.

CAZZIE
Maybe it's because you're an idiot.

DANZINGER
(thinks, then)
No, that ain't it. It's a mental block. I can't remember what's port or starboard after thirty years at sea.

CAZZIE
"At sea?" That's what you call what you do? Being "at sea?"

DANZINGER
Well, I --

CAZZIE
(interrupts)
Cruising around City Island in that greasy, filthy boat of yours yelling

to women, "Hey, you wanna make my fishing pole longer?" That's what you call it? Being "at sea?!"

DANZINGER
Well, if you want to make it sound ugly like that.

LUNTZ enters carrying two large burlap bags from the boat.

LUNTZ
(sarcastic)
Thanks for helping me.

DANZINGER
We were talkin' nautical stuff.

Cazzie begins to examine the contents of the burlap bags, feeling and sniffing the contents lovingly.

CAZZIE
Good, good... you got it.

LUNTZ
And it wasn't easy. The Coast Guard almost caught us a coupla times.

DANZINGER
We were nervous as hell.

LUNTZ
What's the penalty for carryin' this stuff anyway?

CAZZIE
Who cares? They've got to catch you first.
(smelling)
Mmm... aw, man... this stuff is beautiful!

LUNTZ
All buds and flowers.

CAZZIE
Yeah.

DANZINGER
Primo stuff.

CAZZIE
You bet.

DANZINGER
Must be worth a lotta money to the right people.

CAZZIE
Uh huh.

LUNTZ
No stems or seeds.

CAZZIE
I know.

LUNTZ

No twigs, no leaves... just one hundred percent pure... roses.

Cazzie lifts out colorful handfuls of stemless roses.

DANZINGER

You were right, Cazzie. The big, yellow house in Darien. Nobody home, two, three hundred roses bushes just burstin' with flowers.

CAZZIE

You pick all these by hand?

DANZINGER

At first. But our hands were gettin' all cut up so we switched.

CAZZIE

To what?

DANZINGER

A machete.

CAZZIE

Good, good.

LUNTZ

This rose garden...

CAZZIE

Yeah?

LUNTZ

It don't look like a rose garden no more.

CAZZIE

Fuck 'em, they're rich.

DANZINGER

Yeah, fuck 'em.

LUNTZ

Fuck 'em.

CAZZIE

Fuck 'em.

LUNTZ

What do you want with all these roses anyway, Cazzie?

DANZINGER

Can you tell us now?

Cazzie looks around to make sure he isn't being overheard. Danzinger and Luntz look around as well then lean in close to Cazzie.

CAZZIE

Potpourri.

DANZINGER
(knowingly)
Aha, potpourri.

LUNTZ
(knowingly)
Potpourri.

DANZINGER
The ol' potpourri caper.

LUNTZ
Sounds like it.

DANZINGER
That oughta make a lotta dough.

LUNTZ
Potpourri always does.

DANZINGER
Potpourri. What the hell is potpourri?

CAZZIE
Fancy smellin' dried flowers and spices rich people keep around the house so it smells nice.

DANZINGER
What's wrong with spray cans?

LUNTZ
Yeah, what's wrong with spray cans?

CAZZIE
(mocking the rich)
It ain't "fancy" enough. It's not "natural." Assholes.

DANZINGER
Assholes.

LUNTZ
Assholes.

CAZZIE
Assholes.

Donna enters from the house carrying two cups of coffee.

DONNA
I thought I heard you guys. You're up early.

Danzinger and Luntz instantly segue into their very best behavior at the sight of Donna.

DANZINGER
Good morning, Miss DeMarco.

LUNTZ

I hope the noise of our craft did not wake you from a restful slumber.

DONNA

No, no... I've been up for a while. Coffee?

Danzinger and Luntz take their coffee.

DANZINGER

Thank you, Miss DeMarco.

LUNTZ

Thank you, ma'am.

DONNA

I wish you guys would just call me Donna.

DANZINGER

Please, we could never.

LUNTZ

It wouldn't be right.

DONNA

Oh, my God. Look at all the flowers. What's all this for?

LUNTZ

(sweetly)
Potpourri.

DANZINGER

(angrily at Luntz)
I was gonna tell her!

LUNTZ

I'm sorry.

DANZINGER

(sweetly to Donna)
It's potpourri.

DONNA

Potpourri? Who needs so much potpourri?

CAZZIE

We do. We're gonna make a fortune. I was in Bendell's on Fifth Avenue last week.

DONNA

What on earth were you doing in Bendell's?

CAZZIE

I had to pee! And while I was there I saw Calvin Klein Potpourri is selling like hotcakes for twenty-eight dollars. Twenty-eight dollars for a stinky gold box that holds an eighth of an ounce. That's three and a half thousand dollars a pound! Marijuana don't sell for that much.

DONNA

Cazzie, what are you up to?

CAZZIE

I'm gonna dry out these rose petals, get some red cedar shavings from the boat yard, eucalyptus, lavender, citrus peels, crap you find in the garbage. I'm gonna make Calvin Klein Potpourri.

DONNA

Oh, God, Cazzie, no! Not again!

CAZZIE

I found a guy in Jersey who's gonna print up the boxes for next to nothin'! I'll make a fortune. And it's legal. One hundred percent legal.

DONNA

Except for the boxes that say Calvin Klein and it's not.

CAZZIE

Boy, you sure love pissin' on my dreams, don't you?

DONNA

You're breaking the law. Cazzie, if they catch you, they'll put you in jail this time for sure.

CAZZIE

Aw!

DONNA

This isn't like selling pedigree puppies that are really mutts. These designer guys play rough.

DANZINGER

She's right. They've got a lotta lawyers.

CAZZIE

All I'm selling is stuff that smells nice! End of discussion!

DONNA

People don't pay big money because it's "stuff that smells nice." They pay big money because it's stuff that smells nice that Calvin Klein made.

CAZZIE

Oh, yeah, right, sure... Calvin Klein makes his own potpourri. He goes down to the factory personally. "Hey, we need another ton of cloves over here! More nutmeg!" We're through talkin' about this. End... of... discussion.

DONNA

You're going to get in trouble. You'll get arrested again and they'll look at all the other charges and they'll send you to jail for God-knows-how-long! You said this was going to end! But it never does... it only gets <u>worse</u>!

Donna exits into the house crying.

                          DANZINGER
God, she's upset.

                          LUNTZ
   (sadly)
Miss DeMarco cried and we were involved.

                          CAZZIE
She'll be all right when she sees the bucks roll in. You guys want a piece of this? I'll need someone to run loads to Boston, Philadelphia...

                          DANZINGER
Eh... I dunno...

                          LUNTZ
Seems kinda risky.

                          CAZZIE
Risky? Potpourri isn't a crime, it's a <u>smell</u>! Since when did you two become old ladies? Huh!

                          DANZINGER
Ten percent.

                          CAZZIE
For both.

                          DANZINGER
Each.

                          CAZZIE
You always split ten.

                          LUNTZ
Not this time.

                          CAZZIE
I'm not offering more. Take it or leave it.

                          DANZINGER
We'll leave it.

Ambrose enters eating an apple. He stands in the shadows and observes the following.

                          CAZZIE
Why are you breaking my balls like this? You guys have always split ten percent. Why's this different?

                          LUNTZ
Because when we're hangin' out at scummy, little bars, talkin' to truck drivers, tough guys and mobsters fresh outta prison, and they ask us "What scam are you guys runnin' these days?" We're gonna have to say "potpourri."

                          DANZINGER
Ten percent.

                              LUNTZ

Each.

                            DANZINGER

Our manhood is at stake.

                              CAZZIE

Deal. Now meet me here with the boat six AM Sunday. I know another house on the water in Sands Point with azaleas like you wouldn't believe. Go on, get outta here.

Danzinger and Luntz exit to the boat followed by engine sounds and exhaust fumes. Cazzie stores the bags under an overturned dingy as Ambrose surveys the backyard.

                             AMBROSE

Do you know what this backyard needs?

                              CAZZIE

Gasoline and a match.

                             AMBROSE

Grass. It cries for grass.

Ambrose inspects the ground more closely for a few beats.

                          AMBROSE *(cont'd)*

I'm going to plant grass here.

                              CAZZIE

You're gonna what?

                             AMBROSE

Plant grass. This backyard could be really pretty with some work.

                              CAZZIE

Ambrose, we're in the Bronx. There's nothin' pretty about anything. This isn't a backyard. It's a graveyard for old boat parts. Every time it rains we get another crop of rust. Besides, where you gonna find the time to do all this gardening? The church is probably gonna send you somewhere, right?

                             AMBROSE

Uh, well... I uh dunno 'bout that....

                              CAZZIE

You're still on vacation, is that it? Sabbatical, that's what they call it, right?

                             AMBROSE

I'm not on a sabbatical, Cazzie.

                              CAZZIE

You're not?

AMBROSE
No. This isn't a vacation. I was going to tell you when we go to church on Sunday.

CAZZIE
I don't go to church.

AMBROSE
Then I should tell you now.

CAZZIE
Tell me what?

AMBROSE
I'm not a priest anymore.

CAZZIE
What?

AMBROSE
I'm not a priest. Not for several months now.

CAZZIE
You left the order? After dad and I worked so hard to put you through seminary school? It cost eighteen thousand dollars and you just <u>quit</u>?!

AMBROSE
I didn't quit.

CAZZIE
Huh?

AMBROSE
I was kicked out.

CAZZIE
They kicked you out? From being a priest? We gave the church eighteen grand and then they kicked you out?

AMBROSE
Yes.

CAZZIE
They don't kick <u>anyone</u> out. They don't even kick out child molesters.

AMBROSE
Well, they kicked me out.

CAZZIE
But it's like temporary, right? Just for a while.

AMBROSE
According to the document they gave me…

CAZZIE
Yeah?

AMBROSE
It's… "Forever and for all time in perpetuity."

CAZZIE

That sounds kinda permanent.

AMBROSE

It's irreversible. I'm not a priest any longer. I can never be a priest ever again. I feel so degraded and humiliated. There's no describing my agony and shame.

There is a silent beat, then.

CAZZIE

Do you think we can get our money back from the seminary?

AMBROSE

I don't think the church offers refunds.

CAZZIE

What did you do? You fix a bingo game or something?

AMBROSE

Well, I was assigned to Tsu Tsng… a small farming village in China. The Cardinal had heard some reports about my parish and he came personally to inspect.

CAZZIE

What did he find?

AMBROSE

That, on harvest days, I tended not to wear my clerical collar. I worked in the fields with the peasants.

CAZZIE

He kicked you out for that?

AMBROSE

I also practice Yoga and Tai Chi purely for relaxation and exercise, but they also carry a religious significance and the Cardinal felt it was inappropriate.

CAZZIE

That's why he kicked you out?

AMBROSE

Not quite.

CAZZIE

Then why?

AMBROSE

I was married.

CAZZIE

That would do it.

AMBROSE

I wasn't "married" married. I married Jun Yi, a young girl. I had to.

301

CAZZIE

Had to?

AMBROSE

No, not that kind of had to. I was saving her from a fate worse than death.

CAZZIE

When you say young you mean...

AMBROSE

She was twenty.

CAZZIE

(brightens)

Ooo. Chinese... twenty... Go slow.

AMBROSE

There's nothing sexy about this, Cazzie. She was raped by a soldier. The Chinese are a very different culture. The soldier was caught and punished. He was given a fine. That's what they do in China. The girl, even though she was completely without blame, she was now "unclean" and of no value to her family. Staying in the village would only bring her family great shame and dishonor.

CAZZIE

But she didn't...

AMBROSE

Jun Yi was expected to go to the nearest big city and become a prostitute. Unless...

CAZZIE

Unless what?

AMBROSE

Unless someone honored her and took her as a wife. This would reverse everything for her and her family. She could stay in the village, with honor, and finish school.

CAZZIE

The Chinese, they're so fucked up.

AMBROSE

I never broke my vow of celibacy. We never had sex. I was the only one in the village with a VCR. Jun Yi and I spent our wedding night watching *Breakfast at Tiffany's*.

CAZZIE

God, Amby... you were married?

AMBROSE

I could not stand by and do nothing. The Cardinal said I should have prayed for Jun Yi. You don't pray for a baby in a burning building. You <u>do</u> something.

CAZZIE

Eighteen thousand dollars right down the drain.

AMBROSE

Would you stop talking about the money? This isn't about money. This is about life with dignity and honor. It's about doing what Christ would <u>want</u> us to do, what is right, what is moral, and good and decent and worthy.

CAZZIE

... closer to twenty thousand, actually.

AMBROSE

I'll pay you back. If it's that important to you, I'll pay you back every last cent.

CAZZIE

(sarcastic)

Sure. That'll be easy. Just get a job down the street at our local Tai Chi center! Or the store that sells sandals and turbans!

AMBROSE

I'll find a way to make a living. I've got a degree in psychology besides my theology degree. I could help people. People right here on City Island.

CAZZIE

People on City Island are already in therapy. It's called vodka.

AMBROSE

Then they really <u>do</u> need my help. I've run a great many twelve-step programs.

CAZZIE

City Island is too small for twelve steps. Seven, eight steps in any direction and you're in the water!

AMBROSE

No one is so far gone they can't be helped. I just had breakfast with Muriel. She's actually a very bright and interesting woman. But she's in a lot of pain, Cazzie. My heart goes out to her. She's crying for help.

CAZZIE

Oh, please.

AMBROSE

I'm serious. I want to help people like Muriel. Her diet is terrible. I'm teaching her how to eat healthy. And she's happy to learn. She's really a warm and sensitive and loving woman... down deep.

Muriel pops her head over the backyard fence.

MURIEL

Hey, Ambrose. I know I'm losin' weight and lookin' better. I just put out the garbage and I caught some guy lookin' at my ass! Yeah, staring right

at my butt!
>   *(makes a fist)*
> I clocked him! He's still unconscious! But my ass is lookin' better!

Muriel laughs and exits, Cazzie shoots Ambrose a look and the lights fade to black.

SCENE 3

It's night one month later. Ambrose and Muriel enter jogging. They are both wearing sweats. Muriel clearly seems to be going through a slow-but-sure transformation. Ambrose and Muriel jog in place as they perform a brief routine in unison.

AMBROSE

Okay... jog right, jog left. Arms up... arms down. Okay and... stop.

They stop jogging.

MURIEL

Whew! I feel <u>great</u>.

AMBROSE

You're making miraculous progress.

MURIEL

I feel so good physically and...

AMBROSE

And?

MURIEL

I don't know. I seem to have a different attitude. Like I don't want to reach down people's throats and rip their guts out anymore.

AMBROSE

That's good, Muriel. It's a good sign.

MURIEL

I think maybe I was tense. Do you think I was tense? I was tense.

AMBROSE

What makes you say that?

MURIEL

I used to yell, I used to scream... I robbed a liquor store.

AMBROSE

I see.

MURIEL

Well, not robbed, like I got a gun and held the place up. I caught the guy smirking at me so I called him an asshole and swiped a beef jerky without payin'.

AMBROSE

Why was he smirking at you?

MURIEL

I bought a magazine. *Large and Lovely Woman*. It's my favorite. I've always had a secret desire.

AMBROSE

Which is?

MURIEL

Naw, I can't.

AMBROSE

Of course you can.

MURIEL

You'll laugh at me.

AMBROSE

No, I won't. I promise.

MURIEL

Well, I've always wanted to be a model. You know... for queen-size fashions. Maybe I could do a spread in *Large and Lovely Woman*. Or I could do one of those fashion shows.
   (picturing herself)
Walk down the runway in some slinky, clingy French thing all dolled up and lookin'... pretty.
   (snapping out of it)
Stupid, huh?

AMBROSE

If it's your dream, it could never be stupid.

They hug as Donna enters from the house dressed in bedclothes.

MURIEL

You're a miracle.

AMBROSE

You're the miracle. Now don't forget to stretch.

MURIEL

Stretch... like a cat waking up from a nap. A non-fat yogurt, then prayers before I sleep.

Muriel exits.

DONNA

Who was that?

AMBROSE

Muriel.

DONNA

I know it was Muriel but what are you doing with her?

AMBROSE

Nothing. She was tired of being out of control, is all. I'm just helping her to take the reins, so to speak.
   (then)
Getting ready for bed?

DONNA

Not until Cazzie comes home.

AMBROSE

Warm enough?

DONNA

In this? Oh yeah. It's flannel. It's from Victoria's Secret. Although, if you look at their catalogue, there isn't much Victoria's keeping secret. Cazzie, he's always saying "How do you manage to find stuff that covers so much?"

(beat)

I just wish he'd call or something. Let me know he's okay. He probably went drinking with his creepy friends after work.

AMBROSE

Cazzie didn't go to work today.

DONNA

No?

AMBROSE

He's in court. All day. He was out here early this morning in a suit. Said he had to be in State Appellate Court.

DONNA

Oh.

AMBROSE

He didn't tell you?

DONNA

No, we've only lived together eighteen years. Why would he tell me where he's going? He probably thinks he told me where he was going. He'll say "I told you. I was standing right over here, you were standing over there." Cazzie never remembers what he said, he just remembers where everyone was standing when he said it. "I was over here, you were over there." So he was in court. He should've been home by now.

AMBROSE

He says it's minor.

DONNA

It's always minor.

AMBROSE

But with all the trouble he's had with the law he's never...

DONNA

Gone to jail? Never. It's amazing. He's got this lawyer, he's incredible. He gets his case postponed, delayed, moved back for this reason, that reason. His lawyer once got a postponement because he forgot his briefcase! By the time Cazzie's case comes up, the cop that arrested him is retired, the prosecutor is dead, it all happened so long ago nobody cares.

AMBROSE

I have to tell you, Donna, I find very little God in Cazzie's life.

DONNA

I have to tell you, Ambrose I find very little <u>sense</u> in Cazzie's life.

AMBROSE

God is sense. He makes perfect sense. But Cazzie, what's going on with him?

DONNA

Well, I think there are laws...

AMBROSE

Yes?

DONNA

And Cazzie breaks them.

(beat)

Well, I guess it could've been worse. I could've been waiting for him with a romantic dinner.

AMBROSE

I guess.

DONNA

You and Jun Yi... did you ever have a romantic dinner together?

AMBROSE

Cazzie told you?

DONNA

It sounds so romantic, Ambrose. Marrying a young girl to save her life. Did you ever have a romantic dinner together?

AMBROSE

Did we ever... Jun Yi and I, we weren't really married. Not in the eyes of the Catholic church.

DONNA

Uh hmm.

AMBROSE

It was entirely platonic. We were not husband and wife, not in the most meaningful sense of the word.

Donna simply smiles knowingly at Ambrose.

AMBROSE *(cont'd)*

We couldn't have a romantic dinner because the marriage was not based on romance. I loved Jun Yi, but in the same way I love all of God's children.

Donna smiles knowingly again.

AMBROSE *(cont'd)*
Of course... there were nights...

DONNA
Uh hmm...

AMBROSE
There were nights, when Jun Yi had made dinner, and I knew the dinner was a lot of work and she could have taken shortcuts, but she didn't. She had gone out of her way... for me. There were nights I was so grateful that I did not have to eat alone... again... grateful that there was this angelic face across the table from me. And every word she said sounded like music. And, if her words were music, then her laughter was a symphony. To look at her strengthened my faith in God because I knew only He could create someone so wise yet naive, so compassionate and truthful and beautiful. There were nights where I could not imagine ever being without her. We never touched the way married people do but there were nights she looked across the table and held my heart in her hand. Yes, we had romantic dinners together.

Cazzie enters from the street wearing a wilted suit and a matching expression.

DONNA
Cazzie.

AMBROSE
Ah, the victor returns.

CAZZIE
Huh? Oh hiya.

DONNA
Where've you been all night?

CAZZIE
I uh... I dunno... I've just been walking around and...

DONNA
What's the matter?

CAZZIE
Nothing.

AMBROSE
You look terrible.

CAZZIE
I'll be okay.

AMBROSE
How did it go in court today?

CAZZIE
Not good.

DONNA
Oh, my God. Did you get hit with a fine?

CAZZIE
It doesn't make any sense.

DONNA
What doesn't?

CAZZIE
Out of all the things I've done. It doesn't make any sense.

DONNA
You're scaring me. What are you talking about?

CAZZIE
I've sold illegal fireworks, counterfeit foodstamps, fake driver's licenses... you know, harmless stuff. Stuff that people need.

DONNA
And?

CAZZIE
And the thing that finally nails me is that frikkin' Calvin Klein potpourri! Damn, his lawyers are tough!

AMBROSE
What happened?

CAZZIE
These are lawyers for a clothing designer. You'd think they'd be easy to beat. You could distract them or... something. "Look! That lighting fixture. It's art deco!" Nothing. They just kept at it. Hammering away. Saying this to the judge and that to the judge. Police reports, witnesses, evidence!

DONNA
(worried)
They used evidence?

CAZZIE
Can you imagine? Like I was a criminal. There are so many people ripping off famous designers they decided to make an example of me.

DONNA
And they gave you a fine?

No reply.

DONNA *(cont'd)*
They gave you a fine, Cazzie? Tell me they gave you a fine!

Cazzie looks at Donna. She braces herself.

DONNA *(cont'd)*
How bad?

Cazzie sighs.

DONNA *(cont'd)*

How bad?

CAZZIE

Copyright and trademark infringement, interstate trafficking of illegal merchandise, unlawful enrichment, operating a business without a license...

DONNA

How bad?

No reply.

DONNA *(cont'd)*

How bad!

CAZZIE

Two to four years.

DONNA

(gasps)
Oh my God!

AMBROSE

God in heaven!

CAZZIE

But my lawyer says with good behavior I could be out in...

DONNA

(interrupts)
I <u>told</u> you! I <u>told</u> you something like this would happen! I asked you! I <u>begged</u> you! "Please! Stop with the con games and scams! You're going to get caught! You're gonna get in trouble!" Two to four years! We were going to get married, damn it! We were going to have <u>children</u>! Haven't you noticed? I'm not eighteen anymore! I want a family! You <u>promised</u> me a family!

CAZZIE

I swear to God, Donna on my mother's grave, the <u>day</u> I get out.

DONNA

I won't be able to have children in four years, you idiot! My biological clock is almost <u>shot</u>! Look what you've done to me, you son of a bitch! You've made me old, unmarried and childless! You had no right to do this to us! Like it's just you! It's not just you! It's not <u>your</u> life, it's <u>our</u> life! How did my life ever get so messed up! What did I ever do to deserve <u>you</u>?

CAZZIE

If you could take maybe two seconds to stop thinking of yourself here.

311

DONNA
I'm a good person. Why am I getting so little out of life! Why do I grovel for tiny things and wind up with nothing? Now you're telling me I'm going to get even <u>less</u>! You said we would get married! You said we would have babies! Lies! All of it was lies! Four years! Oh, God!

Donna breaks down in tears and exits into the house. Neither of the two men know what to say, finally.

CAZZIE
She's just upset.

AMBROSE
Four years, Cazzie?

CAZZIE
If I keep my nose clean - eight, maybe ten months. All I gotta do is behave, do what they tell me and stay away from guys who want to cuddle after the lights go out. You know what I'm talking about?

AMBROSE
Yes, I do. But I worked in a men's prison, and what you're talking about... you know... that happens to younger men.

CAZZIE
Hey, I might not be twenty anymore but I'm gonna make some of those guys crazy. I mean I stay in shape, I have nice eyes and I have a nice smile and...
    (realizing)
What am I <u>doing</u>! I'm trying to convince you I could turn on men in prison!

AMBROSE
Try and relax, Cazzie. Take a deep breath. Inhale...

CAZZIE
Fuck breathing! Listen to me... Ambrose, you've got to stay. You've got to stay and protect Donna.

AMBROSE
I'll stay, Cazzie.

CAZZIE
Even if it turns out I'm away longer than eight or ten months.

AMBROSE
I'm here for you, Cazzie. I'm your brother.

CAZZIE
Watch over Donna.

AMBROSE
Absolutely.

CAZZIE

Sometimes she tends to get emotional.

AMBROSE

I saw.

CAZZIE

Protect her.

AMBROSE

Day and night.

CAZZIE

Take care of her.

AMBROSE

I swear I will. On Mama's grave, I swear.

CAZZIE

And most important of all.

AMBROSE

Yes?

CAZZIE

Make sure she don't fuck no one.

AMBROSE

Cazzie.

Cazzie grabs Ambrose by the lapels and pulls him close.

CAZZIE

Promise me.

AMBROSE

I can't guarantee.

CAZZIE

Promise me.

AMBROSE

Cazzie.

CAZZIE

Do it.

AMBROSE

It wouldn't be-

CAZZIE

Do it!

AMBROSE

I'll try to-

CAZZIE

Swear it!

AMBROSE

Cazzie-

CAZZIE

Swear it!

AMBROSE

You're hurting me-

CAZZIE

I'll fuckin' kill ya! What do I care? I'm already goin' to prison!

AMBROSE

Cazzie…

CAZZIE

Swear Donna won't fuck no one.

AMBROSE

I…

CAZZIE

Swear it!

AMBROSE

Okay! Okay!

A satisfied Cazzie lets go of Ambrose.

CAZZIE

I'm sorry. It's just that the very thought of some guy… in bed with Donna… it makes me <u>nuts</u>.

AMBROSE

When do you have to show up?

CAZZIE

Tomorrow morning. Early. Hardly makes any sense to go to bed.

AMBROSE

You should try and get <u>some</u> rest, Cazzie.

CAZZIE

Naw…

AMBROSE

You want to be fresh your first day of prison.

Cazzie takes a few steps toward the house then stops.

AMBROSE *(cont'd)*

Go to her, Cazzie. She needs to be with you right now.

Cazzie stares at the house for the longest time, then.

CAZZIE

Will you send me cigarettes, stuff like that?

AMBROSE
I'll bring it... every visiting day.
> (beat)

Go on.

CAZZIE
My lawyer, he says the guys who show up first get the better cells.

AMBROSE
Leave that for tomorrow.

CAZZIE
The repeat offenders, the ones who have been in and out a dozen times, they show up the night before.

AMBROSE
Cazzie...

CAZZIE
They get the real good cells.

AMBROSE
No.

CAZZIE
Tell her... tell her I'm sorry.

AMBROSE
Cazzie…

Cazzie exits to the street.

AMBROSE *(cont'd)*
No, Cazzie, don't! Wait!
> (calling)

Cazzie! Cazzie!

Ambrose turns to see Donna standing inside the house behind the screen door. They look at each other and the lights fade to black.

END OF ACT ONE

ACT TWO

SCENE 4

It is morning nine months later and the backyard has been transformed into a tranquil Japanese garden. The rusty barbecue, lawn chairs and boat parts are gone. There is a winding path, a small ornamental bridge and a rock garden of smooth river stones. As we begin Ambrose, dressed in a Japanese Ghi, is leading Donna, Muriel, Danzinger and Luntz in a Tai Chi routine. Their silent ballet is a thing of beauty as they run through their routine flawlessly.

Donna, Muriel, Danzinger and Luntz seem to be in various stages of self improvement. Muriel wears stylish jogging sweats and leg warmers. She has had her hair done and she wears makeup. She is not an unattractive woman. Danzinger and Luntz have shaved, combed their hair and wear fresh clothing, a major improvement for both. Donna sports a new hairstyle.

When the group is done with their Tai Chi routine, they all turn to each other and bow in unison, then applaud and ad-lib congratulations to each other.

> DANZINGER
>
> Yeah!
>
> LUNTZ
>
> Good one!
>
> DONNA
>
> All right!
>
> MURIEL
>
> Woo!
>
> AMBROSE
>
> You're all doing so much better I can hardly find the words to express myself.
>
> LUNTZ
>
> Try "far out!"

They all laugh.

> DANZINGER
>
> "Awesome!"

They all laugh.

> MURIEL
>
> "Praise God!"
>
> DANZINGER
>
> "The Lord loves us!"

                            LUNTZ
All of us.
                           AMBROSE
Amen. Circle time, everyone.

They all sit, in a circle.

                       AMBROSE *(cont'd)*
For circle time today, I asked each of you to write down five positive things about yourselves. It can be one word, a sentence, or even a paragraph. Has anyone done their homework?

The others all raise their hands.

                       AMBROSE *(cont'd)*
Wow... everybody?
                          DANZINGER
Hey, we ain't messin' around.
                            LUNTZ
Only the weak and scared would fail to make a list.
                           MURIEL
Who's gonna go first?
                            DONNA
You, Muriel.
                          DANZINGER
Yeah, Muriel.
                           MURIEL
No no no... not me. Please. I'll go second but not first.
                           AMBROSE
Then who?

After a silent beat Donna raises her hand.

                            DONNA
I will.

They all applaud their support.

                           MURIEL
Yes, Donna.
                            LUNTZ
Go, Donna!
                          DANZINGER
Yeah!
                            DONNA
'Kay. Here goes.

(reading from her slip)

"Five positive things about me, Donna DeMarco: Pretty, good dancer, honest, hair salon manager, in love with Cashmere Marino."

They all applaud.

MURIEL

Woo!

DANZINGER

Yeah!

LUNTZ

Excellent!

DANZINGER

Love it!

MURIEL

What was that last one?

DONNA

In love?

MURIEL

No before that.

DONNA

Hair salon manager?

MURIEL

Yeah, what's going on?

DONNA

My boss is opening a beauty salon in Manhattan and he asked me to be the manager.

The others applaud.

MURIEL

You go, girl!

DANZINGER

Way to go!

LUNTZ

Woo!

MURIEL

I'm so happy for you!

DONNA

Thank you. Thank you so much. I knew my boss was looking for someone. But I didn't push it.

DANZINGER

Never push it.

MURIEL

Let it come to you.

DONNA

So I just stayed positive. I kept a warm, confident glow that drew people to me. I also knew it was out of my hands. God would decide.

DANZINGER

Amen.

LUNTZ

He always does.

MURIEL

Uh huh.

DONNA

God decided I should manage the new salon. And when my boss offered me the job I didn't go "Who me?" like I was surprised or unworthy.

LUNTZ

No way.

DANZINGER

Screw that.

DONNA

I smiled and said "Yes, Mister Vito. I would like that very much." I'm perfect for this job.

MURIEL

You are.

LUNTZ

You're perfect for everything.

DONNA

It means an extra two hours every day commuting to midtown but... I'm ready to take on more.

DANZINGER

You sure are!

LUNTZ

Go get 'em!

Again the group applauds and ad-libs congratulations as Muriel hugs Donna.

AMBROSE

May I have that slip of paper?

DONNA

Of course.

She hands the paper to Ambrose.

AMBROSE

I'd like to save it. It's a testament to how far you've come. Who's next?

MURIEL

Me. I want to go next. If that's okay with everyone.

LUNTZ

Go for it, Muriel.

DANZINGER

Yeah.

Muriel takes out a slip of paper.

MURIEL
(reading)
"Five good things about me, Muriel Grecco, by Muriel Grecco. Large and lovely..." That counts as one thing, not two. "Poet, good for cold winter nights, can bait a hook, potential model."

The group applauds.

LUNTZ

Yeah!

DANZINGER

Woo!

DONNA

That's a great list, Muriel.

AMBROSE

And what was that about a potential model?

MURIEL

I got a call. From a show business agent. She saw my pictures.

DANZINGER

I took 'em.

LUNTZ

He's got a good camera.

DANZINGER

Found it on a bus.

MURIEL

She wants to see me tomorrow. She thinks she can get me into the high-paying, jet-set, super-trendy world of large and lovely modeling!

The group erupts into wild applause.

DONNA

It's going to happen for you, Muriel. I just know it. It's really going to happen for you.

MURIEL

You think so?

DONNA

Yes. Just stay the way you've been. Confident, sincere, friendly... It's going to happen for you.

MURIEL

Oh, Donna!

AMBROSE

We've got time for one more before our prayer.

DANZINGER

(to Luntz)
Do you mind?

LUNTZ

Be my guest.

Danzinger takes out a slip of paper.

DANZINGER

(reading)
"Five positive things about me in one word, a phrase or even a sentence. By Tyrone Danzinger: One, never killed a dog; two, I own a lot of tools; three, I use sunscreen, a lotta guys don't bother but I do; four, I once give a homeless guy three dollars; and five..."

Danzinger looks directly at Muriel.

DANZINGER (cont'd)

"...utterly and hopelessly in love with a woman who takes the clay of my fears and sculpts them into children at play."

Muriel blushes and turns away as the others react silently. Finally.

DONNA

Wow...

LUNTZ

Yikes...

DANZINGER

You said it could be a whole sentence.

AMBROSE

Yes, Tyrone, I did. And a very fine sentence it was. All of your lists were wonderful. You're taking on new challenges, new adventures...

LUNTZ

We're driving Muriel to Manhattan when she meets with the agent.

AMBROSE

Wonderful.

LUNTZ

I've never been to Manhattan.

DANZINGER

You'll love it, Lyle. You're a Manhattan kind of guy.

DONNA

When I manage the salon you can drop by for lunch.

LUNTZ

(emotional)
Oh, my God!

AMBROSE

What?

LUNTZ

(choked up)
I've never dropped by for lunch! It sounds complicated!

MURIEL

It's easy, and it's fun. You'll see.

Danzinger comforts Luntz.

DANZINGER

Also, while we're downtown, Lyle and I are gonna buy a business license.

The others applaud.

AMBROSE

Excellent.

LUNTZ

Yeah!

DONNA

That's great.

LUNTZ

We're goin' legit.

DANZINGER

We found a guy. Buys discontinued shoes, perfume, makeup, books, records, pens by the ton. You buy say, discontinued tooth brushes at ten cents a piece, you sell them at a flea market for a buck, you're making nine hundred percent.

LUNTZ

High volume, low overhead.

DANZINGER

People are getting a product they need at a low price...

LUNTZ

(a previously unknown fact)
Did you know? A lot of people brush their teeth.

AMBROSE

I've heard.

                             DANZINGER
And we're making a legitimate living.

                              AMBROSE
You'll never have to worry about being arrested.

                             DANZINGER
And that's a good thing.
        (eyes only for Muriel)
A man has to think of the future.

Muriel blushes.

                              AMBROSE
Let us join hands for our prayer.

They do.

                          AMBROSE (cont'd)
Lord, You have smiled on each and every one of us. We are eternally grateful for Your generosity. May You give us the strength to carry out Your plan.

                                ALL
Amen.

                              AMBROSE
And now, one minute of silence as we thank the Lord and ask for His blessing.

They all bow their heads in silence. After several beats Cazzie enters from the street. He's wearing a suit and carries a small suitcase. He's fresh out of prison and he looks plenty happy to be home.

                               CAZZIE
Tah-dah!

No response.

                           CAZZIE (cont'd)
        (sing-songy)
I'm home!

No response. Cazzie surveys the group more closely.

                           CAZZIE (cont'd)
What's the matter? Someone drop a contact lens?

No response.

                           CAZZIE (cont'd)
Hey, I'm home.

No response.

CAZZIE *(cont'd)*

I got out two days early. They had so many new murderers they let us non-violent guys out.

No response.

CAZZIE *(cont'd)*

What's going on?

No response.

CAZZIE *(cont'd)*
(yelling)
Hey! I'm home, damn it!

The group is done with its silent prayer.

AMBROSE

Amen.

ALL

Amen.

The group climbs to their feet and Cazzie readies himself for a warm welcome.

CAZZIE

Donna, baby!

Donna and the others engage in a series of individual hugs, none of which involve Cazzie.

VARIOUS

You're so strong.

Good luck.

I learn so much from you.

God bless you.

Your courage is amazing.

Meanwhile.

CAZZIE

What the fuck is going on? Don't rush over here all at once or nothin'. I only just got out of prison. No, I didn't get raped, thank you. Not that I didn't have any offers!

The group is finally done with its meeting.

LUNTZ

Hey, everyone... it's Cazzie.

Cazzie opens his arms expectantly.

CAZZIE
(to Donna)
Heh heh heh! C'mere, sweet meat.

Danzinger and Luntz cross to Cazzie. Danzinger hugs Cazzie.

DANZINGER
Welcome home, Cashmere.

CAZZIE
Who are you?

DANZINGER
It's me.

CAZZIE
Danzinger?

DANZINGER
Tyrone.

CAZZIE
Tyrone? I didn't even know you had a first name.

DANZINGER
Well, I do and it's Tyrone. Some of my friends even call me Ty.

CAZZIE
Ty?
(examines Luntz)
And who's this? Biff?

Danzinger and Luntz share a laugh. Luntz hugs Cazzie.

LUNTZ
Hi, Cazzie.

CAZZIE
What happened to you guys? Where's your grease?

Muriel crosses to Cazzie and hugs him.

MURIEL
Welcome home, Cashmere Marino.

CAZZIE
(surprised)
Muriel... you're a woman.

DANZINGER
One heck of a woman.

CAZZIE
What's going on with you people? What happened to the backyard?

LUNTZ
It's a Japanese garden now.

MURIEL

We built it together.

DANZINGER

Every Japanese garden tells a story.

MURIEL

This one tells the story of two snow geese separated by a storm and...

CAZZIE

(sarcastic)
Yeah yeah yeah! Of course it does. Any fool could see that!

Ambrose crosses to Cazzie and hugs him.

AMBROSE

Welcome home, brother.

CAZZIE

Yeah yeah. Nice to see you, too. You know I came over the drawbridge and it was covered with rust. Whoever the city got to fill in for me while I was gone screwed up bad. I'll skin the son of a bitch alive. Donna, are you ever gonna say hello or what?

DONNA

Hi, Cazzie.

Donna crosses to Cazzie and gives him a cool, standoffish hug.

CAZZIE

Hello! Tyrone hugged me better than that!

DONNA

That's the best I can do, right now.

CAZZIE

(brightening)
Oh, I get it. Too many people around, huh? Well, we'll try a hug when everyone leaves because that was like hugging a Republican. Better yet, let's skip the hugging, go right upstairs and --

AMBROSE

(interrupts)
Uh... why don't we let Cazzie and Donna get reacquainted?

MURIEL

I'll make us all some camomile tea.

LUNTZ

With the little cookies?

MURIEL

Uh hmm.

DANZINGER

Love the little cookies!

Ambrose, Danzinger, Luntz and Muriel all exit as an astonished Cazzie watches on.

CAZZIE

What the hell happened to them?

DONNA

They're just happy.

CAZZIE

Happy? This is the Bronx. No one's happy! Miss me?

DONNA

Well, it's not like I haven't seen you, Cazzie. I visited you every week.

CAZZIE

I know. And after five months I made the warden's list and was able to get conjugal visits.

DONNA

Uh... yeah.

CAZZIE

Except on those conjugal visits... you and I... we didn't do much conjugating.

DONNA

I wasn't ready.

CAZZIE

I was in prison. I was plenty ready.

Donna reacts hurt.

CAZZIE *(cont'd)*

I know. It's probably not easy for a woman to have sex with her man in a prison. The bars, graffiti, guys screaming, a toilet right next to the bed. It's not what some gals would call romantic. C'mon, let's go up to our bedroom. We'll make up for lost time.

Cazzie takes Donna by the hand and leads her to the house. She stops.

DONNA

Cazzie.

CAZZIE

What?

DONNA

It's not our bedroom any more.

CAZZIE

Huh?

DONNA

It's your bedroom.

CAZZIE

Our bedroom, your bedroom, I don't care if we call it the garage as long as we're having sex in it. C'mon. I'm so horny the crack of dawn isn't safe.

DONNA

Cazzie!

CAZZIE

(annoyed)

What!

DONNA

I moved out of the house. I'm living with Muriel now. I took my clothes and my books... and my copper pans that I bought with my own money... and my mother's furniture and some other things and, for the time being, I've moved in with Muriel. Muriel is renting me a room. For now. It's not forever... but for now. You know... me living at Muriel's.

There is a long silent pause, then.

CAZZIE

I'm not getting laid, am I?

DONNA

That's not what this is about.

CAZZIE

Oh, I'll learn what this is about. Eventually. I don't doubt that. That's the long term objective of this conversation. But for now, at this moment, the short term objective is I'm not getting laid, am I?

DONNA

This isn't a matter of -

CAZZIE

I don't know what's goin' on.

DONNA

Cazzie -

CAZZIE

But I do know I'm not getting laid.

DONNA

This isn't about sexual blackmail.

CAZZIE

Hello! There's words I don't even understand! This is tried and true from caveman times! Before, even! When a woman uses words a man doesn't even understand... he's not getting laid.

DONNA

Cazzie -

CAZZIE

Just tell me it's true. My body has certain expectations. Tell my blood it can go back to where it was before.

DONNA

God, you're home not even five minutes and you're already bullying me.

CAZZIE

Do you want to tell me what this bullshit is all about?

DONNA

It's not bullshit, Cazzie. It's my life.

CAZZIE

Excuse me. Do you want to tell me what's going on in your life?

DONNA

Yes.

CAZZIE

Good.

DONNA

But you have to promise me not to interrupt or to bully me or make fun of me. Because, if you do -

CAZZIE

Yeah?

DONNA

I'll just stop talking and go back to Muriel's.

CAZZIE

You will, eh?

DONNA

Yes, I will.

CAZZIE

I'm in prison ten months and this is what I come home to.

DONNA

Well, you're going to have to listen, Cazzie, because I've been in prison a lot longer.

CAZZIE

Okay. I'm listening. I'm not making fun or anything. I'm just listening.

DONNA

Okay. The first thing I want you to know, Cazzie, is that I love you. I love you very, very much. I have always loved you, ever since high school I have been in love with you.

CAZZIE

You love me so much you moved out?

DONNA

Don't do that.

CAZZIE

Sorry.

DONNA

I have always let you be the leader in our relationship. As long as you were feasting at the table of life I was content to sit at your side and eat the crumbs. I'm sorry.

CAZZIE

Huh?

DONNA

I'm sorry because I misled you. My needs are not crumbs. My needs are every bit as important as yours. My needs are the bread of my life and I have been starving for years. I need to be taken seriously. I need to be listened to. I need for you not to laugh at me even if I do say something stupid. When you're driving like a maniac -- and you do drive like a maniac -- and I beg you to slow down, I need for you to slow down... not laugh at me! I need to know everything you're thinking and feeling because that's what I have given you every day of my life. I don't want to be treated like crap. I want to be treated like someone special. What I want, in my heart, is not silly or frivolous or stupid... it's real. I've covered it up to please you and it's been killing me. This time away from you has been good for me. I've had time alone and I know things about myself. I'm a good person. I'm warm and intelligent and attractive. What I want in my life is to be treated with respect and affection. I'm special and I'm beyond being just some guy's girlfriend. What I want, what I deserve... is marriage and children.

Cazzie rolls his eyes knowingly.

DONNA (cont'd)

No no no... this isn't what you think it is, Cazzie. This is not an ultimatum for you to marry me. If you think I'm trying to get you to say those magic words "Oh, okay... I guess I'll marry you" you're wrong. You've got to want to marry me, Cazzie. Because it's right. Because you can't have it any other way. Because you love me that much. Because it's hurting you inside not to be married to me. I'm getting ready to have what I deserve. I will be married to someone who adores me and gives me babies. It might be you... it might not. If you're not ready to be with me... then I'm getting ready to be without you. I don't want that to happen. But if it does, I'm not afraid of it. Not anymore. I'm done now.

There is a long pause, then.

CAZZIE

I'm really not getting laid.

DONNA

This isn't about sex. This is about us.

CAZZIE

So what was it?

DONNA

What was what?

CAZZIE

What was it I did to you that would make you talk to me like this?

DONNA

Talk to you like... I didn't talk bad to you.

CAZZIE

I treat you like, and I quote, "crap?"

DONNA

Well, you do.

CAZZIE

Taking you in like I did? After your mother died? That was treating you like crap?

DONNA

I wasn't an orphan. I could've lived with my cousin Connie.

CAZZIE

Taking care of you when you were sick?

DONNA

I took care of you, too.

CAZZIE

Giving you a car? I guess that was treating you like crap? Huh? Giving you a car?

DONNA

It was a Chevy Vega, and speaking of crap, the car was crap. General Motors can kiss my ass before I ever buy another one of their cars.

CAZZIE

But you didn't "buy" the car, did you? I gave it to you. That was treating you like crap? Converting the back bedroom into a sewing room for you... boy I really treated you like crap then.

DONNA

Converting? You moved in an old chair and threw a quilt on it!

CAZZIE

I put up a shelf!

DONNA

Excuse me, Bob Villa.

CAZZIE

Your family reunion. In Boston! Who drove you all the way there, then -

DONNA

I'm not getting into this.

CAZZIE
I wasn't finished.

DONNA
Yes, you were! See what you're doing? You're not going to listen to anything I say. Instead you're going to pick out one little thing and harp on it, pick on it, blow it way out of proportion. I said "you treat me like crap" and you're going to confront me on that so we don't have to talk about the real issue... the bigger thing!

CAZZIE
Which is what!

DONNA
You don't cherish me!

CAZZIE
The fuck I do! If I didn't cherish you, would I take you to Atlantic City when I go? Huh? Who gave you a hundred bucks in quarters? Huh? Huh!

DONNA
This is baby-arguing. Who did what for who and when. "I took you here, I gave you this." It's for babies. Don't you get any of what I've said, Cazzie?

CAZZIE
All I know is I just got out of prison and I gotta hear this.

DONNA
When's a good time for this? Next week? There's never a good time. If you can't tell how hurt I am, if you can't see the pain I'm in, I've been with the wrong man all these years.

CAZZIE
I treat you like crap. The world treats me like crap. Ever hear me complain? Huh? I just take it because I know, deep in my heart, life sucks.

DONNA
Is that all you can say? You treat me like crap because the world does the same to you? Don't you have anything else to say?

Donna looks to Cazzie but he turns away. Finally.

DONNA *(cont'd)*
I got offered a job downtown. A good one. I'm going to take it. There's an apartment nearby. I'm getting a U-Haul tomorrow. I'm moving downtown.

Donna begins to exit to Muriel's, but stops.

DONNA *(cont'd)*
You know, I dreaded this very moment for eighteen years. And now that it's here it's pretty bad.

(beat)
But it ain't <u>that</u> bad.

Donna exits. Cazzie begins to pace in amazement and he backs into some wind chimes. He tries to silence them but they only make more noise. He winds up angrily yanking them down. He gives them a mighty heave into Long Island Sound.

After a few beats, Ambrose enters.

AMBROSE
Howdy. You and Donna finish talking? Guess so. Get this. I was at the park and there were two boys about ten playing soccer. It turns out City Island has no children's soccer team. If I could get five or six other kids who -

CAZZIE
What did you do?

AMBROSE
Nothing yet. I need five or six more children, then I'll -

CAZZIE
What did you do to Donna?

AMBROSE
Donna? I did nothing. I just have a little group. No name for it actually. Just a few people who want to -

CAZZIE
I asked you to look out for her.

AMBROSE
And I did. Her diet was terrible. She also wasn't getting enough exercise for a woman her age.

CAZZIE
I asked you to take care of my woman!

AMBROSE
I did. I took very good care of her. And, as far as I can tell, she had sex with no one.

CAZZIE
Well, if you took such good care of her...

AMBROSE
Yeah?

CAZZIE
Why is she leaving me?!

AMBROSE
Oh, did that happen?

CAZZIE

Yes, that pesky little thing happened! She gave me nine miles of self-improvement psycho babble and now she's getting a U-Haul.

AMBROSE

Cazzie, it's not my place to say anything -- this is between you and Donna -- but I can say this without breaking any confidences. Donna is in a lot of emotional pain. I think if you -

Cazzie lunges at Ambrose and grabs him by the lapels.

CAZZIE

What did you do to her!

AMBROSE

(gasping)
Nothing.

CAZZIE

She's not the same!

AMBROSE

(gasping)
She's better.

CAZZIE

She's leaving me!

AMBROSE

(gasping)
So?

CAZZIE

So that don't look like "better" to me!

AMBROSE

Cazzie -

CAZZIE

You poisoned her mind against me!

AMBROSE

(gasping)
No, I just... Cazzie, let go. You're choking me...

Cazzie lets go.

AMBROSE *(cont'd)*

I didn't poison her against you. We never talked about you. We talked about her... Donna. How she felt about herself and her life. Not you.

Cazzie gets ready to fight. He takes off his jacket and tie and rolls up his sleeves.

CAZZIE

Last time I was here everything was fine. Now my backyard is full of paper lanterns hangin' over a Chinese bridge, fat, ugly people are eating little cookies and my woman is gone!

CAZZIE
What are you going to do?

CAZZIE
You'll see, Mister Self Improvement. I'm gonna teach you to never mess with what's mine again!

Cazzie takes a swing at Ambrose but Ambrose manages to step away from it easily with a martial-arts move.

CAZZIE (cont'd)
Son of a bitch!

AMBROSE
This is called denial.

CAZZIE
This is called an uppercut!

Cazzie tries to hit Ambrose a second, third and fourth time but Ambrose makes a slick defensive move each time.

AMBROSE
Give it up, Cazzie... I'm a third degree black belt in Tai Chi. There's no way you can hurt me.

CAZZIE
Oh, yeah?

Cazzie grabs a rung from the stair banister and rips it out. He swings the weapon at Ambrose.

AMBROSE
Put that down.

CAZZIE
I will. Right after the ambulance gets here.

Cazzie tries to hit Ambrose again and again and again but, each time, Ambrose deftly slips out of the way.

AMBROSE
Give it up, Cazzie.

CAZZIE
You dirty...

AMBROSE
Just stop!

CAZZIE
Frikkin'...

AMBROSE
Stop!

CAZZIE
C'mon! Fight like a man!

AMBROSE
No, I won't hit you back.

CAZZIE
Asshole!

AMBROSE
You can't make me angry.

CAZZIE
Loser!

AMBROSE
Call me all the names you'd like.

CAZZIE
Weirdo. Freak. Jackass.

AMBROSE
Whatever.

CAZZIE
At least I never left my woman!

AMBROSE
What?

CAZZIE
You left yours half way around the world!

Ambrose punches Cazzie in the stomach with a punch Cazzie never saw coming. Cazzie doubles over in pain.

CAZZIE *(cont'd))*
Argh!

AMBROSE
Oh my God! I hit someone! Look what you made me do!

CAZZIE
(gasping)
I'm sorry...

AMBROSE
I've never hit anyone!

CAZZIE
Could've fooled me.

AMBROSE
You're not supposed to strike anyone in Tai Chi.

CAZZIE
Get your money back for the lessons.

AMBROSE

You made me angry. I struck you out of anger.

CAZZIE

You gang bangers are all alike.

AMBROSE

You can't treat Donna the way Daddy used to treat Momma. Momma may have loved Daddy but mostly... she was afraid of him. You can't do the same. You can't try to dominate her. It's not love. It's fear.

CAZZIE

Get out of my sight.

AMBROSE

I...

CAZZIE

(screams)

Get out!!!

Ambrose sadly exits as a wounded Cazzie slowly climbs to his feet.

SCENE 5

It's early the next morning. Cazzie enters from the street. He's carrying an extremely large and heavy cast iron gear. Cazzie's coveralls are smeared with grease, as is his face. Cazzie staggers to a corner of the yard where he drops the ancient piece of machinery and covers it with leaves and dirt and whatever else is handy. Satisfied, Cazzie now staggers exhausted to a chair where he sits. From time to time, we hear the faint SOUNDS of angry car horns in the distance.

DONNA (O.S.)
I'll see if he's ready...

Cazzie quickly picks up a newspaper laying nearby, opens it and pretends to read as Donna enters from the street. She breaks her stride and stiffens when she sees Cazzie. Donna expects a confrontation, but Cazzie merely smiles. Donna reacts curious then crosses to the back door. She knocks. Ambrose enters from inside the house.

AMBROSE
Oh, hi... I was just coming over. Have you started?

DONNA
Yeah. Muriel went to the A&P to get some more boxes. Tyrone and Eugene are trying to move my mother's piano but it's so heavy.

AMBROSE
I'll help. Old pianos... they weigh a ton.

Donna and Ambrose begin to exit back to the street.

CAZZIE
Need help?

AMBROSE
Excuse me?

CAZZIE
I asked if you need any help.

AMBROSE
Uh...

DONNA
It'll be okay. We have everyone we need.

CAZZIE
Your mom's piano is pretty heavy.

DONNA
We'll get it on the truck.

CAZZIE
Sure you don't need some help?

DONNA
Positive.

CAZZIE

Once the truck is loaded, you're headed downtown?

DONNA

Uh huh. If I get any mail you can give it to Muriel.

CAZZIE

You're not leaving me your new address?

DONNA

So you can stalk me? I don't think so. I like to <u>watch</u> those police reenactment shows on TV... not <u>live</u> them.

CAZZIE

Then this is goodbye.

DONNA

I suppose it is.

CAZZIE

Goodbye forever.

DONNA

If you want to put it that way.

CAZZIE

Don't you want to say goodbye?

DONNA

Goodbye.

CAZZIE

Not like that. A real goodbye.

Cazzie offers his hand. Donna looks to Ambrose.

AMBROSE

It's a good sign. It shows a lot of emotional maturity on Cazzie's part.

CAZZIE

No sense in parting mortal enemies.

Donna crosses to Cazzie hesitantly.

CAZZIE *(cont'd)*

We'll make a clean break of it. Remember the good times, forget the bad.

AMBROSE

That's very healthy talk.

DONNA

(suspicious)
Too healthy.

CAZZIE

It didn't work out. Now we say goodbye.

DONNA
I'm not kissing you. Not even a little peck...

CAZZIE
I don't expect you to.

DONNA
You'd only turn it into some sloppy mouth kiss with your tongue down my throat.

CAZZIE
Goodbye, Donna. Good luck with your new life.

Donna shakes Cazzie's hand.

DONNA
Goodbye, Cazzie. Good luck with your old life.

Muriel enters excitedly. She's carrying two or three empty boxes.

MURIEL
You should see! City Island Avenue... it's backed up for blocks!

AMBROSE
Are those all the horns we've been hearing?

MURIEL
There must be a hundred cars. They're backed up from the bridge to the A&P.

Danzinger and Luntz enter from the street.

DANZINGER
You guys hear the car horns?

LUNTZ
Something's going on.

Luntz walks to the water's edge and peers into the distance.

DANZINGER
Joey Bovasso was driving his plumbing truck back home. Said City Island Avenue is at a standstill.

LUNTZ
Hey, the bridge is up.

AMBROSE
It's what?

LUNTZ
The drawbridge. It's up.

Donna, Ambrose, Muriel and Danzinger join Luntz and see for themselves.

DANZINGER
It's up all right.

MURIEL
I don't see any boats going through.

AMBROSE
Look at the cars waiting to get on the island.

DANZINGER
Look at the cars waiting to get <u>off</u> the island.

LUNTZ
Hey, Cazzie… if someone's filling in for you today he's screwing up bad.

Cazzie's smirk tells Donna everything.

DONNA
There's no one filling in for Cazzie today.

DANZINGER
There has to be. Why else would he be home when the bridge is up?
    (catching on)
Oh, no.

AMBROSE
Cazzie, you didn't.

CAZZIE
    (innocent)
I didn't what?

MURIEL
You raised the bridge and left it up?

CAZZIE
Why would I do a thing like that?

LUNTZ
So Donna can't get off the island.

MURIEL
You're disgusting.

DANZINGER
Well, it's not gonna work, Cazzie.

CAZZIE
What are you talking about?

LUNTZ
We'll break into the control booth and lower the bridge ourselves.

DANZINGER
We've seen the levers. Up… down… It's not exactly heart surgery.
    (to Luntz)
Come on, Eugene.

LUNTZ
Right behind you, Tyrone.

Danzinger and Luntz go to exit but stop when...

DONNA

No.

DANZINGER

What?

DONNA

Cazzie's already thought of that. He's fixed it so you can't lower the bridge.

MURIEL

How could he do that?

DONNA

I don't know, but he did. Didn't you, Cazzie?

Cazzie only smiles.

DONNA (cont'd)

He broke a switch or he took a fuse that's hard to replace.

CAZZIE

(realizing)

A fuse!

DONNA

And you could break into the control booth and fiddle with the dials and buttons from now until Christmas... but the bridge isn't going to budge. Is it, Cazzie?

Cazzie only smiles.

MURIEL

(time to get tough)

All right, all right, all right... this is cute, Marino, but enough is enough. Four hours from now I'm due in midtown Manhattan. Manhattan... that's on the other side of the bridge! I'm meeting with an agent. A modeling agent. Hear me? Mod-del-ing! She's gonna represent me in the high paying, jet-set, trendy world of large and lovely modeling. Now, I'm going home, I'm gonna plug in my electric curlers and file some dead skin off my feet. I'm gonna do my makeup and iron my outfit, get my hair ready, then come back out... and so help me God... when I'm ready to go...

CAZZIE

Yeah?

MURIEL

(explodes)

That bridge better be down!!!

CAZZIE

Sorry.

MURIEL

He won't do it.

LUNTZ

Muriel, Tyrone and I can take you to Manhattan in our boat.

MURIEL

(sweetly)
Well, that would be nice, Eugene, especially if I wanted to look...
(explodes)
... like I was hit by a typhoon! Do you know what I'd look like! Two hours in an open boat! I have a beauty standard to maintain!

Danzinger crosses to Muriel and comforts her.

DANZINGER

Shh... easy...

MURIEL

I'd look like a sheep dog!

DANZINGER

Muriel, please...

MURIEL

Like I spent the night in a blender!

DANZINGER

Muriel...

Muriel pulls herself together.

MURIEL

I'm sorry. I... I fell off my center.

LUNTZ

It's all right.

MURIEL

I've waited my whole life for this day!

DANZINGER

Cazzie, while Muriel is meeting with the agent, Eugene and I were gonna go downtown to City Hall. We were gonna get a business license.

CAZZIE

Aha.

LUNTZ

We're goin' legit.

DANZINGER

We're going to sell the boat, get a small truck, work the flea markets and street fairs selling discontinued items.

LUNTZ

We're gonna be the kings of toothbrushes and discontinued cosmetics.

CAZZIE

Aha.

DANZINGER

We go back a long time, the three of us, Cazzie. To junior high. Remember the day we met, in the cafeteria?

CAZZIE

Yup, my slice of pizza fell on the floor face down. You ate it.

DANZINGER

That was a long time ago. We've done a lot of business, too. We made a lotta dough, made you a lotta dough.

CAZZIE

That you did, Danzinger. That you did.

LUNTZ

A lot of times the cops arrested us we never even thought of givin' them your name. We never said nothin'.

CAZZIE

I appreciate that.

DANZINGER

So I'm asking you, as a friend, as someone who's known you for almost twenty-five years... please, let the bridge down.

CAZZIE

Tyrone.

DANZINGER

Yes?

CAZZIE

Eugene.

LUNTZ

Yeah?

CAZZIE

Go to hell.

Chaos breaks out. Muriel and Luntz threaten to fight Cazzie. Cazzie springs to his feet and threatens to fight back. Ambrose and Danzinger try to stop a fight from happening. Donna screams to various people to stop.

CAZZIE *(cont'd)*

Hey!!!

They all stop.

CAZZIE *(cont'd)*

I'm so good-and-Goddamn-glad all of you got in touch with your...
    (with disgust)
... feelings... I guess now the world is supposed to lay down at your

feet because you know what it's like to feel yourself feeling your feelings. Well, I gotta feeling for you. Try <u>frustration</u> with a side of <u>agony</u>! You might've changed, but life didn't. It still sucks! You don't believe me? Well, I built a monument to how much it sucks. A five hundred ton, cast-iron drawbridge that nobody's goin' over. Nobody! I spent ten months in prison, the worst ten months of my life! I come home and my girlfriend, the woman I almost married a dozen times, tells me <u>she's</u> the one who's been in prison because I'm not <u>nice</u> enough to her. I can go to hell, huh? I can go to hell? No. All of <u>you</u> can go to hell! You want to get off City Island. Well, we all want something. It doesn't mean we're gonna get it.

Cazzie sits down and resumes reading his newspaper.

AMBROSE
Cazzie, they'll arrest you.

CAZZIE
I don't care.

AMBROSE
They'll find out what you did and put you right back in prison.

CAZZIE
Fine. I won't have to learn everyone's name again. There's Spike, Lenny the Enforcer, Nazi Nick, Blade, Psycho, lovely guy.

DONNA
What are you thinking, Cazzie? That I'll be trapped here on City Island for so long that I'll change my mind? Realize how much I'll miss you and stay?

CAZZIE
Sounds like a plan.

DONNA
Well, that's the single stupidest, most pathetic thing I've ever heard in my life.

CAZZIE
Well, if it's such a stupid plan...

DONNA
Yeah?

CAZZIE
How come you're still here?

DONNA
I don't believe it!

CAZZIE
I know you. You're not goin' anywhere without your mother's furniture. Especially the piano. And your stuff. The seven thousand cubic yards of stuff that you own. You could never leave without your precious stuff.

DONNA
You know... I was prepared to leave this island and still love you, Cazzie.

CAZZIE
Yeah, right sure. Leave me and love me. Very popular concept. Very "now." Simply everyone is leaving the person they love.

DONNA
Now, I'm just going to leave and not love you at all.

CAZZIE
You're bluffin'.

DONNA
This is not a poker game! It's my life! Tyrone, Eugene... would you take me to the other side of the bridge in your boat?

DANZINGER
Certainly.

LUNTZ
One ride comin' up.

Danzinger and Luntz exit to the unseen dock.

DONNA
I'll go to the other side of the bridge, Cazzie. I'll get the bus at Orchard Beach, take the bus to the subway. I'll be downtown in two hours.

Danzinger and Luntz enter in a panic.

DANZINGER
Our boat sank!

LUNTZ
It's in six feet of water!

Danzinger and Luntz look at each other, then realize what's happened. They turn to Cazzie with hatred.

DANZINGER
You!

LUNTZ
You!

CAZZIE
Something wrong?

DANZINGER
You sank our boat!

CAZZIE
It was an act of mercy, believe me.

LUNTZ
You actually sank our boat!

CAZZIE
It's not like I put a hole in it or anything. I just scooped a lotta water into it. You just gotta scoop it out.

DONNA
Cazzie, this is City Island! There's a thousand boats here! I can get anyone to take me to the other side of the bridge.

CAZZIE
Not someone who wants to remain in the good graces of Cashmere Marino.

DONNA
Cazzie, you've been living on this island your whole life. It's time you knew.

CAZZIE
What?

DONNA
Nobody likes you. No one could give a crap about remaining in your good graces. The quickest way for me to get another boat is to tell someone it's a chance to screw you.

CAZZIE
We'll see about that.

DONNA
Yes, we will. I'll be on the other side of the bridge in ten minutes.

Donna exits followed by Danzinger, Luntz and Muriel. Cazzie and Ambrose watch them exit.

CAZZIE
Well, so far this is going pretty well, don't you think?

AMBROSE
Are you serious? Are we on the same planet? You have the whole island furious with you, you're losing the only friends you've ever had, you're hours away from going back to prison and the person you love the most in the world is minutes away from leaving you forever.

CAZZIE
What's your point?

AMBROSE
My point is... things looked better for Hitler when he was in his bunker.

CAZZIE
I guess it was just too much to expect any sympathy or cooperation from my own brother.

Cazzie goes back to reading his newspaper. Ambrose surveys his brother sadly for a few beats.

                        AMBROSE
I understand so little of this. So very, very little.
                        CAZZIE
It's to be expected. You've never had sex. That we know of.
                        AMBROSE
But still I know men, I know women...
                        CAZZIE
You <u>think</u> you know women.
                        AMBROSE
I know some things about men and women. I know how desperately they need each other. I know how you talked about Donna when you met her. When we were boys in high school. We would lay in our beds at night with the light out and you would carry on and on about Donna DeMarco, the most beautiful girl you've ever seen and how you would crawl over ten miles of broken glass just to touch the cuff of her bluejeans. Surely a goddess like her could never know that a nothing like you existed. The time she first spoke to you, you kept me awake until two in the morning going over every last detail of the simple "Hi" she gave you on the bus. The way her eyes sparkled, her hair bounced, the way her fingers curled around her loose-leaf binder. I know men and women feel that way about each other. I just don't know why it changes.

Ambrose takes out a slip of paper.

                        AMBROSE *(cont'd)*
Here, I almost forgot. I asked the group to make up a list of five wonderful things about themselves. This was Donna's.

Cazzie takes the piece of paper and reads it.

                        CAZZIE
Uh huh.
                        AMBROSE
The last one. Number five. Read it.

Cazzie nods.

                        AMBROSE *(cont'd)*
Out loud.

(no reply)

Can't do it?

                        CAZZIE
        (reading)
"In love with Cashmere Marino."
        (recovers, then)

348

Well, all the more reason to keep the bridge up.

AMBROSE

But she loved you <u>before</u> you put the bridge up.

Donna enters with an uninflated life raft and a bicycle pump. She goes about the task of blowing up the life raft during the following.

DONNA

Don't try and stop me. If you do I'll get another one of these and blow it up somewhere's else. Martin's Marine has a hundred of these so don't try and stop me.

CAZZIE

What are you doing?

DONNA

The other shore is only a few hundred yards away. I can make it in this, easy.

CAZZIE

That's insane.

DONNA

Uh uh... staying here is insane. Doing this... totally logical.

CAZZIE

But your stuff...

DONNA

I'll make do without it. I'll come back and get it later. After the bridge is down and you're in prison.

CAZZIE

But, in these waters, even a couple hundred yards can be treacherous. Using a stinky little boat like that you could get you in trouble. Real trouble. You don't know what it's like. These waters are tricky. There's currents running around here, quick and silent. You think you're moving one way, but you're really moving another. Before you know it you're too far away to... I know what I'm talking about. I've been in these waters in a boat too small. When Papa ran his fishing boat -- years and years ago, when these waters were still clean enough to fish -- he had a lifeboat he towed from his fishing boat. This lifeboat, it was just a little dingy, it wasn't much bigger than that damn thing. It was my birthday and, when Amby or I had a birthday, we always got the same treat from Papa. He would let us stay home from school and take us out on the Ruth Ann to fish with him. On this one day, it was the day I turned twelve, I wanted to do something different. I didn't want to ride out to where we were going to fish in the big boat. No, I had a different idea. I would ride in the dingy. I didn't even ask Papa. I just got in the dingy and waited for him. I sat there and I waited, in my rubber boots and my hat with the Goddamn flaps that Mama made me wear, holding the lunch she made me in a brown paper bag. I sat there in the thick morning fog waiting for Papa. He saw me. Never said a word. Just got in the Ruth Ann and pulled out into the Sound. And there I was, twenty feet back, being towed in this six-foot dingy. First thing I realized was the Ruth Ann gave off a ton of fumes and I thought I was going to be sick. But I also felt so special, so free... to be riding in my own boat. One separate from my father. I was twelve, it meant a lot to me. It must've been a strange sight... a commercial fishing boat pulling out into Long Island Sound with a twelve-year-old boy sitting in the lifeboat... only no one could really see that anyway because the fog was so damn thick. Well, don't ask me why, but because I was twelve, and because I knew everything there was to know in the world, I got bored and I decided it would be "fun" to hold on to the rope that was towing my lifeboat. See, I'm twelve, I'm becoming a man but I'm still a fuckin' idiot so I hold on to the tow rope with one hand and untie it with the other. Well, the rope is wet, it's November, my hands are freezing, I'm being towed at maybe fifteen knots so the rope... it slips through my hands like it's made out of butter. I never held on to that rope for even a brief second. It just... zing... right out of my hands. And I watch my father and his boat waddle off into the fog as I come to rest in the middle of Long Island Sound in a six-foot boat with no motor, no oars, nothin'.

DONNA

Didn't you yell?

CAZZIE

Like a son of a bitch. "Papa! Papa!" I never yelled so loud in my life. But he's in a commercial fishing boat, the engine's as loud as a factory. He's watching his compass, his radar, listening to shortwave, maybe once in a while he'll look back to check but by the time he did look back I was miles away in the fog. I'm in this little wooden boat in a thick fog surrounded by this enormous silence. There were no sounds at all, that's what frightened me the most. No sounds. I was so lonely and frightened I just cried. I sat in that little boat and cried. I was so ashamed of crying. I was twelve on that day. That was too old to cry. I tried singing songs but I sang them as I cried. Twice I heard other boats go by. Jesus, did I scream! But the fog, it plays tricks with sound. Those boats could've been ten feet away, they could've been ten miles away. Six hours later the fog finally lifts, and I see my father's boat, coming right at me. Holy shit, was I one happy kid, lemme tell ya. He tossed me a line, I tied it to the dingy, like it should be, I climbed on board his boat and he never said a word to me. Nothing. He probably thought I didn't need a sermon, I had learned my lesson but good.

AMBROSE
I remember this. Tell her the rest, Cazzie.

CAZZIE
Not much else to tell.

AMBROSE
Tell her.

CAZZIE
Well, we rode back to City Island together. I sat in the wheelhouse, next to the little heater, sipping hot coffee from his thermos, just glad to be alive and safe and warm.

AMBROSE
Then you got hack to City Island and...?

CAZZIE
We got back.

AMBROSE
And?

CAZZIE
And... I expected my father to dock his boat where he usually does but he didn't.

AMBROSE
Where did he go?

CAZZIE
Somewhere else. Listen...

AMBROSE
If you don't say it I will.

CAZZIE
He goes down to Martino's Dock... and he unloads a load of fish! He went fishing! His son was lost somewhere in Long Island Sound and he went fishing! I was somewhere in the fog for six hours and he took the time to drop nets and and and fish! I've tried to understand that. I've tried to make excuses for it every time I think of it. He couldn't find me in the fog anyway, his fish-finder told him it was an easy catch, maybe he didn't drop his nets, maybe the fish just jumped into his fuckin' boat, but the fact still remains, my father fished while I was missing!

DONNA
No wonder you're so fucked up.

CAZZIE
I saw him walking back to his boat from Martino's office counting his cash. Oh, his face was lit up. Like a Christmas tree! His face didn't light up like that when he found me alive. But money, now that put a smile on his face. That's what I learned on my twelfth birthday. Nothing's more important than money. Nothing! I wanted my father to love me

so desperately. And, if I couldn't have my father love me... then I would have plenty of <u>what</u> he loved... money. I put everything aside for money. The making of it, earning it, keeping it, counting it, saving it, stealing it. I sacrificed everything. My self-respect, having friends, my family, my health, my sanity, my religion and ultimately... you. I thought everyone loved like my father loved. The love of things. I sought to earn money and things and you never wanted any of it, did you?

DONNA

No.

CAZZIE

You tried to tell me every day we were together, didn't you?

Donna nods yes.

CAZZIE (cont'd)

But I was too caught up in my mission. A few more thousand dollars, just a little more, then just a little more after that and I would have enough. I worked my whole life to give you so very much. And all you ever wanted was so very little.

(pause)

Donna, we could drive to Maryland. Today, right now. There's no waiting period in Maryland. We could be married by lunch time. We could honeymoon in Atlantic City and start trying to make a baby tonight. And every day that we're together, for the rest of our lives, I will let you know how sorry I am for these past years.

Donna thinks for several beats, crosses to Cazzie and the two hug.

DONNA

You don't ever have to say you're sorry.

They hug again.

DONNA (cont'd)

Well, maybe a little.

They continue to hug until Ambrose, Danzinger, Luntz and Muriel enters carrying a broken surf board.

DANZINGER

Here we go, here we go.

LUNTZ

We found this.

DANZINGER

Just lie down on it.

LUNTZ

Keep your toes out of the water.

DANZINGER

Sharks love that.

MURIEL

Don't stand.

LUNTZ

Try not to fall off. If you do...

DANZINGER

Just keep swimming.

CAZZIE

What does she need that for?

DANZINGER

To get to the other side of the bridge.

LUNTZ
(mocking)
Duh!

CAZZIE

But the bridge is coming down. In just a few minutes.

AMBROSE

What?

MURIEL

It is?

Cassie crosses to where he hid the gear. He uncovers it and lifts it up.

CAZZIE

Sure. The bridge was scheduled for a little maintenance. One of the gears needed work.

DANZINGER

What's goin' on?

LUNTZ

Somethin' ain't right here.

CAZZIE

Everything's fine. The bridge is comin' down and Donna and I are driving to Maryland to get married. Today.

Muriel screams with delight. She and Donna hug as the men congratulate Cazzie.

DANZINGER

Great news, Cazzie. Great news.

LUNTZ

What should we get you for a wedding present?

CAZZIE

How 'bout you carry this gear?

Cazzie dumps the gear into Danzinger and Luntz's arms.

                        CAZZIE *(cont'd)*
C'mon, we've got a drawbridge to fix. People want to get on and off this island. I'll be back for you in fifteen minutes, Donna. Is that enough time?

                        DONNA
Yes, it's fine. I'll pack a bag. Should I pack a bag for you?

                        CAZZIE
No. You shouldn't have to do that. You pack your own bag. I'll pack mine.

                        DONNA
Okay.

Donna and Muriel exit to the street excitedly.

                        MURIEL
Do you have a white dress?

                        DONNA
This is my wedding, not science fiction.

                        MURIEL
I've got to lend you something so you'll have something borrowed.

They're gone. Cazzie turns to Danzinger and Luntz.

                        CAZZIE
Hurry up, you two!

Danzinger and Luntz happily exit as Cazzie yells after them.

                        CAZZIE *(cont'd)*
I'm getting married!

They're gone. Cazzie turns to Ambrose.

                        CAZZIE *(cont'd)*
I'm getting married.

                        AMBROSE
Scared?

                        CAZZIE
No. Yes. I'm excited. But I'm also scared out of my mind. It's the right thing to do, Amby. I know it is. I've got to let go and let life take me a few places.

                        AMBROSE
It's a lot easier trip.

The two brothers look at each other for a few beats then hug. They break.

CAZZIE

Thank you.

AMBROSE

I did nothing.

CAZZIE

You did everything. Take care of the house while I'm gone.
(goes to exit, but stops)
Don't be runnin' babes in and out of here at all hours, okay?

AMBROSE

Shucks.

CAZZIE

And after we're married, Amby...

AMBROSE

Yeah.

CAZZIE

We want you to live with us for as long as you like. Forever if you need.

AMBROSE

I'll get a job and find a place.

CAZZIE

Here on the island.

AMBROSE

Of course. But after you get back...

CAZZIE

Yeah.

AMBROSE

I need to go back to China.

CAZZIE

What for?

AMBROSE

Someone I love is still there. I need to bring her back.

Cazzie stares at Ambrose amazed, hugs him, smiles and exits running as we hear more car horns.

CAZZIE

(calling)
Coming!
(beat)
All right! Stop!

The lights slow fade to black.

THE END

OF MEN AND CARS

CAST

(in order of appearance)

JIM

DAD

MOM

FRANKIE TWO FINGERS

GIRL NEXT DOOR

RUSSO

ANNA

DOMINIC

SALESMAN

MAN

WOMAN (NY)

POT HEAD

COLLEGE GIRL

WARREN

SOLDIER

DUMB GUY

SHRINK

JACK

DOROTHY

WOMAN (LA)

SALESWOMAN

MAN

OF MEN AND CARS can be performed with four chairs to represent a number of cars over the years and a cast of six or seven. The act break is optional.

ACT ONE

The set is four identical chairs arranged to represent a number of different four-door sedans throughout the years. As we begin we find DAD repairing his Ford with a large pair of pliers. After a few beats JIM enters and watches Dad for several beats.

JIM
I've owned the car I currently drive for three years and it occurred to me the other day I've never looked at the engine. So I got the car's manual, found out how to open the hood and dammit... I looked at the engine. I'm glad to report it was there. All six cylinders. Or is it eight? I've got to look that up. Anyway, I know it's a gasoline engine because I have put gasoline into my car. The car's a hybrid which means it also has electric motors *somewhere* powered by batteries *somewhere* and a computer *somewhere* that tells me where I can buy frozen yogurt. Dad's car didn't do any of that. It was a 1939 Ford. Dad liked Fords.

DAD
Dependable. Gets you home.

JIM
As a four-year-old it was always great fun to watch Dad fix his fifteen-year-old car every time it broke down.

DAD
It didn't break down! It just needs maintenance!

JIM
'kay.

DAD
The exhaust pipe.

JIM
What's that?

DAD
It runs from the manifold to the muffler.

JIM
What's a man fold?

DAD
(points)
It's over there.

JIM
What's a mudler?

DAD
(points other way)
There.

								JIM
'kay.
								DAD
The exhaust pipe needs an L-bracket.
								JIM
What's that?
								DAD
A bracket shaped like an L.
								JIM
What's a L?
								DAD
A letter shaped like this.

Dad shows Jim with a finger and a thumb.

								JIM
'kay.
								DAD
The old one broke.
								JIM
Why?
								DAD
Potholes.
								JIM
Why?
								DAD
The city don't give a crap.
								JIM
Why?
								DAD
It's part of the oath they take when they're elected.
								JIM
'kay.
								DAD
Bracket broke and I'm replacing it.
								JIM
You buy a new one?
								DAD
No, they cost a fortune!
								JIM
There's man at the gas station.

                          DAD
    Carmine charges a fortune!
                          JIM
To Dad the repair of anything always cost the same amount of money...
a fortune.

Dad gives the underside of his car a few more whacks.

                          DAD
    Done!
                          JIM
    You fixed it?
                          DAD
    I replaced the bracket with some wire.
                          JIM
    What kind?
                          DAD
    Thick.
                          JIM
    How thick?
                          DAD
    A wire hanger.
                          JIM
    Where'd you get it?
                          DAD
    Your mother's closet. Don't tell her.
                          JIM
    'kay.
                          DAD
    Good boy.

Jim picks up a small piece of metal.

                          JIM
    Is this what broke?
                          DAD
    Yeah.
                          JIM
    What does it cost?
                          DAD
    No idea but whatever it is, it's too much. Listen to me, Jimmy. To reach
    into your wallet and take out money to replace a piece of metal when
    you've got half a ton of metal crap hanging around doing nothin' is
    insane! It's wasteful! It's more than that, it's a sin! It's a mortal sin in the

eyes of the Catholic church to waste money buying a bracket you don't have to. If I went to confession I'd have to tell the priest "Forgive me Father, I bought an L-bracket for my thirty-nine Ford!" He'd say...

(bad Italian accent)

"How mucha you pay?" I'd tell him it was sixty cents and he'd say...

(bad Italian accent)

"Wassa matter! You no have no wire somewheres?"

JIM

Why's he talk like that?

DAD

Because he's Italian! All these priests are Italian! You'll know what I'm talking about when you turn seven and start confessing your sins.

JIM

What are sins?

DAD

Sins are evil acts that make the devil happy. If we don't confess them before we die we're sent to hell forever where you burn in fire and little guys poke you with sharp sticks.

JIM

Dad had a sunny streak a mile wide.

DAD

Wasting money is sinful. In the depression you had to get by with whatever you had. People had nothing. Nothing! Everyone had one pair of shoes, one pair of socks, an undershirt if they were lucky, and no one ever rode on a bus or went to the movies.

JIM

Why not?

DAD

It cost a fortune! Breakfast was some oatmeal slop, dinner was a big potato and that was it! You bought nothing because there was no jobs, no money, nothing. If something broke, you fixed it. If you needed parts you either made them or found them. And it was all because we had a depression!

JIM

Do we still have it?

DAD

No.

JIM

If we don't have it.

DAD

Yeah?

JIM
Why don't you buy stuff?

DAD
Good God! It's like talking to a brick wall! I give up!

As Dad exits, he shouts to Mom.

DAD *(cont'd)*
Do something with your son! Tell him money doesn't grow on trees!

We hear MOM and Dad yell at the same time.

MOM *(O.S.)*
Leave him alone for Christ sake, he's only four! He doesn't know about money! He can't even count to ten! He doesn't understand half the crap you say! You get all worked up and pick on the kid! Get a beer and relax before you drive me crazy!

DAD *(O.S.)*
I'm just trying to learn him we're not made out of money! He has no idea that things cost money and someone's gotta earn it before you spend it! To him money is just there! Like we're millionaires! Next time the car has trouble he'll want me to buy a new one!

JIM
Thinking of times like that makes me feel terrific. No, I don't need therapy. In the Bronx people who yell at you are people who love you. Watch...

Jim calls to offstage.

JIM
Dad! Why did you yell at me?

DAD *(O.S.)*
Because you're worth it, God damn it!

JIM
See?

(then)
The Bronx was like a romantic comedy full of nutty people falling in love and yelling. A borough of blue collar dreams. For me dreams began and ended in a place called City Island, a small island off the coast of the Bronx. The most remarkable thing about City Island is that in four hundred years it has avoided the deadly trap of becoming trendy.

FRANKIE TWO FINGERS enters. He stands in place and surveys activity offstage.

JIM *(cont'd)*
There's a "fraternity of men" that live on City Island and they like things the way they are. My Dad's Army friend Frankie Two Fingers was one of them. Frankie and his friends wanted City Island to stay just the way it was.

Frankie speaks to an unseen neighbor.

> FRANKIE
> Hey! This house you're buildin'! Is it gonna look trendy? 'Cause me and my friends, none of us like trendy. If this house looks trendy, there's gonna be problems. And is that a second story you're buildin'? No, I don't think so. It'll block my view. You block my view, there's gonna be problems. You want a second-story, make a *basement*. Build *down*, not *up*. You pick a color yet?
> (beat)
> I don't wanna look at no stupid color, you understand? Show it to me before you put it on.

Frankie begins to exit, then stops.

> FRANKIE *(cont'd)*
> One other thing, this section of curb, that's my parking space... even when I'm not here.

Frankie exits.

> JIM
> Today City Island looks pretty much the way it did in the fifties. Tiny homes, ancient trees, narrow streets, all of them leading to the water... water that turns inky black at night offering a floor for the lights to dance on. I knew my girlfriend would like it there. That's where I was headed the first time I drove a car. I was four years old. Yeah. I stole my father's car when I was four. But I wanted to take my girlfriend somewhere romantic. What can I tell you? I was a player.

THE GIRL NEXT DOOR enters. She carries a coloring book.

> JIM *(cont'd)*
> Her name was The Girl Next Door. First name The Girl, last name Next Door. She had a coloring book and a box of sixty-four crayons. On the side of the box was a sharpener. A *sharpener*! She was beautiful and she came from money! You don't let a woman like this get away.

Jim approaches The Girl Next Door.

> JIM *(cont'd)*
> Hi.

> GIRL
> Hi.

> JIM
> I'm Jim.

> GIRL
> I'm The Girl Next Door.

JIM
Told you.
> *(then)*

What are you coloring?

GIRL
Pictures.

JIM
What kinda pictures?

GIRL
Kittens.

JIM
I love kittens.

GIRL
Me too.

JIM
I had one.

GIRL
What happened?

JIM
It ran away.

GIRL
So did mine.

JIM
You'll notice we're both four, standing on the sidewalk, not one adult in sight. If it were present day, we'd both be on the six o'clock news by now.
> *(then)*

You want to color in my Dad's car?

GIRL
'kay.

Jim and The Girl Next Door sit in the back seat.

GIRL *(cont'd)*
It's nice in here.

JIM
Yeah. Sometimes I hide in the back seat and I scare my father when he gets in.

GIRL
How.

JIM
Like this.
> *(loudly)*

JIM *(cont'd)*
YAAAAH!!!

GIRL
'kay.

JIM
He doesn't like surprises.

GIRL
Why not?

JIM
He was in the war.

GIRL
What's a war?

JIM
I don't know. But it makes people nervous.

GIRL
'kay.

JIM
You color good.

GIRL
Thank you.

JIM
How do you stay inside the lines?

GIRL
When I think I'm going outside the line...

JIM
Yeah?

GIRL
I stop.

JIM
Why's the kitten purple?

GIRL
I like purple kittens.

JIM
So do I.
  (then)
Even though I was four I knew it wasn't worth disagreeing with women over trivial things.
  (beat)
Or important things.

GIRL
I like this car.

JIM
My Dad lets me drive it whenever I want.

GIRL
Really?

JIM
Yeah. Wanna go somewhere?

GIRL
'kay.

Jim and The Girl Next Door get out of the back seat and into the front seat.

JIM
Where you want to go?

GIRL
I don't know.

JIM
How about City Island?

GIRL
What's that?

JIM
It's a nice place.

GIRL
'kay.

Jim fiddles with the dashboard.

GIRL *(cont'd)*
What are you doing?

JIM
Finding the thing that makes it go.

GIRL
'kay.

Jim keeps trying.

SFX: LOUD CAR HORN

JIM
That's the horn.

GIRL
Yeah.

JIM
Loud.

GIRL
Yeah.

                              JIM

Funny.

                              GIRL

Yeah.

                              JIM

This is the cigarette lighter.

Jim shows the Girl his hand.

                              JIM *(cont'd)*

See? I had to get a band-aid.

                              GIRL

Eww!

Jim tries again.

MUSIC: "HOUND DOG" BY ELVIS PRESLEY

                              JIM

That's the radio.

                              GIRL

Yeah.

                              JIM

That's Elvis Presley.

                              GIRL

Yeah.

                              JIM

My Dad hates him.

                              GIRL

Mine, too.

The MUSIC fades.

                              JIM

Now, the key to Dad's car only turned the car on, it didn't start the engine. If I pushed the ignition button, it would make the starter motor run. This wouldn't start the engine but, if the car was in gear, and it was, it would go forward powered by the starter.

    (pushing buttons)

This one doesn't work... this one doesn't do anything. I wonder what this one does?

Jim pushes a button.

SFX: GEARS GRINDING LOUDLY

The sounds continue as Jim and The Girl Next Door sway wildly and scream with horror in SLOW MOTION.

JIM & GIRL

Noooo!

Ahhhh!

Stop!

SFX: MILD AUTO CRASH

The Girl Next Door jumps out of the car and exits crying.

GIRL

Mommy! Mommy!

JIM

We traveled about forty feet and stopped when we hit Mister Russo's fig tree. The car was fine but Mister Russo had just planted the fig tree and he was not pleased.

RUSSO enters.

RUSSO

(furious)

My fig tree! Look what you did! I just planted this! Holy crap look what you did! Cost me twelve dollars! It's dead! You killed it!

JIM

Mind you I'm semi-conscious and bleeding.

RUSSO

Oh, my God! I don't believe this! Look at the dent! Look how the bark is scraped off! Un bambino colpito così giovane!

(new thought)

Burlap! I need burlap!

Russo screams to off stage.

RUSSO *(cont'd)*

Anna! Where's that roll of burlap!

ANNA (O.S.)

I dunno!

As Russo exits.

RUSSO

Dumb bitch!

JIM

For the next three years Mister Russo wrapped burlap around the wound on his tree and changed it every other month. At night you could hear him screaming at his wife and kids.

RUSSO *(O.S.)*
You're so frikkin' stupid it's pathetic! Blah blah blah! Shut your mouth! I'm so tired of listenin' to your crap!!

ANNA *(O.S.)*
Drop dead! I'm stupid because I married *you*! Jerk! Go to hell, Carmine! Blow it out your ass! Eat crap and live!

JIM
Mister Russo was hated by everyone who knew him including his own family. When the neighborhood found out I damaged his stupid fig tree I became a minor celebrity.

DOMINIC enters.

JIM *(cont'd)*
Even my friend Dominic was impressed.

DOMINIC
You go driving?

JIM
Yeah.

DOMINIC
In the car?

JIM
Yeah.

DOMINIC
Your Daddy's car?

JIM
Yeah.

DOMINIC
You hit this tree?

JIM
Yeah.

DOMINIC
I hate this tree.

JIM
Everyone does.

DOMINIC
You drive alone?

JIM
No.

DOMINIC
With someone?

JIM

Yeah.

DOMINIC

Who?

JIM

The Girl Next Door.

Dominic points to a place far away.

DOMINIC

The one over there?

JIM

No, the one next door.

DOMINIC

Oh.

JIM

Yeah.

DOMINIC

She's pretty.

JIM

Yeah.

DOMINIC

I like her.

JIM

We listened to music.

DOMINIC

What kind?

JIM

Elvis.

DOMINIC

My father hates Elvis.

JIM

Mine too.

DOMINIC

Yeah.

JIM

I'm going to marry her.

DOMINIC

Who?

JIM

The Girl Next Door.

DOMINIC

Okay.

JIM

Then I'm going to drive us to City Island.

DOMINIC

Why?

JIM

So we could be happy.

DOMINIC

Can I come?

JIM

Okay.

Dominic exits.

JIM *(cont'd)*

The Girl Next Door, that's where she went and stayed... forever. Next door. Our relationship lasted all of twenty minutes. As I became an adult I was astonished to learn I would have relationships with women even <u>shorter</u> than that. And without crashing a car.

Dad enters and begins driving the car as Jim rides shotgun.

JIM *(cont'd)*

Dad, he pretended to be angry but I could tell he wasn't. I think, down deep, he was proud of me. His four-year-old son had logged his first forty feet.

DAD

More like fifty actually. Maybe sixty.

Russo enters carrying some burlap.

JIM

Dad especially liked the fact I hit Russo's stupid fig tree.

DAD

He planted it on city property.

JIM

What's that?

DAD

Dirt he doesn't own! Just dug a hole and put it there!

JIM

Mister Russo is putting a band-aid on his tree again.

DAD

He's an idiot.

Russo yells at Dad.

RUSSO
If this tree dies you're buyin' me a new one!

DAD
Eat me!

RUSSO
You drunken, shanty Irish, piece of crap!

DAD
Shut your yap up, you fat ass WOP!

Russo and Dad yell at the same time.

RUSSO
You're kid's a maniac! He's out of control! He's all over the neighborhood doin' all kinds of shit! Where the hell are *you*? Nowhere! Inside drinkin' beer you shanty Irish pig! I spend money makin' the neighborhood look better and this is the thanks I get? Your idiot kid tryin' to kill my tree?

DAD *(cont'd)*
My kid's a maniac? My kid? How's Tony doin'? Huh? He outta jail yet? Can't find someone to kill the witness? This neighborhood was fine until *you* moved in! Go learn to read and write, see what that's like! You want to make the neighborhood better? Move the hell out! And take your stinkin' fig tree with yuh!

Russo exits.

JIM
This was back in the days when America was great.
   (beat)
Dad dealt with the incident by giving me small lessons in the art of driving.

DAD
And the pedal on the left is the clutch. You press the pedal down, select a new gear, pedal up... Did you feel that? That surge in speed?

JIM
I guess.

DAD
It's because we went from second to third gear.

JIM
'kay.
   (then)
I had no idea what he was saying but it was still nice, the two of us driving on a warm day, windows down, listening to the Yankees on the radio. And if the Yankees weren't playing there was always music.

Jim turns on the radio.

MUSIC: "GOOD GOLLY MISS MOLLY" BY LITTLE RICHARD

DAD
What is that!

JIM
Music.

DAD
You like that?

JIM
Kinda.

DAD
That's not music. That's screaming. Nothing more than noise. Turn it off.

JIM
Why?

DAD
Because I said so.

JIM
Why?

DAD
Because it's awful!

JIM
No, it's fun.

DAD
Rock and roll is music of the devil.

JIM
No.

DAD
It's a plot by the Communists to make everyone in America insane so we have no idea what's going on when they invade us.

JIM
I don't know what that means.

DAD
Daddy can't drive a car and listen to that at the same time! We might have an accident!

JIM
'kay.

Jim turns off the radio.

JIM *(cont'd)*
Dad was a co-pilot on a B-17. Safety was a big thing with him.

DAD
You cannot properly operate a motor vehicle *and* listen to rock and roll.
JIM
I also think driving through the neighborhood, a neighborhood he had lived in his entire life, brought memories to him that didn't mix with happy music.
DAD
I knew a girl lived in that building.
JIM
What girl?
DAD
Emily, she was in my English class.
JIM
She still there?
DAD
No, her father lost his job, they got thrown out.
JIM
Where they go?
DAD
No idea. Some of her stuff was in the garbage.
JIM
What kind of stuff?
DAD
Girl stuff. I took some of it, put it in a box, saved it for a while but...
    (beat)
Goldberg lived there.
JIM
Who's that?
DAD
Friend.
JIM
What was his first name?
DAD
Don't know. Everyone just called him Goldberg.
JIM
You still friends?
DAD
No.
JIM
Why?

DAD

Dead.

JIM

What happened?

DAD

Juno.

JIM

What's that?

DAD

The beach where he died.

JIM

Where?

DAD

France.

JIM

He drowned?

DAD

Some guys did. Most got shot.

JIM

By who?

DAD

Germans.

JIM

The war thing?

DAD

Yeah, the war thing.

JIM

What about the other guy?

DAD

Which one?

JIM

I forget his name.

DAD

DeRosa?

JIM

Yeah.

DAD

He died somewhere else.

JIM

Where?

DAD

South Pacific.

JIM

Where's that?

DAD

It's a place far away with blue water, white sand and palm trees.

JIM

Is it nice there?

DAD

Nice? Well, I haven't been there but... Yeah! I guess so! It's gorgeous! Hula girls and dolphins! It's a God damn paradise! DeRosa *loved* it!

JIM

'kay.

DAD

Light me a butt!

JIM

'kay.

Dad hands Jim a cigarette.

DAD

Here's matches. Don't put your finger on the red part.

JIM

'kay.

DAD

Bend forward.

JIM

Why?

DAD

So you're out of the wind.

JIM

'kay...

DAD

When you rub the match on the black thing...

JIM

Yeah?

DAD

Do it *away* from you.

JIM

'kay.

DAD

So you don't burn yourself.

JIM

'kay.

DAD

And when it's lit don't inhale!

JIM

I won't.

(then)

I lit Dad's Camels until I was sixteen. Then I started smoking and Dad didn't let me light his Camels anymore. He was disappointed in me.

DAD

It's a filthy, disgusting habit. I have no idea why you picked it up!

JIM

The do-as-I-say-not-as-I-do method of parenting was very popular back then. Popular... not effective. Dad also didn't want me to drink.

DAD

Not even a little.

JIM

'kay.

DAD

Not even a sip!

JIM

'kay.

DAD

Stay away from booze.

JIM

Yeah.

DAD

It won't do you no good.

JIM

'kay.

DAD

It takes your money, makes you stupid, ruins your life.

JIM

That also didn't work. But I took care of that when the time came. All it took was a thousand AA meetings.

SFX: BAR NOISE

JIM *(cont'd)*

Every trip with Dad included a stop at a bar. To a kid bars can be fun for the first ten minutes. But the thrill wears off after two or three hours of cigarette smoke and guys talking bull. Maybe Dad and his Army pals were trying to drink away memories of the war. Either that or they just didn't want to go home. By the time I was ten I could beat most anyone at pinball.

Frankie enters and joins Dad and Jim.

JIM *(cont'd)*
I also got to spend quality time with Frankie Two Fingers.

FRANKIE
You don't *give* yourself a nickname. A lotta guys try it but it's frowned on. A nickname is something that is *given* to you by others as a sign of affection and respect. Like your father's... Lone Wolf.

JIM
That's his name?

FRANKIE
Nickname. Those who really know him call him that.
 (to Dad)
Right, Lone Wolf?

DAD
He's only six, he won't understand.

FRANKIE
It comes from the nose art on your Dad's bomber.

JIM
What's that?

FRANKIE
Nose art is pictures on the front of an airplane meant to scare the enemy.

DAD
You know he's six! Do you have to?

FRANKIE
Your father's bomber had this big picture of a wolf with big teeth eating a Messerschmitt!

DAD
That's enough.

FRANKIE
It must've scared the crap out of every Kraut pilot who saw it.

DAD
Enough.

FRANKIE
The crew on the plane was called the Wolf *Pack*.

DAD
Cut it out!

FRANKIE
The *Lone* Wolf comes from-

DAD
Enough!

FRANKIE
What!

DAD
I said enough! He's six, he's heard enough!

FRANKIE
All right, all right!

DAD
He's a little kid!

FRANKIE
I can see that!

DAD
Then *act* like it!

FRANKIE
What's with you!

DAD
I tell you to stop - you stop!

FRANKIE
All right!

DAD
You want to waste time; tell him how you got Frankie Two Fingers, you dumb frikkin' grease ball!

JIM
You only have two fingers?

FRANKIE
No. Every bartender in the Bronx knows I drink Wild Turkey. But I don't want no single shot.

Frankie holds out two fingers horizontally.

FRANKIE *(cont'd)*
This means I want a double.

JIM
What's a double?

DAD
It's what drunken losers order.

FRANKIE
Drop dead!
   (to Jim)
It's twice as much as what amateurs drink. I walk into any bar, I shoot the bartender one of these...

>   *(gestures again)*
>
> And I got a double Wild Turkey without sayin' nothin'. Every bar I go to knows who the hell I am and what the hell I want!

DAD

> *(sarcastic)*
>
> Thanks, Frankie, this is important information every six-year-old should know!

FRANKIE

Sorry.

> *(to Jim, gesture)*
>
> Frankie Two Fingers.

DAD

> I gotta hit the head.
>
> *(to Frankie)*
>
> You do more Wolf talk and I'll kill you.

Dad exits.

FRANKIE

> *(to self)*
>
> I love this bar, it's so convivial!

JIM

Frankie also took the time to explain the science of nut machines to me.

FRANKIE

You put your nickel in?

JIM

Yeah.

FRANKIE

Okay, stop right there. Don't do nothin'.

JIM

I want to get some nuts.

FRANKIE

I know. But I'm gonna show yuh how to get *more* nuts. You'd like that, wouldn't yuh? Huh? Gettin' *more* nuts? Huh?

JIM

Okay.

FRANKIE

Listen, the nuts all fall down into a chamber, it's like a little cup. You put in a nickel, turn the knob, the cup turns upside down and the nuts come out the thing.

JIM

That's what I was going to do.

FRANKIE

But there's a trick. If you shake the machine like this, see?

Frankie mimes violently shaking a nut machine.

SFX: NUT MACHINE BEING SHAKED

FRANKIE (cont'd)

Shake it, shake it, see? What's gonna happen?

JIM

(timid)

I dunno...

FRANKIE

What's gonna happen!

JIM

(frightened)

I don't know!

FRANKIE

More nuts is gonna drop down into the cup!

JIM

Okay!

FRANKIE

So when you turn the knob what's gonna happen?

JIM

Leave me alone!

FRANKIE

What's gonna happen?

JIM

I don't know!

FRANKIE

You're gonna get more nuts! Go 'head! Turn the knob! Turn the knob!

Jim turns the knob.

FRANKIE (cont'd)

Hah! Look at all the nuts yuh got!

JIM

Go away!

FRANKIE

Look at that! More nuts! A lot more nuts!

JIM

Daddy!

As Frankie exits.

                          FRANKIE
Hey! You should see all the nuts the kid got!

Jim watches Frankie exit, then.

                            JIM
I liked Frankie. He was the only adult I knew who never asked me how school was going. He helped Dad get Mom a fur coat for very little money. On the Fourth of July Frankie could get you fireworks even though they were illegal. Someone owed Dad money. Dad called Frankie and the next day Dad had eighty percent of it. When we left the bar Dad made me promise not to tell Mom we had been there. And he knew she would ask me. I believe this was part of a secret plan the two of them had cooked up.

Dad and Mom enter separate from Jim.

                            MOM
What can we do to make our child feel guilty, dishonest, neurotic, depressed and worthless?

                            DAD
Why don't I take him to a bar?

                            MOM
Okay...

                            DAD
Then make him promise *not* to tell you.

                            MOM
No matter how much I badger him?

                            DAD
Yeah!

                            MOM
So, if he tells me the truth.

                            DAD
He betrays me.

                            MOM
And if he lies.

                            DAD
He betrays *you*.

                            MOM
Exactly.

                            DAD
There's no way he can feel good about any of it.

                            MOM
He'll be *so* screwed up!

DAD

We can only hope!

Dad exits. Mom crosses to Jim.

MOM

Where did you go?

JIM

The park.

MOM

What did you do?

JIM

Play catch.

MOM

What else?

JIM

Nothing.

MOM

You sure?

JIM

Yeah.

MOM

You telling me the truth?

JIM

Yeah.

MOM

Your father stop anywhere?

JIM

No.

MOM

Stop at a bar?

JIM

No.

MOM

Stopped at a bar, didn't he!

JIM

No.

MOM

If you love Mommy you'll tell her the truth.

JIM

Okay.

                           MOM

Did he?

                           JIM

No.

                           MOM

Why do you smell like peanuts?

                           JIM

I ate some.

                           MOM

Where?

                           JIM

I dunno.

                           MOM

You don't know where you ate peanuts?

                           JIM

Yeah.

                           MOM

Did Daddy get them?

                           JIM

Yeah.

                           MOM

Where?

                           JIM

Store.

                           MOM

What store?

                           JIM

One that sells peanuts.

                           MOM

Did you see that hoodlum Frankie Two Fingers?

                           JIM

Yeah.

                           MOM

Where!

                           JIM

At the store.

                           MOM

What store?

                           JIM

The one that sell peanuts.

MOM

Ach!

Mom exits.

JIM

The Bronx shares a rich history with organized crime and a lot of gangsters gave up their best friends. But not me. I never *once* ratted out Dad. And it wasn't that I chose Dad over Mom. That part of their plan never worked. What I chose was riding in Dad's thirty-nine Ford as opposed to staying home. They were great cars, lots of chrome, big steering wheels, radios that crackled, and no seat belts so you could stand up and see better. Two months after I hit Mister Russo's fig tree Dad woke me out of a sound sleep at midnight.

Dad enters.

DAD

Jimmy! Get up!

JIM

What?

DAD

Get up!

JIM

What's the matter?

DAD

Nothin'. C'mon! The Westchester Lumber Yard is on fire!

Jim and Dad cross to the car and Dad drives.

JIM

No one in the house turned on the TV. This wasn't going to be on TV. If you wanted to see it... you had to *go* there. That's pretty much the motto of the fifties. It was August and even though it was midnight it was still hot. Dad kept the windows down and we could smell the fire way before we got there. We pulled up as close as we could, behind all the fire trucks and police cars, and there it was...

SFX: A CRACKLING FIRE THROUGHOUT, AND AN OCCASIONAL SIREN.

JIM *(cont'd)*

This gigantic red and yellow fire tickling the sky as a couple hundred tons of stacked lumber went up in flames. Dad sat me on the roof of his Ford so I could get a better view.

Dominic enters.

JIM *(cont'd)*

Dominic and his family showed up! They put him on the roof with me.

DOMINIC
You wear pajamas?
JIM
Yeah.
DOMINIC
Me, too.
JIM
Yeah.
DOMINIC
Davy Crockett.
JIM
Yeah.
DOMINIC
What's yours?
JIM
Hopalong Cassidy.
DOMINIC
I like him.
JIM
Me, too.

Jim and Dominic mime guns and shoot each other.

JIM & DOMINIC
Kew! Kew! Kew! Kew!

Jim and Dominic laugh.

DOMINIC
You see the fire?
JIM
Yeah.
DOMINIC
It's big.
JIM
Yeah.
DOMINIC
What happened?
JIM
Daddy said someone played with matches.
DOMINIC
Okay.

JIM

When you play with matches this happens.

DOMINIC

Yeah.

JIM

Big fire.

Frankie enters.

DOMINIC

Did people die?

JIM

I don't know.

(then)

Frankie Two Fingers showed up. What the hell was Frankie doing at the lumber yard at midnight? City Island was ten, twelve miles away. For all I know he started the fire. Dad and Frankie stood with some other guys while Dominic and I listened to some serious man talk.

Dad and Frankie stare at the fire.

DAD

Naw... they can't put it out.

FRANKIE

No?

DAD

No way. Best they can do is save the Woolworth's next door.

FRANKIE

Yeah.

DAD

Yeah.

FRANKIE

Keep it from spreading.

DAD

What's on the other side?

FRANKIE

Parking lot.

DAD

So that side's okay.

FRANKIE

Yeah.

DAD

So just let it burn.

                        FRANKIE
It's all they can do.
                        DAD
Yeah.
                        FRANKIE
It's what they call a containment.
                        DAD
Contain the fire.
                        FRANKIE
Save the Woolworth's.
                        DAD
All they can do.
                        FRANKIE
Yeah.
                        JIM
Flames were shooting a hundred feet into the air, there must have been a dozen fire trucks, fifteen to twenty police cars, a couple of ambulances and maybe two hundred people who showed up just to watch this catastrophe and in the middle of all this some guy was selling ice cream! Yeah, a Good Humor truck showed up! Dad bought ice creams for me and Dominic!
                        DOMINIC
What flavor you got?
                        JIM
Vanilla.
                        DOMINIC
Me too.
                        JIM
I got chocolate on the outside.
                        DOMINIC
Me too.
                        JIM
It has a stick.
                        DOMINIC
Yeah.
                        JIM
So you can hold it.
                        DOMINIC
Yeah.
    (beat)
Know what?

JIM

What?

DOMINIC

I once had my ice cream and and and... it fell off the stick!

JIM

Wow!

DOMINIC

Yeah!

JIM

Yeah.

DOMINIC

It fell and fell and fell!

JIM

We sat on the roof of Dad's Ford, in our pajamas, eating ice cream watching the Westchester Lumber Yard burn to the ground.

DAD

They got a lotta plywood in there.

FRANKIE

I'll bet.

DAD

Plywood's pressed together with glue.

FRANKIE

Yeah.

DAD

That glue is petroleum based.

FRANKIE

So it's making it worse.

DAD

Burns hotter.

FRANKIE

Yeah.

JIM

The fire was three or four blocks wide, everything in its path was doomed, I saw a building burn and crumble.

Dad and Frankie stare silently at the fire for several beats; their faces glow from the flames, finally.

DAD

If you stood on a sidewalk in Dresden...

FRANKIE

What?

DAD

If you stood on a sidewalk in Dresden, you think it looked like this, down there?

FRANKIE

I don't know. I never looked back.

DAD

Neither did I.

FRANKIE

I was too busy pissin' my pants.

DAD

First the flak... then the fighters.

FRANKIE

They were pissed.

DAD

Bombing targets was one thing but Dresden...

FRANKIE

I felt bad about it. I did. But after the war, when I found out what they did.

DAD

I know.

FRANKIE

Bastards. Lost Wallace that day.

DAD

Went quick.

FRANKIE

Better that way.

DAD

Came right through the windshield.

FRANKIE

Didn't see it comin'.

DAD

Gone in a blink. The port side had a hole the size of a suitcase, wind screaming into the cockpit, left rudder was twenty percent, blood all over me and the cockpit, Wallace next to me, dead, looking up at the ceiling.

(breaking up)

God forgive me! I pushed him over so I wouldn't have to-

FRANKIE

I would have done the same. Anyone would've. Thing is, you got it back. 17's were made to get back.

DAD
Yeah.

FRANKIE
Lone Wolf.

Dad and Frankie watch the fire for several silent beats again, finally.

DAD
Frankie.

FRANKIE
What?

DAD
Don't call me that no more.

FRANKIE
'kay.

Frankie exits slowly. Jim and Dad watch him go.

JIM
Frankie Two Fingers died when I was ten.

DAD
He went swimming off City Island and drowned.

JIM
I looked up Frankie's obit in college. They found him in the water but he didn't drown.

Mom enters and joins Jim and Dad in the car. Dad drives.

JIM *(cont'd)*
Sundays we would drive to Long Island to visit Uncle George, Dad's brother. On the way home Mom and Dad would talk about Uncle George.
    (then)
What's a schmuck?

MOM
None of your business!

DAD
Don't say that word again!

MOM
It's not a nice word.

JIM
Daddy said it.

DAD
It's a grown up word.

MOM
Not a word for children.
JIM
Then I won't say it.
MOM
Good boy.
JIM
Why is Uncle George a word I can't say?
DAD
Because the day after Pearl Harbor he enlists in the Coast Guard!
MOM
Let it go, Roy.
DAD
Said the Coast Guard stays right here... doesn't get sent overseas.
MOM
Well, everyone had a different role to play and-
DAD
After he joins your uncle finds out the Coast Guard operates *landing craft*.
MOM
Enough!
DAD
For invasions.
MOM
Oh, stop!
DAD
And if you survive the *first* landing you go back and get *more* troops!
MOM
You need to stop!
DAD
The Krauts and Tojo got all day to kill yuh.
MOM
I'm going to get out of this car!
DAD
But they kept him here. Thanks to your Uncle George the Japs never made it past Newport!
JIM
Where's that?
DAD
Oregon.

                             JIM
Is that in America?

                             DAD
Sort of.

                             MOM
I don't know why you-

                             DAD
It's a luxury resort.

                             MOM
It's not a resort. The Navy kept some-

                             DAD
It's a luxury *resort* in Oregon so remote even the Japs couldn't find it.

                             MOM
The proper word is "*Japanese.*"

                             DAD
Your Uncle George spent the war getting a suntan. Now you know what a schmuck is.

                             JIM
Why do we visit him?

                             MOM
He's family.

SFX: THE CAR STRUGGLING IN ONE GEAR

                             DAD
Every time I ask him what he did I get a load of bull. "I coordinated various operations and oversaw all personnel who-"

                             MOM
What's that noise?

                             DAD
It's me talking. He spent four years waving a flashlight.

                             MOM
The car, it's making a noise!

                             DAD
What?

                             MOM
The car.

                             DAD
What about it?

                             MOM
It's making a noise!

> DAD
> Wait... wait... Yeah.

> MOM
> What is that?

> DAD
> I dunno, it's...

> MOM
> What is it?

> DAD
> I don't know!

Dad struggles with the gear shift, then.

> DAD *(cont'd)*
> Damn, it's the clutch... I can't get out of first gear.

> MOM
> Will the car catch on fire?

> DAD
> No.

> MOM
> Will it explode?

> DAD
> No.

> JIM
> Mom had a heightened sense of danger.

> MOM
> Can we get it fixed?

> DAD
> It's late. All the gas stations are closed.

> MOM
> We'll have to stop and stay in a motel.

> DAD
> Are you kidding? It'll cost a fortune!

> MOM
> How are we going to get home?

> DAD
> Just like this.

> MOM
> In first gear?

> DAD
> As long as we stay on Northern Boulevard and off the highway we're okay.

MOM
Can't you go any faster?
DAD
No!
MOM
We can't drive home doing one mile an hour!
DAD
We're doin' seven!
MOM
That's insane!
DAD
We're fine.
MOM
You can't!
DAD
We're fine.
MOM
You're driving over the Whitestone Bridge doing one mile an hour!
DAD
Seven! Seven!
MOM
It's suicide!
DAD
We're fine. It'll take longer but we'll get there. It's a good car. It will get us home.

Jim, Dad and Mom exit the car and examine it.

JIM
And it did. Dad was right about Fords. A thirty-minute drive took three hours but we made it home traveling one mile an hour.
DAD
Seven!
MOM
Why's it smoking?
DAD
That's what happens to a transmission when you burn it out.
MOM
Thank God we're not dead!
DAD
It was time for a new car anyway.

MOM

Volkswagens are cute.

Dad slowly turns and stares at Mom until she fully understands what his stare means.

MOM *(cont'd)*

Sorry.

Mom exits.

JIM

Dad never owned a new car. He said if you gave him one he wouldn't take it.

DAD

They're not broken in. All the gears are still learning what they're supposed to do.

JIM

Dad was part of the generation that married the same woman for life, drank the same beer for life, and drove the same brand of car... for life.

DAD

Ford.

JIM

How come?

DAD

Dependable. Gets you home.

JIM

Doesn't break down?

DAD

If it does... it still gets you there.

JIM

Like this one did?

DAD

Yeah.
    (choked up)
Like this one did.

The lighting changes to resemble the hanging light bulbs of a used car lot at night.

JIM

Where we goin'?

DAD

Bruckner Boulevard, there's a mile of used car lots.

JIM

But it's freezing!

DAD
February is the best month to buy a used car.

JIM
Why's that?

DAD
It's winter. None of these guys have sold a car in months. They're desperate for cash.

JIM
What are we looking for?

DAD
This one.

JIM
Why this one?

DAD
It's a Ford.

A SALESMAN enters.

SALESMAN
Smart choice.

DAD
Sticker says five hundred and thirty. The thirty is like a dead tree branch. You push it and it falls off.

SALESMAN
No, it's part of the price.

DAD
You and I both know that five hundred and thirty means five hundred. I'm here on Friday with cash.

SALESMAN
Five hundred?

DAD
No, four hundred and eighty.

SALESMAN
What happened to five hundred?

DAD
It fell off with the other thirty dollars.

SALESMAN
Four hundred and eighty...

DAD
It's too cold for this, yes or no, c'mon!

SALESMAN
Okay, four-eighty it is... if it's cash.

DAD
Friday after work, I'll be here.

The Salesman exits as Dad takes a large wad of bills out of one pocket and distributes them into other pockets.

JIM
You think getting the salesman to lop off fifty bucks was it? Not even close! What you're about to see is the most diabolical used car buying maneuver ever invented. Dad is stuffing bits of cash into all of his pockets. How many pockets in your pants, Dad?

DAD
Two in the front, two in the back.

JIM
Vest?

DAD
Three.

JIM
Shirt?

DAD
One.

JIM
Sport coat?

DAD
Two outside. Two inside.

JIM
That makes twelve. Dad had most of the money in one pocket, the rest was stuffed into eleven other pockets. And that was only part of his plan.

DAD
You remember your line?

JIM
Yes.

DAD
What is it?

JIM
(lifeless)
You promised to take me to the circus.

DAD
You gonna say it like that?

JIM
No.

DAD
How you gonna say it then?

JIM
(bigger)
You promised to take me to the circus!

DAD
Good. Remember to look angry like I'm always letting you down.

JIM
But you never let me down.

DAD
That's why you have to act. Acting is just normal people pretending they're not happy.

JIM
Okay.

DAD
Try it again.

JIM
(angry)
You promised to take me to the circus!

DAD
Pretend it's Christmas morning and there's no presents for you under the tree. Then think of that when you say your words.

JIM
Dad was the Lee Strasberg of used car buying.

DAD
And remember… you don't say your words until I say "I'll come back Monday."

JIM
I know.

DAD
Good.

Dad and Jim stroll back to the used car lot.

JIM
Returning Friday after three o'clock was part of the plan. Banks closed at three o'clock. How many were open Saturday? None! Sunday? Are you kidding? ATM's? What the hell is an ATM!

The Salesman approaches and Dad takes out a wad of money and puts each bill in the hand of the Salesman.

DAD
Okay… four hundred and eighty. Here we go. Twenty, forty, sixty, eighty, one hundred… Twenty, forty, sixty, eighty, two hundred… twenty, forty, sixty…

Dad runs out of money.

DAD *(cont'd)*
How much is that?

SALESMAN
Two hundred and sixty dollars.

DAD
Yeah, hold on.

Dad takes out bills from various pockets.

DAD *(cont'd)*
Yeah, here's a ten. And another. Makes two hundred and eighty...
(then)
Damn wife... helped herself to my wallet...

JIM
Dad loved Mama... but this is war and there are no rules.

DAD
Three hundred, another twenty, and another, couple more, three eighty... Listen, pal... I'm gonna have to run to the bank.

SALESMAN
The banks just closed.

DAD
That's right. I'll go to the bank in the morning.

SALESMAN
Tomorrow's Saturday.

DAD
Damn, and Sunday's no good. Crap! Well, in that case...

Dad and Jim turn and look at each other, then.

DAD *(cont'd)*
I'll come back Monday.

JIM
You promised to take me to the circus!

DAD
That's right. And I already bought the tickets. Cost a fortune. Yeah... well, let me think... maybe... maybe Tuesday... dunno...

JIM
I had never seen anyone die but I think the salesman's face gave me a good idea. His pride, his dignity was replaced with the tranquil look of surrender.

SALESMAN
Tell yuh what. To hell with Tuesday! Why don't we just call it three eighty?

                              DAD
Done.

Dad and the Salesman exit.

                              JIM
Once every three or four years it was the same thing, wait until February, find a car, come back Friday with cash stuffed into eleven pockets, give me a line of bull about Monday, then sit back and watch the magic happen. My reward? When I turned eighteen, Dad taught me how to drive. The first five lessons were in the Orchard Beach parking lot which was equal in size to Rhode Island. After that came lessons on actual streets. Sunday mornings, seven A.M. The roads were empty at seven A.M.

Dad enters and sits in the car with Jim who readies to drives.

                              JIM *(cont'd)*
Getting up when the world was still asleep was just the first step.
     (then)
Should I start the engine?

                              DAD
We don't take off until we run a checklist.

                              JIM
This is a Ford Galaxy, not a bomber.

                              DAD
Both can kill you.

                              JIM
Okay.

                              DAD
You check the gas?

                              JIM
Yeah.

                              DAD
Oil?

                              JIM
Yeah.

                              DAD
Tires?

                              JIM
Yeah.

                              DAD
Windshield?

                              JIM
Clean.

DAD

Backlight glass?

JIM

That's the windshield in the *back* of the car.

DAD

Hello!

JIM

Clean.

DAD

Go to mass?

JIM

Yeah.

DAD

Which one?

JIM

Six o'clock.

DAD

Saint Francis?

JIM

Saint Claire's.

DAD

Why?

JIM

Closer.

DAD

Saint Claire's is a new church.

JIM

I know.

DAD

Saint Francis is an old church.

JIM

I know.

DAD

Go to Saint Francis.

JIM

Why?

DAD

God's been there longer.

JIM

Gotcha.

DAD

Confession?

JIM

Yeah.

DAD

When?

JIM

Yesterday.

DAD

Penance?

JIM

Three Hail Marys.

DAD

Next time do ten.

JIM

Check.

DAD

You receive at church this morning?

JIM

Yes.

DAD

When you got home did you drink a large glass of water to make sure the sacred body of Jesus Christ our Lord and Savior went down all the way?

JIM

Yes.

DAD

And after that did you eat anything?

JIM

No.

DAD

You sure?

JIM

I'm sure. My stomach is totally empty.

DAD

Good. Remember, Jimmy; never mix the sacred body of Jesus Christ our Lord and Savior with bacon or donuts.

JIM

Right.

DAD

Okay, ready?

JIM
Ready.

DAD
Hold on, I forgot my cigarettes.

Dad exits.

JIM
Pretty soon I was the most dangerous animal on the planet. I was an eighteen-year-old boy with a driver's license.

MUSIC: "FUN, FUN, FUN" BY THE BEACH BOYS.

JIM (cont'd)
I know, I'm playing surf music and I'm in the Bronx! I don't care! Later on I think I'm going to play some Motown and sing along!

Dominic enters and rides with Jim.

JIM (cont'd)
As soon as I got my license I picked up Dominic. We drove up and down Arthur Avenue for hours yelling out the window.
　　(calls out the window)
Yo! Henry! Yo!

DOMINIC
Why you yellin' to him?

JIM
I know him.

DOMINIC
Henry's an asshole!

JIM
So?

DOMINIC
So you don't yell to assholes! It makes you look bad! People gonna think *you're* an asshole! You want people to think you're an asshole?

JIM
No.

DOMINIC
Then don't do that! Turn up the radio. I like this song. You like this song?

JIM
I like this song.

DOMINIC
Me, too. I like this song.

Jim turns up the radio. Jim and Dominic shout above the music.

                    DOMINIC *(cont'd)*

Make it louder!

                         JIM

It won't go any louder!

                       DOMINIC

What?

                         JIM

It won't go any louder!

                       DOMINIC

Why not!

                         JIM

I dunno!

                       DOMINIC

What kinda radio is this?

                         JIM

What?

                       DOMINIC

What kinda radio you got?

                         JIM

The one that comes with the car!

                       DOMINIC

It sucks!

                         JIM

What?

                       DOMINIC

It *sucks*!

                         JIM

What?

Dominic turns off the radio.

                       DOMINIC

I said it sucks. No one gets laid with a radio like this. You need a bigger amp and more speakers.

                         JIM

C'mon, stuff like that costs money.

                       DOMINIC

I know a guy, he can put it all in, twenty bucks.

                         JIM

The whole thing?

405

DOMINIC

Woofer, tweeter, all of it top quality, even a thing what plays eight-track cassettes.

JIM

Woa.

DOMINIC

Just don't ask where it came from.

JIM

What do I tell my father?

DOMINIC

Tell him it's for him. Makes the ballgame sound better.

JIM

Yeah, maybe.

DOMINIC

Slow down.

JIM

What?

DOMINIC

It's Camilla. Slow down. Slow down. Look how tight her jeans are. Lookit. Mama! What I'd give!

(calls out the window)

Camilla! Them blue jeans look really tight! You need help takin' them off... call me!

Dominic snorts and chuckles.

JIM

(sarcastic)

Oh, that was slick.

DOMINIC

Did you see the look on her face!

JIM

She was pissed.

DOMINIC

She looked pissed but she wasn't. She wore them jeans to see if anyone likes her ass... and someone did.

JIM

You yelled out a car window and said something dirty to her. She hates your guts.

DOMINIC

It gives me a reason to talk to her. I'll beg her to forgive me when I see her at twelve o'clock mass tomorrow.

JIM

What makes you think she'll forgive you?

DOMINIC

We'll both be standing in *church*! Under the statues and shit! She's *got* to! I could fill a bucket with what you don't know about women!

JIM

Hold on, there's Brenda.

DOMINIC

Who?

JIM

Brenda Doyle.

DOMINIC

Where?

JIM

Left side.

DOMINIC

Wadda yuh gonna do?

JIM

Quiet!

DOMINIC

Wadda yuh gonna do?

JIM

Watch.

DOMINIC

Wadda yuh gonna do?

JIM

Hold on... hold on...
    (calls out the window)
Yo! Brenda! How'd you do on the Spanish test?
    (pause)
Great!

Dominic looks at Jim astounded.

DOMINIC

What... the fuck... was *that*!

JIM

I was sayin' hi to Brenda.

DOMINIC

Spanish test?

JIM

Well...

DOMINIC
(bigger)
Spanish test?! She's got tits like bazookas and you're asking her *that*?

JIM
I'm not going to yell at her about her tits! She's got three older brothers who can beat the crap out of me!

DOMINIC
So? Camilla's whole family is in the mob! It didn't stop *me*!

JIM
That's because you're crazy.

DOMINIC
Maybe, but Camilla knows I risked my life to tell her how much I like her ass. That *means* something to a woman. Pull over here, I want to get some pizza. You want some pizza?

JIM
Naw.

DOMINIC
I want some pizza. You sure you don't want some pizza?

JIM
I'm sure.

DOMINIC
They got good pizza.

JIM
I know.

DOMINIC
You want some pizza?

JIM
I'm okay.

Dominic gets out of the car.

DOMINIC
While I'm gone if some girl walks by don't say nothin' stupid, okay?

JIM
Okay.

DOMINIC
Think about gettin' the speakers unless you made up your mind to never get laid. Twenty bucks, cassette thing, the works.

Dominic exits.

JIM
Dominic's business came to a sudden end when the police caught up with him. He was offered a choice, a year in prison or the Army. He

chose the Army. A lot of my friends decided to serve our country that way. Dominic started his hitch the same month I started college.

Dad enters.

JIM (cont'd)
At the end of my first semester Dad had a talk with me.

DAD
You need to find some kind of night job after your first semester.

JIM
Why?

DAD
We don't have enough money for your second semester.

JIM
But you said you saved money for college.

DAD
We did, we just didn't think you'd get this far.

Dad exits.

JIM
I got a job driving a cab at night. Luckily I was able to pass the stringent test New York City gives to hopeful cab drivers.

A MAN enters with a clipboard.

MAN
Grand Central Station.

JIM
What about it?

MAN
You know where it is?

JIM
50th Street? 60th?

MAN
Close enough.

The Man exits.

Jim sits in the driver's seat. A WOMAN enters and sits behind Jim.

JIM
Driving a cab in New York was a little rough at first but passengers were nice enough to give me helpful tips.

WOMAN
(enraged)
Slow down you idiot! You tryin' to kill us both! Slow *down*! You're a God

damn pot head, I can smell it! An' stop tryin' to look up my dress in the rear view mirror you *pervert*! I gotta comb with a sharp handle here, I'll run it through your neck!

The Woman exits as a POT HEAD enters.

>JIM

I also learned commerce and negotiating.

>POT HEAD

Man! I need to go like Queens!

>JIM

"Like Queens?" Is that the actual Queens or a facsimile?

>POT HEAD

No, like the real one.

>JIM

I'm sorry, I don't go to the real Queens or the fake one.

>POT HEAD

I'll pay what's on the meter.

>JIM

Is that like a "bonus" on your planet?

>POT HEAD

Also three joints and a Zippo lighter that needs a new flint.

>JIM

I don't need the lighter. We're off the meter. It's twenty in cash, in advance. I want five joints. I smoke the first joint now, if I'm not high by the time we get to the 59th Street Bridge I'll know you're full of crap and you get out of the cab.

>POT HEAD

If I have to get out of the cab...?

>JIM

Yeah?

>POT HEAD

Will you stop?

>JIM

I'll slow down.

>POT HEAD

Cool.

The Pot Head exits.

>JIM

Going to college during the day and driving a hack at night could take a lot out of you but I discovered I could maintain my energy if I got enough sleep, ate healthy food and did all the drugs I could.

Dad enters.

JIM *(cont'd)*
I also spent very little time at home.

DAD
Where you been?

JIM
Friend of mine at the garage got mugged... took him to Roosevelt Hospital.

DAD
Hurt bad?

JIM
Eight stitches.

DAD
Mugged?

JIM
Yeah.

DAD
Colored guy?

JIM
What?

DAD
He get mugged by a colored guy?

JIM
What difference does it make?

DAD
Just curious.

JIM
My friend is black and the guy who beat and robbed him was white.

DAD
Oh.

JIM
You surprised? To you it's not supposed to happen that way.

DAD
Don't be a smart ass. You stink. What's that smell?

JIM
That's the delightful odor of driving a cab for eleven hours.

DAD
You smokin' that marijuana? Is that what I smell? You go into the Army boy they're not gonna put up with that crap.

JIM
Are you kidding? The Army is the Promised Land of Pot. There was less marijuana at Woodstock.

DAD
That's bull. There's no way our troops would go into battle smokin' that stuff.

JIM
Dominic sent me a letter. He said his entire company is drunk or stoned most of the day.

DAD
He should be ashamed. If we lose this war all them other countries are gone.

JIM
"Other countries?" You can't even name them.

DAD
Don't get smart.

JIM
Couldn't find them on a map.

DAD
Stop.

JIM
But you'd spill blood there.

DAD
What a mouth on you! To think I lived long enough to hear crap like this!

JIM
It wasn't just the war. Dad understood less and less about me every day. My clothes.

DAD
Where'd you find *that*?

JIM
My friends.

DAD
Where'd you find *him*?

JIM
Girlfriends.

DAD
Where'd you find *her*?

JIM
My hair.

DAD
You look like crap.

JIM
My music.

DAD
Sounds like crap.

Dad exits.

JIM
We were becoming strangers and Dad was left with one last hope... that the Army would...

(yells to Dad)
What did you hope the Army would do?

DAD (O.S.)
Knock some damn sense into you!

JIM
Right after college I got a letter from my draft board telling me to report for my physical. I didn't take it lying down. I sprang into action and called a girl I knew in my English class.

The COLLEGE GIRL enters and speaks into a phone.

COLLEGE GIRL
No! I will not have sexual intercourse with you because you might get drafted!

The College Girl exits angrily.

JIM
I made a dozen calls like that. They all went the same way. After that I visited Warren, my friend's uncle. Warren was a psychologist, an organic farmer, a spiritual healer, and an anti-war activist.

WARREN enters and drives while Jim rides shotgun.

MUSIC: "GAT KIRWANI" BY RAVI SHANKAR

JIM (cont'd)
He was driving upstate to visit his secret pot farm and said it would be a good time for us to talk.

Jim listens to the music for several beats, finally.

WARREN
Where was I?

JIM
Um... something about no assembly of men or something?

WARREN
There is no assembly of men, women and machinery larger than the United States military. Its size is incomprehensible. The military spends

weeks and weeks plotting out ways to kill the largest number of people as they also wonder why everybody doesn't love them.

(holds up bag)
More soy chips?

JIM

No, I'm fine.

WARREN

The military is powerful and frightening but they live by this myth that everything they do is perfect. It works to your advantage.

JIM

How so?

WARREN

If you're *imperfect* in any way they don't have the time to reinvent you. It's too much trouble. More tea? I've got some in the thermos.

JIM

I'm fine.

WARREN

What they do is process thousands of people daily who have no problem doing whatever they're told. They don't want the hassle of dealing with people who won't do it their way. If you don't really want to go - they don't really want you. But you really have to *not* want to go. The second you give up on that, it's over. The acid I gave you...

JIM

What about it?

WARREN

Hold on.

Warren turns up the volume of the sitar music. Warren becomes lost in the music.

WARREN *(cont'd)*

This part is incredible.
(beat)
Mmm!

JIM

(couldn't mean it less)
Yeah.

Warren is still lost in the music.

JIM *(cont'd)*

What about the acid you gave me?

No reply.

JIM *(cont'd)*

Hello? Warren? Warren?

WARREN

Hmm?

JIM

The acid you gave me.

WARREN

What about it?

JIM

You were going to tell me something.

WARREN

Oh. It comes on like Rainbow with a touch of Pyramid. But it's not.

JIM

Then what is it?

WARREN

Within twenty minutes you'll know you're trippin' on Lightning.

JIM

Lightning, what's that like?

WARREN

It's a laser of total spiritual truth and enlightenment that awakens your conscience to the mysteries of the cosmos. It also relieves minor arthritis pain.

Warren exits.

JIM

LSD wasn't my drug of choice but I wanted to be in prime shape when I got to the induction center. I also didn't sleep for two days. Breakfast was LSD with vodka and a beer chaser. My pulse was a hundred and thirty, my nose was bleeding and I was seeing bugs on the wall that weren't there. So far, so good. I left the house early to catch a bus.

Dad enters in the car.

JIM *(cont'd)*

Dad was on his way to work and stopped before the bus came.

DAD

Hop in.

JIM

I'm taking the bus.

DAD

I'll drive you.

JIM
The bus goes right to the place.

DAD
C'mon!

Jim gets in the car.

JIM
I could've taken the bus.

DAD
What the hell, it's a mile or two out of the way.

JIM
Thanks.

DAD
Piece of cake.

JIM
Good thing I got a lift. The acid was really kicking in. I was seeing trash cans dancing.

Jim tilts his head back and looks out the window.

JIM *(cont'd)*
Woa!

DAD
What?

JIM
That Chevy... it's gigantic.

DAD
That's a billboard.

JIM
Oh. Didn't sleep much.

DAD
Relax. You want to be fresh for your big day.

JIM
Of course.

Jim turns on the radio.

MUSIC: "BACK IN THE U.S.S.R." BY THE BEATLES

JIM *(cont'd)*
Oh, excellent!

DAD
What is that!

JIM
The Beatles.

DAD
Is that them British fags?

JIM
They're not fags.

DAD
Have you *seen* them?

JIM
Yeah, so have a hundred million girls who are dying to screw any one of them.

DAD
Well, their stuff is crap. It's not even music! It's noise, just yelling and screaming!

JIM
You know, you're ruining this song.

DAD
It's already ruined! Turn it off. C'mon!
    (beat)
I said turn it off!

Jim turns off the music.

JIM
Shit!

DAD
And don't use words like that when you get there.

JIM
The word "shit" offends guys who throw hand grenades?

DAD
Knock it off. Just relax. Show your best face. They'll see you've got smarts and probably post you some place nice in the U.S.

JIM
I never understood that thinking. To support a foreign war but hope you get assigned to a post in Malibu.

DAD
Look at that, guys are lined up already.

JIM
Yeah.

DAD
Okay, well... Give me a call after.

JIM

Huh?

DAD

Let me know how it went.

JIM

Okay.

Jim gets out of the car.

JIM *(cont'd)*

As I got out of the car I knew I had to say something to my father, but what?

Jim builds his courage and slowly turns to face his father.

JIM *(cont'd)*

I'm sorry, Dad. I won't let them take me. Your war was Hitler and Pearl Harbor, this war is not. I have a one-way train ticket to Montreal in my pocket and I cleaned out my savings account. If they say I'm good to go, I won't be coming home. Tell Mom... tell her... whatever you need to.

    (then)

But I didn't say that. Instead I said...

    (then)

Bye.

Jim takes a step or two but stops when...

DAD

When do you think you'll be back?

Jim turns and looks at Dad. Finally...

JIM

I don't know.

Jim and Dad look at each other.

Lights fade.

END OF ACT ONE

ACT TWO

Jim takes small steps as he walks, giving us the feeling he's on a very long line. After a beat a SOLDIER enters.

SOLDIER
Double line you stupid fuckin' idiots! Double line! Are you potheads too fuckin' stupid to know what a fuckin' double line looks like!

JIM
Eight hundred of us had gotten the same letter. The Army filed us into two enormous rooms to give us tests.

SOLDIER
Do not turn your tests over until it begins. The questions in your test are multiple choice. Letters A through D. That's A... B... C and D! Do not guess if you do not know the answer! The computer knows if you were guessing even if you get it right!

JIM
Computers were primitive in the sixties, but they already knew how to detect lies.

SOLDIER
The computer can also tell if you are giving wrong answers on purpose!

The Soldier exits.

JIM
They didn't tell me what my grade was but I'm certain is was a zero. Think about it; getting a zero on a multiple choice exam is almost as hard as getting a hundred! Somehow the Army's computer didn't spot that. I was kept behind to take a second test with a small handful of guys most of whom had wet chins and bad haircuts. One of them had eleven fingers.

A DUMB GUY enters and talks with Jim in loud whispers.

DUMB GUY
Pssst! Pssst!

JIM
What?

DUMB GUY
What's the answer to number four?

JIM
Caucasian.

DUMB GUY
Thanks!

419

The Dumb Guy exits.

JIM
This test was different. It had true-false questions like "being criticized makes me angry, sometimes I hear voices." It was pretty much designed to see if you're a psychopath. I thought true-false answers were over simplified so I began to pencil in answers like "maybe" and "sometimes." They took my test away and sent me to see the shrink.

The SHRINK enters holding papers.

JIM *(cont'd)*
The Shrink at the Army Induction Center; I don't remember his name but I know if I wanted to keep a beer cold I'd place it on his heart.

SHRINK
Name?

JIM
Yes.

SHRINK
Yes what?

JIM
Yes, I have one.

SHRINK
And what might it be!

JIM
Jim.

SHRINK
Why are you here?

JIM
I don't know, why are you here?

SHRINK
Let's just move on. Addictive drugs?

JIM
You have some?

SHRINK
No. You checked "yes." What sort of drugs do you use?

JIM
Grass, hash if I can get it, but only when I'm uptight or if I'm bored or if there's a really scary movie on late night TV. You get high, watch that shit, it's a trip.

SHRINK
Any other drugs?

JIM

Vicodin, Demerol, Percocet, Xanax, my father works in a hospital, the pharmacy has locks but they're too busy to use them. Ritalin, Nardil, Valium, but none of it is addictive, I can stop whenever I want. And acid because I'm on a journey to increase my overall understanding of the universe.

SHRINK

Homosexual tendencies?

JIM

Why did you look hopeful when you asked me that?

SHRINK

I looked nothing of the sort!

JIM

I'm sorry but I saw a twinkle.

SHRINK

Maybe that was wishful thinking on your part.

JIM

No, I saw a little somethin' there.

SHRINK

You saw no such thing!

JIM

Then why even ask me?

SHRINK

Because you checked "yes" *and* "no."

JIM

Well, I like getting women naked...

SHRINK

Uh huh.

JIM

And I like having sex with them...

SHRINK

Okay.

JIM

But when we're done...

SHRINK

Yes.

JIM

I like to wear their clothes. It's why I tend to date women my size.

SHRINK

I don't understand.

JIM

A woman much smaller than me...

SHRINK

Okay.

JIM

If I put her stuff on, it gets stretched out of shape. She'll get pissed off about that. You put on her panties, it stretches out the waist band, she'll never let you forget it.

SHRINK

Aha.

JIM

And I dated this large woman, a woman way tall, really big.

SHRINK

Okay.

JIM

Her clothing just *swam* on me. I looked ridiculous.

SHRINK

So you enjoy feeling like a woman?

JIM

No! I enjoy *looking* like one. *Feeling* like a woman? What the hell is that? That's sick and twisted! It's insulting! Are you on fire?

SHRINK

Am I *what*?

JIM

It looks like you're on fire.

SHRINK

I can assure you I am *not* on fire.

JIM

You look like a tree that's on fire and all the animals and insects living inside you are running out trying to save their lives. But the fire is at the top of you and the bottom of you and they are in the middle with nowhere to go. The four-legged ones run around crying for their mothers. The birds and insects try to fly away but the fire sucks them back and they can only flap their wings, fall to the ground and die. They beg for their right to live a natural life but you chose to let your flames consumed them!

    (instantly pleasant)
But... apparently... it was only my imagination.

SHRINK

Have you ever been institutionalized?

JIM

(*furious*)

Yes! Yes! I was put into an institution by my father when I was ten!

SHRINK

And where was this?

JIM

(*more furious*)

Little League! I *hated* it! He stood behind a fence and yelled at me for three fuckin' years! We're winning twenty-two to nothin', I'm comin' around third base and what's he do? He yells "Slide!" Yeah! Head first! "Slide!" He wants to make sure we *obliterate* a teamed called "The Blue Birds." Broke my wrist *and* my shoulder! Nine years later and I *still* can't lift my right arm more than this!

Jim raises his right arm only slightly above his shoulder.

JIM (cont'd)

Which has totally shot any chance I had of joining the Nazi party!

SHRINK

Show me again.

JIM

Hmm?

SHRINK

Your right arm.

Jim raises his arm.

JIM

Like this?

SHRINK

Does it hurt?

JIM

No, it just won't go any higher. Thanks, Dad.

SHRINK

Have you seen one of our doctors?

JIM

No.

SHRINK

I'll be right back.

The Shrink begins to exit then stops.

SHRINK (cont'd)

Um... if I send you to a doctor...

JIM

Yes?

SHRINK

Are you wearing any...

JIM

No, not today.

SHRINK

Good.

The Shrink exits.

JIM

All my plans, all my work, failing the test, pills, booze, dropping acid, no sleep, listening to sitar music for three hours... didn't need any of it. Turns out the forward elevation of my right arm was less than ninety degrees which made me unfit for military service. It's ironic when your absurd plans bathed in utter nonsense are replaced with logic. I left the Army Induction Center still high on acid, I'm not sure how I got home. I think I took a Zeplin.

Dad enters.

DAD

How'd it go?

JIM

Hmm?

DAD

You were supposed to call me.

JIM

I was?

DAD

I told you to call me when you were done.

JIM

Why?

DAD

To let me know how it went.

JIM

Oh.

DAD

So?

JIM

Hmm?

DAD

How'd it go?

JIM

Oh.

(pause)

They classified me as 4-F.

DAD

What's that?

JIM

Unfit for military service.

DAD

What!

JIM

Yeah.

DAD

Unfit?

JIM

Yeah.

DAD

Why?

JIM

My right arm.

DAD

The shoulder thing?

JIM

Yeah. I can't get it high enough.

DAD

Why the hell would they need people to get their arms high!

JIM

So the enemy can see you when you surrender?

DAD

Cut the crap! It's not funny!

JIM

I wasn't trying to be funny.

DAD

Did you raise it all you can?

JIM

Yeah.

DAD

Did your best?

JIM

Yeah.

DAD
Did you hold back?

JIM
No.

DAD
You hold back a little? Get yourself deferred?

JIM
If that's all you had to do, *no one* would be in the Army. They took X-rays. I spent ten minutes with a doctor.

DAD
That's not very long.

JIM
Everyone else got ten *seconds*. The doctor OK'd a guy with eleven fingers!

DAD
What did the doctor ask you?

JIM
He said "Can you raise your arm any higher?"

DAD
What'd you say?

JIM
I said "No."

DAD
How did he know you weren't faking?

JIM
He *pushed* it.

DAD
What happened?

JIM
He heard a grinding sound.

DAD
Did he say anything?

JIM
Other than I can expect arthritis in a few years?

DAD
Yes!

JIM
He said a couple of things.

DAD
Like what?

                                JIM

He said "If you were winning twenty-two to nothing why did your father tell you to slide?"

                                DAD

He can drop dead! What else!

                                JIM

He said therapy might help.

                                DAD

The arm?

                                JIM

Yeah.

                                DAD

Exercise?

                                JIM

Yeah.

                                DAD

Loosen it up.

                                JIM

Something like that.

                                DAD

You could do arm exercises.

                                JIM

Yeah.

                                DAD

Raise your arm, stretch it out.

                                JIM

Yeah.

                                DAD

Bit by bit.

                                JIM

Sure.

                                DAD

And if you did that...

                                JIM

Yeah?

                                DAD

You could go back, try again.

                                JIM

    (couldn't mean it less)
Great idea.

DAD

Ask them to test you again.

JIM

Beg them to test me again!

DAD

Atta boy!

JIM

"Here yuh go, Sparky! Take a look at this right arm *now*!"

DAD

Do some of that uh…

JIM

Therapy.

DAD

Yeah. You know what your problem is?

JIM

I don't have a girlfriend.

DAD

Your arms, you need to build muscle. You're out of shape, flabby, you lay around like a sack of potatoes all day long.

JIM

This from a man who owns five TV's with remote controls.

DAD

Build up the strength in that arm, get it to go higher, go back and show them!

Dad exits. Jim yells after him.

JIM

That's what I'm thinkin'! Do a thousand pushups a day!
    (beat)
Gonna take a nap first!
    (beat)
Then I'll do the pushups!
    (then)
It was time to get a place of my own but I didn't have the cash. Then some drug dealer left a roll of hundreds in the back seat of my cab and I did. I got an apartment over the Carnegie Deli in midtown Manhattan. The Carnegie is Ground Zero for comedians. It's where I met Jack. He was half of a comedy team.

JACK enters.

JIM *(cont'd)*

I was writing for the team when Jack gave me bad news about his partner.

JACK
He got the lead in a play!

JIM
Bobby?

JACK
Yeah!

JIM
Then he's in trouble!

JACK
I know! He can't act!

JIM
I own a *sofa* who acts better than Bobby!

JACK
Lumber has more charisma!

JIM
Well, this is your chance to work alone.

JACK
I can't work alone!

JIM
Why not?

JACK
If it goes bad I got no one else to blame!

JIM
Yeah.

JACK
It gets worse. Bobby and I are supposed to start a tour on Monday.

JIM
That's three days from now.

JACK
A week in Chicago, a week in Philly, then Boston and New York.

JIM
Man, you better find someone fast.

JACK
Already have.

JIM
Who?

JACK
I'm lookin' at him.

JIM
What!

JACK
Why not? You wrote half our stuff. You've seen us a hundred times, you can step right in.

JIM
No. No way. Sorry. Won't happen. Please, pick someone else. Night clubs, travel, that's not me. I'm not gonna trudge all over the country, work in dark, smoky night clubs making drunk people laugh while I live in cheap motels and eat all my meals in greasy diners. Sorry. No way in hell.

JACK
It's a tour of Playboy Clubs.

JIM
(without missing a beat)
And yet seeing America might be fun.

JACK
We split a grand each week, they throw in airfare, hotel and dinner at the club.

JIM
Hell, if I'm going to do this in three days we'd better start rehearsing.

JACK
You remember everything Bobby does?

JIM
Sure.

JACK
Don't do it that way. We leave Monday.

Jack gets in the car.

JIM
As a Catskill comic once told me "Being a comedian is a lot like being a hooker. First you do it for close friends for free. Then you figure what the hell, I might as well make money doing this!" Jack and I cashed in the airline tickets and bought a car. Yeah, a Ford. Dependable. Gets you home.

Jim joins Jack in the car. Jim drives.

MUSIC: "MERCURY BLUES" BY ALAN JACKSON

JIM *(cont'd)*
We never missed a gig, forty-six states, all of it by car.

JACK
South Carolina, how much more?

JIM
Four, five hours.

JACK
We gonna keep listening to this Hee Haw crap?

JIM
It's not crap, it's what most people listen to down here.

JACK
What's this song about anyway?

JIM
Not sure. Most country songs are about trucks, infidelity or dogs.

JACK
I think this South Carolina thing was a bad idea. If I see a sign that says "Jews Go Home" we turn back.

The MUSIC fades.

JIM
Trust me, you're going to love it. Southern girls love to have sex with losers.

JACK
You're just saying that to make me feel better.

JIM
Best of all the south has family-style restaurants.

JACK
What's that?

JIM
You've never been to one?

JACK
No, for Jews the South starts and ends with Miami.

JIM
We'll stop at the first one we come to. They have these long tables that seat twenty or thirty people and you sit wherever you want.

JACK
With other people?

JIM
Yeah.

JACK
Strangers?

JIM
Yeah.

JACK
At the table with you?

JIM
Yeah.

JACK

That's disgusting.

JIM

Stop. They serve seven, eight things.

JACK

Like what?

JIM

It's the South so it's barbecued ribs, mac and cheese, fried chicken, ham, biscuits, collard greens, big pitchers of ice tea.

JACK

It's getting better.

JIM

It's home cooking.

JACK

Is it kosher?

JIM

No. They bring the food on huge platters, big bowls, you take all you want, when it runs out they bring more.

JACK

And there's other people sitting at the table with you, like a family?

JIM

Right.

JACK

Is there arguing?

JIM

No.

JACK

How can it be a family dinner without arguing?

JIM

They do the best they can.

JACK

It's not a family dinner unless someone's telling me I'm wasting my life.

JIM

Same here.

JACK

Do they at least have an elderly woman crying "Why can't we have a nice dinner just once?"

JIM

Never happens. But it's all you can eat.

JACK

"All you can eat." That's a Jewish prayer.

JIM
They're all over the South.

JACK
Family style... that wouldn't work in New York.

As Jack exits.

JACK *(cont'd)*
Where's the lasagne! Hey! We're outta lasagne! Who do I have to kill or fuck for more lasagne!

JIM
Every other week, I'd call the Bronx and check in.

Mom enters with a phone. Jim uses a phone.

MOM
Where are you calling from?

JIM
Montana.

MOM
What's that like?

JIM
Cold.

MOM
Who are you touring with?

JIM
Blue Mountain Rascals.

MOM
I never heard of them.

JIM
Big in Montana.

MOM
Do you have a sweater?

JIM
Yes.

MOM
Underwear?

JIM
Yes.

MOM
Do you have enough socks?

JIM
Yes.

MOM

If you need more socks I can mail you some.

JIM

I'm okay, I just want to say hi.

MOM

Hold on, your father wants to say hello.

Dad enters and uses Mom's phone. Mom exits.

DAD

Where are you calling from?

JIM

Montana.

DAD

What's that like?

JIM

Cold.

DAD

Who you touring with?

JIM

Blue Mountain Rascals.

DAD

Never heard of them.

JIM

Big in Montana.

DAD

You have a sweater?

JIM

Yes.

DAD

Underwear?

JIM

Yes.

DAD

Enough socks?

JIM

Yes.

DAD

If you need more socks your mother can mail you some.

JIM

I'm okay, I just want to say hi.

Dad and Jim hang up their phones.

JIM *(cont'd)*
Jack and I learned a lot from being on the road those four years... mostly we didn't want to do *another* four. After that we stayed in New York. We didn't need the car anymore so I gave it to my father.

Dad examines the car with wonder.

                            DAD
You're shittin' me!

                            JIM
No.

                            DAD
Mine?

                            JIM
Yeah.

                            DAD
To keep?

                            JIM
Yeah.

                            DAD
And it's a Ford.

                            JIM
Yeah. Ford. Dependable.

                            DAD
Gets you home.

                            JIM
I know.

                            DAD
The inside smells a little.

                            JIM
Sorry.
    (then)
Getting rid of the smell of booze and marijuana wasn't easy.

                            DAD
A little air freshener will fix that. And you don't want it?

                            JIM
Naw.

                            DAD
Why?

                            JIM
I live in Manhattan. There's nowhere to park it.

DAD

Aha.

JIM

You have a garage.

DAD

And you don't need it?

JIM

No.

DAD

Not going on the road?

JIM

No, there's plenty work in New York. Jack's doing commercials, I'm writing for some comedians and a few underground papers.

DAD

When are you going to stop wasting your life and get a real job?

JIM

When are you going to stop drinking, smoking and gaining weight?

DAD

Never mind about me, it breaks my heart to see you waste your life.

JIM

I'm going to tell you something about me and I don't think you're going to like it.

DAD

You're a homo?

JIM

No. What I do makes me happy.

DAD

You're completely out of your mind.

As Dad exits.

DAD (cont'd)

Thanks for the car.

JIM

(calls after Dad)
You're welcome!
(then)
It wasn't long after that I got a call from my agent.

DOROTHY enters. Jim and Dorothy speak on phones.

JIM (cont'd)

Hello.

DOROTHY
Where the hell have you been!

JIM
Dorothy?

DOROTHY
I've been calling you for days!

JIM
I was at the Lakeview Hotel.

DOROTHY
Where the hell is that?

JIM
The Catskills and don't ever stay there.

DOROTHY
Why the hell not!

JIM
There's no view of the lake because there *is* no lake!

DOROTHY
And what the hell were you doing in the Catskills?

JIM
Writing gags for Lenny Hersch. When I wasn't doing that I was telling women I was a lawyer.

DOROTHY
Well, I got a call from Steve Crowley in Hollywood.

JIM
Crowley, isn't he the guy who has that talking dog show?

DOROTHY
Yes, it's in the top ten. His new show is a talking donkey.

JIM
Oh, there's a stretch.

DOROTHY
Don't be a schmuck! I sent your material to him. He's looking for writers. He loves your stuff, he wants to give you thirteen weeks in Los Angeles as a writer on the show.

JIM
Dorothy, Jeez... I've heard he's a gold-plated prick, a total son of a bitch. All he does is turn out these idiotic shows that appeal to the lowest possible mentality. I'd have to give up my last drop of self respect to work for a no-talent dirt bag like Crowley.

DOROTHY
It pays three thousand a week.

JIM

I'll be there tomorrow.

Jim hangs up the phone.

MUSIC: "LIVING THING" BY ELECTRIC LIGHT ORCHESTRA

JIM *(cont'd)*

I took a Moment to ask myself "What am I made of?" The answer came quickly "Not very much." Oh my God, I've been an Angelino my whole life and never knew it! Los Angeles, a city where the entire population was born in another state. A place where virtually no one keeps the hair color they were born with. A city where people, on average, can name only two Mexican friends but eight Mexican restaurants.

The MUSIC fades.

JIM *(cont'd)*

My postman saw I get a weekly check from a studio, now I have his head shot. I have a girlfriend who's on her third name. I've been invited to seven parties but, so far, no one will give me the address. Scientology has told me if I join I can fast track to level six. I watch the news every night to make sure tomorrow's going to be eighty degrees and sunny. I know three guys named Bob and they all spell it different. Jack, my ex-partner, he's here now. He's on a sitcom so he can't be seen talking to me in public.

Jim gets into his car.

JIM *(cont'd)*

All of these things were part of my west coast indoctrination but I became an official Angelino when I got t-boned in Beverly Hills.

SFX: HUGE CAR CRASH

A WOMAN with trendy sunglasses enters. A shaken Jim gets out of the car.

WOMAN

Good Gawd! Bummer!

JIM

I know...

WOMAN

Wadda rush!

JIM

Uh huh.

WOMAN

I think my car really violated your car's space.

(then)

WOMAN *(cont'd)*
Are you like okay?

JIM
I don't think so.

WOMAN
That's odd.

JIM
Why?

WOMAN
Because you look *fabulous*.

JIM
Do I?

WOMAN
Incredible.

JIM
Thank you.

WOMAN
The red thing, on your face, is that a tribal marking? Native American? Apache? Kiowa maybe?

JIM
No, it's blood.

WOMAN
Well, for a man with a head injury you look fantastic.

JIM
Thanks.

WOMAN
Do you work out?

JIM
No.

WOMAN
Then I hate you.

The Woman exits.

JIM
My car was totaled. I was going to buy something sensible at a used car lot but I never made it past the BMW dealership.

A SALESWOMAN enters.

SALESWOMAN
Sweet lookin' car.

JIM
Sure is.

                    SALESWOMAN
Looks like she's doing sixty just sitting there.
                         JIM
Yeah.
                    SALESWOMAN
And this model, that color, total babe magnet.
                         JIM
You think?
                    SALESWOMAN
Trust me, I *know*. Do me a favor, will you?
                         JIM
What?
                    SALESWOMAN
Stand closer to the car.
                         JIM
Stand...?
                    SALESWOMAN
Closer. Just a few feet. Go ahead. Just get closer.

Jim takes awkward steps toward the car.

                    SALESWOMAN *(cont'd)*
Now smile.
                         JIM
Hmm?
                    SALESWOMAN
Smile.

Jim smiles.

                    SALESWOMAN *(cont'd)*
You just got better looking.
                         JIM
What's the sticker say?
                    SALESWOMAN
It says "Hello, handsome, forty-five thousand and I'm yours."
                         JIM
Forty.
                    SALESWOMAN
For this car?
                         JIM
Yeah, I'll be back tomorrow with forty-thousand.

SALESWOMAN
And how will you pay the other five?

JIM
I'm offering forty.

SALESWOMAN
Aha.

JIM
And?

SALESWOMAN
No.

JIM
Forty thousand, *cash*.

SALESWOMAN
We don't take cash.

JIM
Why not?

SALESWOMAN
Takes too long to count.

JIM
Forty-one thousand.

SALESWOMAN
No.

JIM
Forty-two.

SALESWOMAN
No.

JIM
Okay, okay, forty-three.

SALESWOMAN
Let me check with my manager. He says no.

JIM
You didn't even ask him!

SALESWOMAN
Didn't have to.

JIM
Forty-four. Final offer.

SALESWOMAN
You're gonna walk away over a thousand dollars?

JIM
Yes! And you can stand there and watch me do it!

The Saleswoman looks far off and points.

                    SALESWOMAN
> That your car?

                    JIM
> It's a rental.

                    SALESWOMAN
> You're gonna drive away in *that* and feel *good* about it?

                    JIM
> *(sighs)*
> I'll be here tomorrow with a bank check for the forty-five.

                    SALESWOMAN
> Excellent. We'll put tax and license on your credit card.

The Saleswoman exits.

                    JIM
> I'm glad my Dad didn't see that. Sunday night I always made sure to call home.

Dad enters and talks to Jim on the phone.

                    DAD
> Where are you calling from?

                    JIM
> My apartment.

                    DAD
> What's that like?

                    JIM
> Filthy.

                    DAD
> You have a sweater?

                    JIM
> Yeah.

                    DAD
> Underwear?

                    JIM
> Yes.

                    DAD
> Enough socks?

                    JIM
> Yes.

                    DAD
> You sure?

JIM
They have stores that sell them here.

DAD
If you need more socks your mother can mail you some.

JIM
I'm okay, I just want to say hi.

DAD
Working?

JIM
Danny the Donkey, yeah.

DAD
The show is kinda stupid.

JIM
That's our goal.

DAD
What else?

JIM
Gotta girlfriend.

DAD
One of them hippie sluts?

JIM
(sarcastic)
Yes, Dad... total hippie slut.

DAD
She Catholic?

JIM
Yeah.

DAD
Good. What else?

JIM
Bought a car.

DAD
What kind?

JIM
BMW.

DAD
Made in Germany.

JIM
Yeah.

DAD
Hitler killed my friends so you could do that?

JIM

It's a beautiful car, Dad.

DAD

Why not a Ford? Dependable. Gets you home.

JIM

I checked out some Fords.

DAD

And?

JIM

They look like shoe boxes, no styling.

DAD

You don't buy a car for style. You buy a car for dependability. You don't have a family yet but someday you will. And you want to know when you put your family in that car you're all going to make it home. There's a lotta fancy gadgets and wiring in BMWs that can screw up. Then you're at the mercy of some Kraut mechanic! You should get your money back. Tell them there's a *thousand* things wrong with it.

JIM

Nothing's wrong with it!

DAD

Pull some wires! Drop a bag of sugar in the gas tank! Didn't I teach you nothin'!

Dad hangs up and exits.

JIM

After that the Bronx and Los Angeles didn't talk for a couple of months.

Mom enters. She and Jim talk on the phone.

JIM *(cont'd)*

Mom finally broke the silence.

MOM

James, this is your mother.

JIM

I could tell.
 (then)
She called me James. This is serious.

MOM

Are you coming to New York anytime soon?

JIM

Yeah, next month, the show is down.

MOM

It's having a hiatal?

JIM
It's call a hiatus, Ma. Hiatal is a hernia.

MOM
Then you're coming home?

JIM
Yeah, I'll be back in New York, sure.
(then)
I stay in a hotel. It works out better than way.

MOM
You need to come visit.

JIM
I always come visit.

MOM
Your father.

JIM
What about him?

MOM
He wants to go fishing.

JIM
Why?

MOM
He likes fishing.

JIM
He can go fishing whenever he wants.

MOM
He wants to go with you.

JIM
Why?

MOM
Jesus Christ you're such a smart fancy pants writer but you don't know crapola! He misses you! Do you understand? He misses his son. He's trying to work up the courage to ask you. Don't tell him I called you and if you say no to him I'll never speak to you again. Did you get the socks?

JIM
Yeah.

MOM
Good. Love you.

Mom hangs up the phone and exits.

                              JIM

June came, I flew home, and I mean *home*, to the Bronx. I slept in my old room, the first time in years. Oh, the girls who had been in that room! If the walls could talk!
   (beat)
Actually the walls would have very little to say. In any case I didn't get much sleep.

Dad enters and gets in the car, Jim drives.

                         JIM *(cont'd)*
Dad and I were out the door at three AM. We were headed for Montauk to meet up with two buddies from his bombardment group. A day of war stories and tuna fishing was at hand.

Jim turns on the radio.

MUSIC: "SURRENDER" BY CHEAP TRICK

                              DAD
Aw, what is that?
                              JIM
A little music.
                              DAD
It's three in the morning and you're going to do *that* to me?
                              JIM
It's just music!
                              DAD
It's not music! It's noise! It's screaming!
                              JIM
It's a song on the top ten list.
                              DAD
It should be on the top of a garbage list. Change the station!
                              JIM
Won't do any good. All the disc jockeys who play Bing Crosby have died!
                              DAD
You like this? This is what Hollywood has done to you?
                              JIM
I've always been like this!
                              DAD
That's the problem with your generation. You listen to garbage when you can be talking to each other.

JIM

For God's sake!

DAD

I see you once a year now. It would kill you to talk?

JIM

Okay. Fine.

Jim turns off the radio. Silence. Finally.

JIM *(cont'd)*

Look at this. It's three AM and there's already traffic headed the other way to the city.

DAD

Every day.

JIM

All these people bought homes out here thinking they'd be living the dream.

DAD

Is it any better in Los Angeles?

JIM

No. In fact it's worse. Is it good anywhere?

DAD

No. But that's life. Traffic gets worse and then you die.
    (beat)
You like it out there?

JIM

I don't know. Kinda. Weather's nice, never gets cold.

DAD

Name another good thing.

JIM

Tacos.

DAD

What else?

JIM

It's a very different place. Hard to describe.

DAD

Try.

JIM

No one cares about the process, only the results.

DAD

I don't understand.

JIM
Okay. I went to a party where someone was celebrating the article he did for Architectural Digest. He's a photographer. All eight pages had been blown up so people could walk around and look at them while drinking champagne.

DAD
Fancy schmancy.

JIM
Pictures of a massive estate in Beverly Hills that was in danger of being torn down. The new owner was at the party, he told me it took three years, five million dollars and two hundred different craftsmen to bring the house back to what it was.

DAD
Looked good?

JIM
Breathtaking. If I lived in this house I don't believe I could ever leave it. Later that night, when people left, I noticed more of them congratulated the photographer than the owner.

DAD
So?

JIM
So, if you think the photographer deserves most of the credit... you need to move to Los Angeles as soon as you can.

DAD
Gotcha.
   (beat)
But you like your work?

JIM
Yeah, the writers are all funny people. Funnier than the show.

DAD
Eh... sometimes the show is funny.

JIM
You watch the show?

DAD
I tape it and watch it in the morning. It's on too late.

JIM
Nine-thirty?

DAD
Yeah. When you going to name a character after me?

JIM
You want that?

DAD

Yeah.

JIM

Why?

DAD

It would be nice.

JIM

Like... what kind of character?

DAD

I don't know, someone funny like a mailman or something.

JIM

Okay.

DAD

No one stupid. Just a regular guy.

JIM

Gotcha.

DAD

But handsome. And one of the stars on the show...

JIM

Which one?

DAD

Doesn't matter.

JIM

Okay.

DAD

One of the stars might say something like "Okay, Roy. Thanks for the mail, Roy. See you tomorrow, Roy." I mean, I'm not a writer or anything but something like that.

JIM

No, that's actually better than what *we* write. Consider it done.

DAD

Good.

JIM

Okay.

DAD

When it's on I'll stay up late and watch it.

JIM

Deal.

DAD

I'll call Joe and Danny, tell them to watch.

JIM
Are those your air corps buddies we're fishing with?

DAD
Yeah. We'll be talkin' over old times today, guys we knew...

JIM
Sure.

DAD
You'll probably be bored out of your mind.

JIM
Naw, we'll be on a boat, I'll be busy vomiting. I just hope you're not embarrassed when they learn your son is a life-long civilian.

DAD
Embarrassed... no.

Dad looks out the window then at Jim, finally.

DAD *(cont'd)*
Glad actually.

JIM
Of what?

DAD
That they didn't take you.

Jim thinks for a few beats, then.

JIM
You're telling me... you're *glad* the Army didn't want me?

DAD
Yeah.

JIM
I gotta hand it to you.

DAD
What?

JIM
You hid it very well.

DAD
That was eight, nine years ago, and I was all...
   (stops, sighs)
I feel different now.

JIM
The war's over.

DAD
Wars are never over.

Again, Jim thinks for a few beats, then.

JIM
You should know, if they had not found the problem with my arm... I mean, if they accepted me that day...

DAD
I know.

JIM
What?

DAD
I know.

JIM
Know what?

DAD
Canada.

JIM
What?

DAD
You would have gone there.

JIM
How in the hell did you know?

DAD
Your mother found the ticket in your pants. Showed it to me a couple years ago.

JIM
She held on to it for-

DAD
The woman don't throw out nothin'. You did what you had to do. It's okay, I understand. Your mind was made up all along.

JIM
No. I was like a lot of guys, I wasn't sure what I was going to do for years. But right after I got my letter from the Draft Board...

DAD
Yeah.

JIM
Dominic came home.

DAD
God...

JIM
I know.

DAD
I went the first day.

JIM
I went all three. On the last day Dom's mother asked if they could open the coffin so she could kiss her baby goodbye.

DAD
Good God! Good God! Please, tell me they didn't!

JIM
They told her his body was too damaged to view.

DAD
No, c'mon! Dammit!

JIM
After they buried Dominic I got drunk with one of the Army guys. He told me the coffin contained *most* of Dominic.

Dad blesses himself.

DAD
Aw, Jesus, Mary and Joseph! I loved that kid! He was crazy but I loved him!

JIM
Everyone did. And we lost him. I was done.

Silence, then.

DAD
We went there, you know.

JIM
Where?

DAD
Montreal. Your mother and I.

JIM
When?

DAD
Last year.

JIM
Why?

DAD
Your mother said it would be a sin not to use the ticket.

JIM
You guys used the train ticket Mom found?

DAD
Yeah.

JIM
Which means you had to buy *another* one way ticket.

DAD
Yeah.

JIM
And a round trip ticket.

DAD
Plus hotel and meals.

JIM
Just to use the one way ticket!

DAD
Yeah.

JIM
What did all that cost you?

DAD
About six hundred dollars.

JIM
You spent six hundred dollars to justify the use of a forty dollar one-way ticket?

DAD
They don't give refunds.

JIM
You took the train to Canada?

DAD
You wouldn't have liked it there.

JIM
Why not?

DAD
First of all everyone there is Canadian.

JIM
What else?

DAD
Cold and clammy.

JIM
When did you go?

DAD
July.

JIM
That's the screwiest story I've ever heard.

DAD
It made sense to your mother, made her happy. We had a good time.

JIM
That's hysterical. You should tell your buddies.

                              DAD
Joe and Danny?
                              JIM
Yeah.
   (beat)
Were they in the same bomber group?
                              DAD
Affirmative.
                              JIM
Same plane?
                              DAD
No.
                              JIM
Are they going to be calling you... what was it Frankie Two Fingers told me...?
                              DAD
I dunno.
                              JIM
What was it?
                              DAD
I forget.
                              JIM
How could you forget?
                              DAD
It was a million years ago.
                              JIM
There was a wolf painted on the plane and... Lone Wolf! That's it, right?
                              DAD
I dunno.
                              JIM
That was it, wasn't it?
                              DAD
It was a long time ago.
                              JIM
Lone Wolf, they still call you that?
                              DAD
No. No one does.
                              JIM
Why not? It's a cool nickname. The plane got shot up, the pilot was killed but you were able to fly it back and-

DAD
It's not how I got the name.

JIM
Lone Wolf, you got the plane back.

DAD
I did. But it's not what the nickname means.

JIM
What does it mean?

DAD
When we landed at Ridgewell...

JIM
Yeah.

DAD
I was the only one alive on the plane.

JIM
What!

DAD
They were all gone.

JIM
My God! How many?

DAD
All of them. Flynn, our navigator, I saw him get hit, he bled out. Lizowski, the bombardier, I looked back, he was on the deck. I could see his legs. They were moving. For a while. The intercom was shot. I tried yelling to the back of the plane but there was a hole in the fuselage, well there were a *lot* of holes in the fuselage; the noise was... there was no way we could hear each other. Holes the size of grapefruits, bullet patterns all over, they shot the crap out of us. Barzetti, Taylor, Brody, Fat Freddy, Drucker... you didn't have to check. These guys were gone. Lone Wolf, worst nickname ever.

JIM
Who gave you that nickname?

DAD
Some asshole.

JIM
Why didn't you tell him to shove it?

DAD
The war... it was so dark and screwed up. We knew half of us would be dead before our tour was over. The only thing that helped was booze and dark humor. We were all twenty-four going on a hundred.

JIM

Like Frankie used to say... nicknames are things given to you out of respect and affection.

DAD

Yeah.

Silence.

JIM

We didn't say anything for the next half hour. I was about to break the silence but a piece of metal under the car beat me to it.

SFX: THE SOUND OF A CAR THUD AND A GRINDING CRASH

Jim and Dad shift left and right until the sounds stop.

JIM *(cont'd)*

Something went really wrong. Sixty miles an hour, we heard a crack and felt a thud as sparks started flying from the bottom of the car. We chewed up the road for a hundred yards, turned sideways, ran into the dirt and came to a stop.

DAD

What happened?

JIM

Don't know.

DAD

We hit something?

JIM

I don't think so.

DAD

Was it a pot hole?

JIM

We would've felt that.

DAD

Yeah.

JIM

I think something broke.

DAD

Left side of the car is down.

JIM

Yeah.

DAD

Flat?

JIM
Could be.

DAD
Blow out.

JIM
Yeah.

Jim and Dad get out of the car and look.

JIM *(cont'd)*
Oh, no!

DAD
Holy crap!

JIM
The whole wheel!

DAD
It broke off!

JIM
How could that happen?

DAD
Broken sway bar... maybe a tie rod.

JIM
What are we going to do?

DAD
I don't know. I don't know.

JIM
We were about thirty minutes from Montauk. The boat had been paid for. There were no refunds. Dad's buddies would go fishing whether we showed up or not. And our day of fishing was over before we got there. We would have to find a tow truck, get the car towed, rent a car and drive back to the Bronx. At least that's what I *thought* was going to happen.

A MAN approaches.

MAN
Anyone hurt?

JIM
Hmm?

MAN
You guys okay?

DAD
Yeah. We're okay.

MAN
You guys chewed up the road pretty good.

DAD
Looks like it.

MAN
Front left tire gave way?

DAD
Yeah, I think it was a sway bar.

MAN
Either that or a tie rod.

DAD
Yeah. Tie rod.

MAN
Or a sway bar.

DAD
Right.

MAN
Looks bad. You put a lotta damage on the undercarriage.

DAD
Yeah.

MAN
Where you headed?

DAD
Montauk. Pier fifty.

MAN
I go right by the piers.

DAD
Uh huh.

MAN
Want a lift?

JIM
That's very kind of you, sir but my Dad and I-

DAD
(interrupts)
Yes.

JIM
What?

DAD
I said yes.

JIM
What about the car?

DAD

Fuck the car.

JIM

What do you mean?

DAD

Leave it. It was a good car. Thanks for giving it to me, Jimmy.

JIM

You're welcome.

DAD

But it's twelve years old, the engine was on its way out, it's worth maybe fifty bucks.

MAN

Not even, look at the damage, it's scrap.

DAD

We'll leave it here and I'll call the cops in Montauk, tell them where it is.

The Man, Jim and Dad sit three across in what is now the Man's truck.

JIM

And that's what he did. Dad took off the license plates and we jumped into this guy's pickup truck! We made it to pier fifty with time to spare.

(then)

You feel bad about the car, Dad?

DAD

Nah.

JIM

It was a good car.

DAD

Yeah, it was.

JIM

Ford. Dependable. Gets you home.

DAD

Except when it doesn't.

The Man turns on the radio.

MUSIC: "BROWN EYED GIRL" BY VAN MORRISON

MAN

You guys mind some music?

JIM

Actually my Dad is kinda-

DAD

No, music is fine.

MAN

Cool.

DAD

Mind if I turn it up?

MAN

Go for it.

Dad turns up the music and the three men listen as they make their way to Montauk. The MUSIC plays for several beats then the MUSIC and LIGHTS slowly fade.

THE END

www.ingramcontent.com/pod-product-compliance
Lightning Source LLC
Chambersburg PA
CBHW070714160426
43192CB00009B/1182